Object-Oriented Analysis & Design

About the Author

Andrew Haigh has worked in the computer software industry for 15 years, graduating with a B.Sc. in Computer Science, Aston University, England. While in England, Andrew was a member of the British Computer Society, and the object-oriented programming and systems, specialist group. He also became a Chartered Engineer, a professional title awarded by the Engineering Council of Great Britain.

It was while working for Digital Equipment Co. that he was introduced to object-oriented programming and quickly became the European advocate for Trellis, a pure object-oriented programming environment, giving presentations and training on the product. After leaving Digital, Andrew became a consultant and worked on object-oriented projects for financial institutions in London.

In 1995 Andrew joined Computer Associates, moving to the USA in 1997 to take up the position he currently holds as a development manager working on Jasmine ODB, Computer Associates object-oriented database.

Object-Oriented Analysis & Design

Andrew Haigh

Osborne/**McGraw-Hill**

New York   Chicago   San Francisco
Lisbon   London   Madrid   Mexico City
Milan   New Delhi   San Juan
Seoul   Singapore   Sydney   Toronto

Osborne/**McGraw-Hill**
2600 Tenth Street
Berkeley, California 94710
U.S.A.

To arrange bulk purchase discounts for sales promotions, premiums, or fund-raisers, please contact Osborne/**McGraw-Hill** at the above address. For information on translations or book distributors outside the U.S.A., please see the International Contact Information page immediately following the index of this book.

Object-Oriented Analysis & Design

1234567890 CUS CUS 01987654321

ISBN 0-07-213314-7

Publisher	Brandon A. Nordin
Vice President & Associate Publisher	Scott Rogers
Editorial Director	Wendy Rinaldi
Acquisitions Coordinator	Tim Madrid
Technical Editors	James Saliba
	Kin Leung
Copy Editor	Susan Cohen
Proofreader	John Gildersleeve
Indexer	Claire Splan
Computer Designers	Carie Abrew
	Lauren McCarthy
Illustrators	Michael Mueller
	Alex Putney
	Beth Young
Series Design	Roberta Steele

This book was composed with Corel VENTURA™ Publisher.

To Karen, Daniel, and Sarah for
their continued love, patience,
and encouragement.

Contents at a Glance

Contents

Acknowledgments

If it had not been for Mark Bohlman, for asking me to come to America, the chain of events behind this book would never have started.

Ada Graham, for asking me to interview graduate and work experience candidates.

The many graduate and work experience candidates whose lack of knowledge inspired me to write this book.

My thanks are extended to Wendy Rinaldi, my acquisitions editor at Osborne/McGraw-Hill, for working so hard to get this book started; both of us gave birth this year to something new and special.

Karen Haigh for helping to replace the 'they should already know this' with 'just in case they didn't know.'

Kin Leung and James Saliba for technical editing.

I would also like to thank all the people that I work closely with at Computer Associates.

Introduction

When I was originally asked to undertake the interviews of graduate and work experience candidates, I naturally asked questions on subjects I knew well. Therefore, when I was informed by a candidate that they knew Java or C++, that was where I started. Having established whether a candidate knew the syntax of these programming languages, I moved the questions onto object-orientation analysis and design. It quickly became apparent that although they could write an object-oriented application, they did not know how to design one. In several instances, candidates did not understand the concepts of object orientation.

An analogy would be teaching people how to use a saw to cut up pieces of wood, and a hammer and nails to join pieces of wood, and then asking them to build a house. Technically, they can build the house, provided they are given a design to follow. However, they would not be able to design a house, at least not one I would be willing live in, nor would they be able to examine an existing house and explain why it was built the way it was.

In a similar fashion, graduating programmers could write an object-oriented application. However, I would not trust it if it was put under any kind of stress, nor would I entrust them with an existing application and ask them to understand how it works and to make enhancements.

This shortfall inspired me to write this book. A book was required that could be used in conjunction with object-oriented programming, to provide a foundation of concepts and analysis and design techniques. In addition, this book provides valuable information for the programmer once development of the application has started; chapters include testing and debugging.

Audience

The audience for this book is anybody who has ever wondered why it takes so long to write a successful object-oriented application, while trying to correctly follow the doctrine of incremental development. The problem is that every time an increment is developed and tested, part of the source code always needs to be rewritten to move the application forward to the next stage in design. Having carried out a full analysis and design of the application requirements, the classes and their associated functionality can be properly implemented. The usual mistake is to write a class to fulfill the needs of the moment and then have to subdivide that class when the requirements of the application change during the incremental development.

What You Will Get from this Book

You will gain an understanding of object-oriented analysis and design using UML v1.4.

What the Book Covers

The book is divided into five parts,

- ▶ Part I, "What Is Object Orientation?"
- ▶ Part II, "Analysis"
- ▶ Part III, "Design"
- ▶ Part IV, "Programming"
- ▶ Part V, "Case Studies"

which contain 11 chapters and an appendix:

- ▶ Chapter 1, "Introduction to Object Orientation"   This chapter provides an introduction to object orientation, a description of object orientation, what an object is, as well as its attributes and methods. This chapter also contains a description of the fundamentals of object orientation.

- ▶ Chapter 2, "Analysis"   Analysis is an important stage of any project, so this chapter covers all aspects of the analysis process. Analysis starts with gathering the information. The next step is to determine what an object is. The chapter then covers all of the basic analysis document types supported by UML v1.4. Included in this chapter is a discussion on use case analysis.

► Chapter 3, "Design Do's"   The idea behind this chapter is to provide you with a collection of the basic constructs used in designing an application.

► Chapter 4, "Design Don'ts"   This chapter takes a novel approach and actually tells you what not to do when designing an application, including some personal dislikes in multiple inheritance and the C++ construct of 'friend'.

► Chapter 5, "Advanced Design"   Having presented a chapter on basic design constructs and a chapter on design constructs to avoid, I now cover some design constructs that are considered advanced and are introduced in this book for future usage.

► Chapter 6, "Testing"   This chapter introduces you to the concept of testing. As normal academic training does not discuss this topic, it is discussed here.

► Chapter 7, "Debugging"   In addition to testing, programmers are rarely taught the concepts behind debugging an application to determine where errors occur.

► Chapter 8, "Porting"   This chapter is a subject close to my heart and is a subject that every programmer should understand. It covers writing an application to support various hardware platforms and multiple natural languages.

► Chapter 9, "Application Lifecycle"   The topic of this chapter covers documenting the source code, creating a good project directory, using the make utility to build the application, and using source code control to manage source code changes.

► Chapter 10, "Case Study 1—Simulated Company"   This first case study covers the stepped development of a simple application, showing how the application is developed and tested at every stage.

► Chapter 11, "Developing a Multithreaded Airport Simulation"   This final case study shows how to develop a multithreaded application. The development shows how to handle problems that occur when the usage of resources is not properly handled and what happens when the threads are waiting on each other.

Finally, the appendix provides you with the philosopher source code that is referenced throughout the book.

What Is Object Orientation?

OBJECTIVES

► Introduce object orientation

► Learn the fundamentals of object orientation

Introduction to Object Orientation

IN THIS CHAPTER:

Understand What an Object Is

Identify Objects

Learn About Classes, Attributes, and Methods

Learn the Fundamentals of Object Orientation

Documenting Your Findings

When computing first started, programmers were working within strict limitations of memory and storage. These programmers produced marvels of engineering. They were able to produce the most programs for the least amount of resources. The programs were all function, no frills, and had no room for anything other than the required functionality.

When more powerful computers became available, with more memory and storage space, programs were written on an ad hoc basis with no regard for any overall design. Soon it became apparent to the programmers that structured analysis and design techniques were needed to bring order to the ensuing chaos. These structured techniques created a revolution; they allowed programmers to write applications that followed formalized methods. A plan could be confirmed with the client and ultimately be tested. Unfortunately, these same structured techniques caused a problem. They did not allow the final application to be very flexible—unless you consider rewriting significant parts of the application flexible. Object-oriented techniques provided the much-needed flexibility, as demonstrated by the following analogy of owning a home.

After a while, no matter how much thought goes into buying a house, it always seems that in time you run out of room. There is never enough room for growing families in most homes' current design. People's requirements for a house change, as do the needs of a business toward existing software applications. As with a house, there are usually only two choices with inadequate software:

▶ You can discard it and purchase new software, which requires retraining. Unfortunately, there is no resale value on old software. In addition, it will usually take longer to write new software than it will to build a new house.

▶ A cheaper option is to build an extension to the existing software. You get the additional functionality with the minimum of retraining.

Old software (or badly designed software) starts to look like the old houses in a country village. The house has grown to accommodate the changing needs of its occupants, with more rooms added on to the existing original house. New extensions were added to fulfill specific purposes. However, each extension was added where there was space to add it, so to get from one room to another becomes an adventure. Some software is comparable to these houses: features have been added not to enhance the design, but merely to enhance the features available. The software is feature-rich, but a nightmare should anybody try to improve functionality or performance. The features that need changing are as difficult to modify as the rooms in an old house, and improvements would probably cost more than the value of the house.

The solution in software is far easier to achieve than carrying out redesign and remodeling on an older house (especially with a preservation order in place!). With software, you just knock it down, learn from your mistake, and try to build better software next time.

In the same way that a modern architect is concerned with how people will live and enjoy the functionality of a house he builds, someone using the object-oriented approach is concerned with how to keep associated information together, providing flexibility and design that are prepared for change. Although structured methodology does not have such a severe learning curve as object orientation, it also does not have the flexibility to build code suitable for the modern business world, nor is it adaptable enough to withstand REPEATED alteration and change.

Comparing Structured and Object-Oriented Techniques

For those of us who used the earlier, structured methods, there will be some mental hardship in trying to master object orientation. However, the benefits of the object-oriented approach far outweigh the hardship of the learning process. By way of contrast, here is an example of a structured design versus an object-oriented design.

Before the object-oriented revolution, everything was designed around a structured systems model. The driving force behind this model was the process, which was all-encompassing. This approach was especially popular, as everything modeled was already a process. Figure 1-1 shows an extremely simple example of an ordering process.

What is not shown on this diagram is the fact that every process has to interface with a database. This database is used so that each process using a key can track a client's order. Typically, this interface to the information store provides a generic

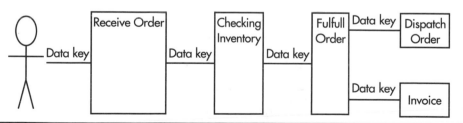

Figure 1-1 *A simple example of an ordering process*

set of information manipulation methods—for example, **setSomething** (the key to information or the value to set). Anything more specific and the interface could end up larger than the application using it.

By contrast, the object-oriented driving force is the information that flows around the system. To start with, associated information is kept together in bundles, and each new order is a new bundle of information in the system. This is like adding a new row to a database table.

Another change is that rather than external processes being adept at manipulating the information directly, each bundle has a set of methods that it exposes as an interface to allow others to manipulate the information in a controlled manner. This is akin to having methods stored in the database that know how to manipulate the information.

So far, we have the basis for an object, an information bundle with the methods used to manipulate the information in a controlled fashion.

The final twist is that if a different order type enters the system, it can adapt. It simply derives a new order from an existing order, changes the amount and type of information stored, and adjusts the methods accordingly. This is how object orientation works, and Figure 1-2 shows how the previous example would now look.

As you can see, it is the object that flows through the system. The concept of a process is now identified by the state of the object—in other words, something that would previously have been modeled in the "Checking" process is now modeled as an object performing checking methods on its own information. Completion of an old process would signal that a new process starts. Using object orientation, an object would signal its change of state from "Checking Order" to "Checked Order."

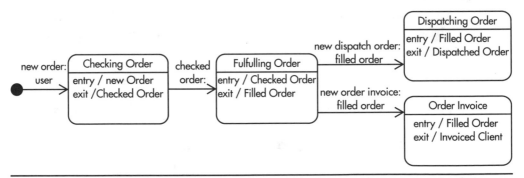

Figure 1-2   *This is how the previous example would look using object-oriented techniques.*

What Is Object Orientation?

Using object-oriented techniques allows users to fully understand the environment they are attempting to model. Identifying the components of the environment and detailing the relationships that exist between them helps to achieve this aim.

Using the example of an air traffic control system, the idea of one controller handing over an airplane to another controller further along the airplane's flight path, as shown here, is easily modeled using object-oriented techniques:

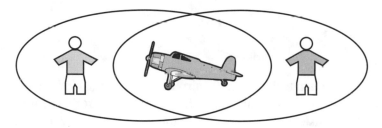

In this example, the first controller simply passes the second controller enough information to allow him to identify the location of the airplane. The information should be enough to allow the second controller to recognize it (its call sign) and advise which frequency to use to make contact. Using object-oriented techniques, this scenario can be modeled exactly:

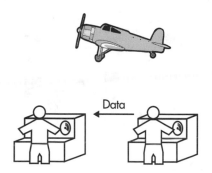

However, if all the second controller needs is some pieces of information, such as altitude and call sign, structured systems can provide the same support. Therefore, in a perfect world, object-oriented techniques offer no advantage.

Now consider the situation in which the air traffic controller needs to clarify some details with the aircrew, such as whether the plane has a full flight crew. If the environment is modeled using object-oriented techniques, the ability to respond to the request is contained in the same object (an airplane) as the initial collection of data items, allowing any request to be easily accomplished. This is shown by enclosing the aircraft in a box.

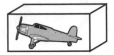

Using object-oriented techniques, the airplane object holds information with reference to its normal crew complement. It can determine for itself if the current crew number is consistent with normal crew limits and can answer appropriately.

In the case of structured systems, the initial information passed to the air traffic controller is just that: information. Any request for clarification needs to be processed by the system on behalf of the conceptual airplane. To answer the air traffic controller's question, the system needs to determine the type of the aircraft, then determine the number of crew for this aircraft, and finally compare this with the actual number on board.

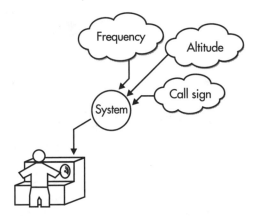

To further complicate the situation (and often provoke additional extensive rework), an aircraft can be used in several configurations, such as freight, passenger, or diplomatic. In each case, the concept of a normal crew complement differs.

An air traffic controller asking questions of an airplane directly does not have to use one piece of information to look up yet another piece of information. In the same way, object-oriented techniques provide a more realistic model, and the interactions between the objects in the system are realistic.

How Object-Oriented Techniques Relate to Users

From the previous example, you can see that the world is full of objects. You can also see that an object-oriented approach is going to be more intuitive for everyone involved. Object-oriented analysis and design techniques have been designed to follow this more natural way of thinking. This means that the terms, definitions, and notations used should be things that everyone can relate to, including the client.

The way that object-oriented analysis and design has been developed, a client can be involved in the analysis of the system from inception to completion, including discovering the objects and producing the object definitions. The clients are also involved in the design of the system, since everyone is using common terms when discussing the interactions that take place between discovered objects. Clients can also be involved in the production of the documentation for the system, as they understand the object definitions of the discovered objects. They will also understand the design phase, based on the interactions between the discovered objects. Finally, the client can follow the objects and the system design into the implementation stage.

Additional Advantages of Object Orientation

Here are some other advantages to be gained by using object-oriented techniques. The topics discussed are source code reuse, the maintainability of the source code, building on existing objects and using pure object-oriented languages.

Reuse

Once a system has been implemented, not only does the knowledge of how the system was designed and implemented stay with those involved, but the objects created can live on after the project as well. For instance, if a library is developed to support a graphical interface as part of a project, rather than redevelop it for future applications, it can be reused.

Reuse appears to be one of the driving reasons for adopting object-oriented methods and languages. This belief is becoming obsessive, to such an extent that people often equate reuse with object orientation.

Reuse helps reduce costs and shorten development times of future projects. It sounds like such a simple thing to do, but it rarely happens as planned, as nobody ever writes code the way you would do it, which always prompts rework.

Software designed using object-oriented techniques does not have to be reused, even though reuse is enabled by those techniques. After all, reuse of software was around long before object orientation. A company selling a library of routines for use by another is enabling software reuse.

Whichever way object orientation is viewed, reuse is not automatic. Code will only be reused if:

▶ There is a managed repository of available code (managed in the sense of having a librarian who is responsible for checking the reusability of code submitted to the repository).

▶ The code is well documented.

▶ The code is easy to use; that is, it has intuitive interfaces that support a wide range of uses. Instead of a date class that just supported the date in the format MM/DD/YY, the class is more likely to be reused if it supported another format such as MM/DD/YYYY, DD/MM/YY, or DD/MM/YYYY.

▶ The repository is well publicized, either widely available on the Internet or released with regular updates in the form of a development kit.

▶ Access to the repository is easy. Making access difficult will deter users and diminish code reuse.

▶ Feedback is encouraged. Code that does not meet the user requirements will produce some feedback. Either the existing code could be enhanced or new code could be written which itself will be entered into the repository.

▶ Using or contributing to the repository is encouraged.

There is a balance to be struck between the cost of implementing reusable code and administering the repository against the cost of buying code libraries with support and licensing that almost do the job.

Maintainability

One of the biggest hurdles in maintaining any source code is trying to understand what each of the components does and how it relates to the rest of the system.

The first element of the problem, what it does, is by necessity a technical one. It would be simplistic to assume that just because someone is technically competent, he or she can easily understand the code written by another programmer. If, for instance, they encounter a nuance in the code they have never seen before, it may take some time to understand the full implications of what they have found. Documentation and commented code become invaluable in situations like this.

The second element of the problem concerns how the code relates to the rest of the system. A piece of code could be a technical masterpiece. It may be well coded, have many useful comments and ample documentation, but if there is no clue as to why it exists, what it does, or how it is used, it may as well be a black box.

This second part of the problem is related directly to the problem domain. Only when enough of the problem domain is understood can the code be put into context. One of the key features of object-oriented applications is that a problem domain expert can be consulted about the objects as they relate to tangibles in the problem domain.

The need for a problem domain expert is shown in the following example:

A team of programmers is asked to maintain a program that plays chess. The system has many complex algorithms. However, it is also designed to play many complex strategies, and it would take a chess Grand Master to know if the system was really playing the way it was designed to play.

Building on Existing Objects

The nice thing about object-oriented techniques is that everything is modular. You start with a collection of objects that when assembled form the basis of the system you are striving to achieve. However, it does not stop there. The design has created a larger module—your application—with defined interfaces that can then be used in an even larger application. What starts off as a simple object that implements a sort routine suddenly becomes a part of ever more complicated systems.

Pure Languages

Analysis will highlight current system needs, while good design will allow the system to grow. Object-oriented analysis and design techniques are conceptual—that is, the objects discovered can be implemented in many ways. Providing that the analysis and design have been true to object-oriented principles, the user can implement the application in almost any language. Obviously, an object-oriented language will give a purer result, whereas using another language will make implementation more difficult to achieve, as these languages are unlikely to support some fundamental features.

For instance, a language such as Visual Basic is object based, but it does not support all of the features of object orientation. This is not to say the language should not be used, just that it will be more difficult to translate the design into a working solution.

Some Disadvantages of Object-Oriented Techniques

No simple object-oriented methodology can cater to every system or project type. The trick is to standardize on one methodology and adapt other available techniques when required. Although Unified Modeling Language (UML) is being followed in this book, additional techniques are also being used, such as CRC cards and scripts, both of which are covered in Chapter 2.

Unfortunately, the available analysis and design tools are expensive and do not always allow the user to include additional notations and techniques. In situations like these, analysts and designers often resort to graphics packages or desktop publishing packages, as I have done in writing this book.

What Is an Object?

An object is a real or abstract item that contains information (the attributes that describe it) and methods that allow it to be manipulated. Any object can be comprised of other objects, which can be comprised of other objects, and so on until the most basic objects of the system have been discovered.

For example, a car can be described as an object, and it has subcomponents, of which the engine is one. The engine can also be described as an object comprised of other objects. The level of detail depends on the requirements of the system.

Identifying Objects

When identifying objects, several valid techniques exist:

► Read through a functional specification and underline all the nouns. This has a tendency to overwhelm the analyst with potential classes. I say potential classes because, for example, if "money" is identified as an object of a payroll application, money in this context is more easily represented as a number. However, in a different context, money may become a class that needs to determine its currency rather than just being an amount. The context—or problem domain, as it is commonly known—is discussed in Chapter 2.

Quick Introduction to Some Necessary Notations

Every object has a class (or object definition) associated with it. Classes will be discussed later in this chapter, but for now, here is the notation used throughout this book. The notation used will be from the industry standard Unified Modeling Language version 1.4.

- ▶ The UML notation for a class is **ClassName**.
- ▶ The UML notation for a nonspecific object of a class is <u>**:ClassName**</u>; the colon delimits the nonspecific object.
- ▶ An object of a nonspecific class is shown as <u>**ObjectName:**</u>. Notice that the class is not specified.

- ▶ Look for tangible things. A tangible thing is something that interacts with other objects within the system, such as:
  - ▶ People (managers, employees, family, friends)
  - ▶ Places (home, work, vacation destinations)
  - ▶ Pieces of paper (shopping lists, legal contracts, birth or marriage certificates)
- ▶ Look for relationships between objects.

An Example of Finding Objects in a Family

A <u>**:Male**</u> object and a <u>**:Female**</u> object form a relationship that can be expressed as getting married. The status of being married can be expressed as attributes of the <u>**:Male**</u> object and the <u>**:Female**</u> object. The <u>**:Male**</u> and <u>**:Female**</u> objects have handles to each other, as shown in Figure 1-3.

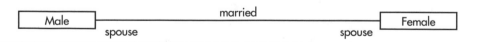

Figure 1-3   *A <u>:Male</u> object marries a <u>:Female</u> object*

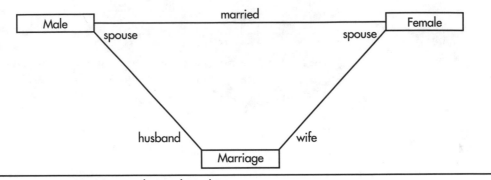

Figure 1-4 A *:Marriage* relationship object

It is usual for an official record to be kept of the marriage. In this context, the relationship *married* would be expressed as the object **:Marriage** , as shown in Figure 1-4.

When a child is born and the married couple becomes a family, a new relationship object emerges, as shown here:

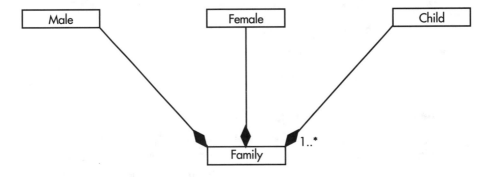

As it is, this model only shows family members, it does not show their relationship to the family. There is a notation in UML for just such a purpose, called a link, which is used to highlight special associations. This link notation is shown here:

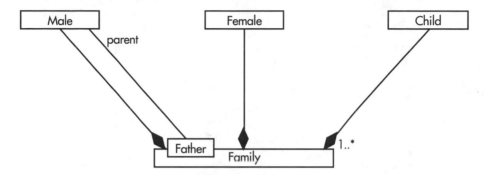

Another Example of Identifying Objects

The next example involves a group of company employees, each carrying out different roles for the company. From an analysis point of view, the problem is how to label each employee.

► Every employee in the company is shown in Figure 1-5. This shows the employees without any adornments—no job title, no project name, no team assignments, or any other special relationships.

► As with any company, there are many project groups, and the employees in some of the groups are shown in Figure 1-6. The project group with horizontal stripes is working on an accounting package, the project group in white is working on the company web page, while the project group working on an inventory package has vertical stripes.

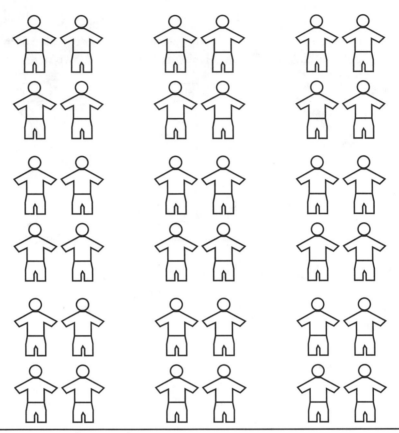

Figure 1-5   *Every employee in the company*

▶   Across all of the projects, there exist three distinct teams. The employees in these teams are shown in Figure 1-7. One team (shown with diagonally striped shorts) is development, the next team (shown with white shorts) is quality assurance, and the final team (with crosshatched shorts) represents support.

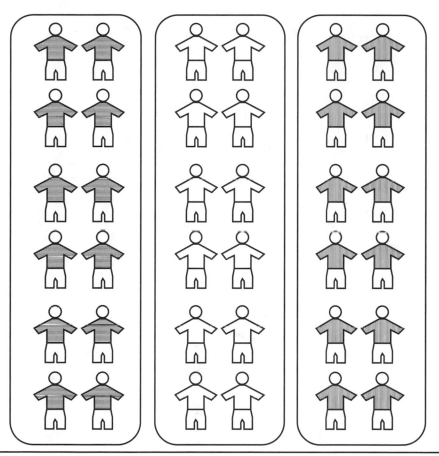

Figuro 1-6 *Employoos in thoir projoct groups*

▶ Each project contains three teams: development, quality assurance, and support. Each team contains four employees, one of whom is chosen to be the team leader. Each of the team leaders is shown in Figure 1-8 as having one half of their shorts drawn in black.

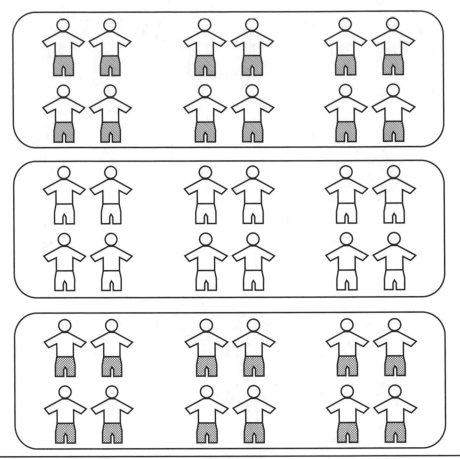

Figure 1-7   *Employees in their teams*

▶   Some of the employees are married. Their relationships may be a consideration.
     For example, it might not be possible to send both partners away to training
     if they have children, unless childcare is provided. Employees with special
     relationships are shown in Figure 1-9.

     Having shown how employees can be adorned to signify their roles within the
     company, the problem becomes how to describe the employee highlighted in
     Figure 1-10.

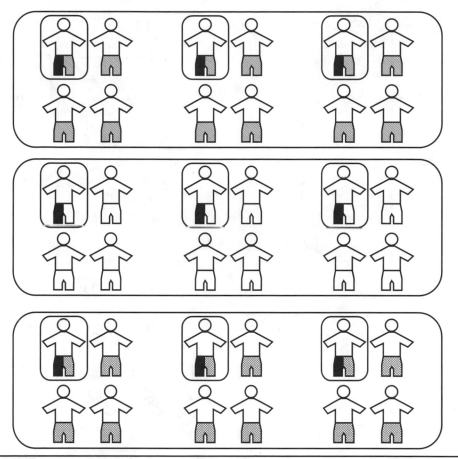

Figure 1-8   *Team leaders*

The highlighted employee could be described as:

▶   An employee

▶   A member of a team—in this case, quality assurance

▶   A member of a project group—in this case, the inventory package

▶   Alternatively, any or all of the above

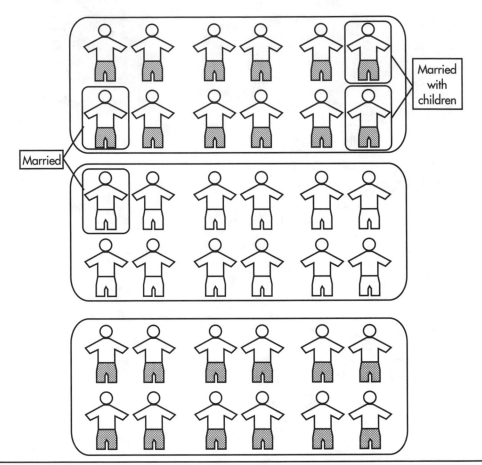

Figure 1-9   *Employees with special relationships*

In summary, anything could and should be considered as an object for the project. It is only when all aspects have been considered that good analysis can take place.

During the analysis phase of the project, it may be possible to combine objects that share common features or eliminate them, but every decision must be made in the context of the project.

There are several solutions to the problem of how to describe the highlighted employee, but each depends on the context of the project. One such solution will be discussed in the section on multiple-inheritance in Chapter 3.

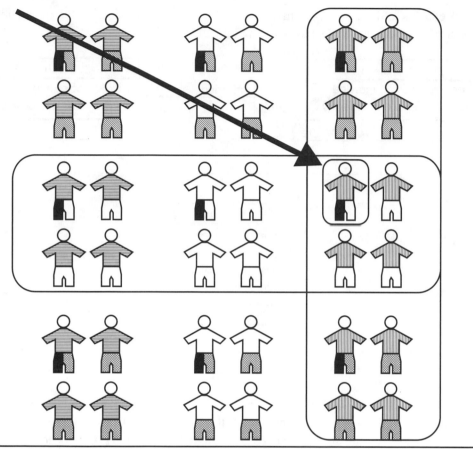

Figure 1-10   *The highlighted employee can be easily described.*

Attributes

An attribute is a characteristic of an object that has value within the context of the system. Refer back to Figure 1-3. The status of being married can be expressed as attributes of the **:Male** object and the **:Female** object, as shown here:

Male
private boolean married = 0
private Female spouse = 0

married

spouse   spouse

Female
private boolean married = 0
private Male spouse = 0

Refer back to Figure 1-4. Attributes of **:Married** could be when the marriage occurred, where, and between which **:Male** and which **:Female**, as shown here:

Male		Female
private boolean married = 0	married	private boolean married = 0
private Female spouse = 0	spouse spouse	private Male spouse = 0

husband   wife

Marriage
private Date when = 0
private Location where = 0
private Male husband =0
private Female wife = 0

An example of an object with attributes is **MyCar:**. The attributes of **MyCar:** are numerous. There is its manufacturer, its model, its age, its color, its engine size, and so on.

What I need to know when I describe **MyCar:** is the possible information required by the listener in response to a question. If the listener only wants to know if I can offer him a ride to the airport, he does not want to hear about **MyCar:**'s color. On the other hand, if **MyCar:** was stolen, the police would definitely like to know its color. Therefore, you see that **MyCar:** has many attributes, each having a value:

MyCar: Attributes: make, model, engineSize, color

As another example of an attribute having a value depending on the context, imagine two small houses built with an adjoining wall. Over time, one neighbor bought the house next door. They took down the adjoining wall and merged the two small houses into one larger house. There now exist the original plans of the two houses and the plans of the new house.

In the context of the new house, the original plans are of no practical use to the current tenant. However, in the context of keeping historical records, the information has immense value as it shows the development of the property.

Methods

A method is how an object allows other objects to interact with it. The methods that are defined for an object are documented and are called the *interface*. The interface is used to dictate the following:

- ▶ What methods an object supports
- ▶ How they are to be used
- ▶ What additional information is required
- ▶ What can be expected to happen (what this method does)
- ▶ What result if any is returned to the caller

Objects interact with each other by sending messages, which invoke published methods, where each method performs a function on the receiving object on behalf of the sending object. The phrase "invoking a method" refers to the sender waiting for the receiver to process the method and then return, whereas the phrase "sending a message" is used as it allows the sender not to wait. This allows for parallel actions to take place.

Each message must match a published interface. The message format provides each method with something referred to as its signature. This method signature is enforced by the compiler and has the following form:

<method name>   <additional information or parameters> : <return data type>

Objects may wish to publish an interface that reuses a method name with different parameters. This indicates that these methods perform the same function, but will do so with differing input. The method signature provides the development tools and the running system with enough information to determine which method is being called.

Adding the methods to the example of **<u>MyCar:</u>** is shown here:

<u>MyCar:</u>	Attributes:	make, model, engineSize, color
	Methods:	startCar(), driveCar(), changeWheel()

Object **<u>Me:</u>** provides the method *IsItYourBirthday()*. For example, asking **<u>Me:</u>** if it is my birthday today could be written as:

```
result = Me.IsItYourBirthday ("TODAY")
```

If my birthday is today, the result returned would be "YES". Otherwise, the result returned would be "NO".

Method Overloading

When a method name is used for different reasons in the same scope, the method is overloaded. The method *Age,* as shown in the following table, is one such example—it is overloaded in three different languages. The choice of which method to use is made based on the method signature used. The return type and the arguments given are checked to determine the correct method to use.

	C++	SMALLTALK	Java
get	int *Age* (void);	*Age* ^N*age*	int *Age* ()
put	*Age* (int newVal);	*Age:val*N*age*=:val	*Age* (int newVal)

Object State

An object state is a condition during the life of an object. For example, a car tire is either inflated or flat, therefore a tire has two states. An object state can be the result of a method or can be used to show an object during the method. A *composite* state is a state composed of *simple* states. Conceptually, an object remains in a state for an interval of time. However, the semantics allow for modeling "flow-through" states that are instantaneous, as well as transitions that are not instantaneous.

A *state machine* is a collection of interconnected rules that can be modeled graphically as state diagrams. It may be used to model an ongoing activity of an object. State diagrams are a part of UML and are discussed in Chapter 2.

Adding state to the example of **MyCar:** gives the description shown here:

MyCar:	**Attributes:**	**make, model, engineSize, color**
	Methods:	startCar (), driveCar (), changeWheel ()
	State:	stopped, running, flatTire

Class

Having discovered an object, the first task is to document it. This is achieved using a class (or object definition). A class is similar to a user manual. It tells the user what can be done with the object and lists the methods available, the parameters they require, and the results they return.

As previously mentioned, an object is defined as something that has:

► Attributes

► Methods

► A state

As several objects are defined, it may become apparent that they all share the same attributes and methods. If this is the case, a class can be defined to describe this collection of objects. Using the previous examples, a person in a company can be defined as an employee of that company, where each person is an instance or object of the **Employee** class definition.

The attributes for **MyCar:Car** shown next are dependent on the car I choose, unless I choose a Ferrari, in which case the color is typically red and is chosen for me. In this case, color ceases to be an object attribute, but becomes an attribute of all Ferraris. It becomes a class (all Ferraris) attribute and not an instance attribute.

The features of an object can be summarized in the class definition, shown below in the UML notation for a class:

ClassName
attributes
methods

The class **Car**, its attributes, and the available methods are shown here:

Car
make, model engineSize, color
startCar(), driveCar(), changeWheel()

The class dictates the methods available, while the implementation dictates how the methods work. In addition, **MyCar:Car** is a named instance (or object) of class **Car**.

The notation for an object is shown next. The class from which the object is instantiated is shown as being contained within the object. The reason for showing the class as part of the notation is to help clarify the origins of the object, as it shows the class from which the object was instantiated. This notation will be extended in future discussions to also include inheritance.

<u>ObjectName:ClassName</u>
attributes
methods

So far, the objects that have been described have been known. That is to say, they are examples of named objects, such as **MyCar:**. There exists a notation in UML for an instance of an object that is yet to be named, an anonymous object, as shown here:

:ClassName
attributes
methods

Fundamentals of Object Orientation

Data abstraction and encapsulation allow the information in the system to exist as well-defined entities, while inheritance provides a mechanism for sharing attributes and methods between related classes. Polymorphism and overriding provide the ability to interchange objects of differing classes without having to recode to handle the classes.

In addition to introducing the concepts of object orientation, this section also emphasizes the need for clear and precise documentation.

Data Abstraction and Encapsulation

Data abstraction is defined as extracting from the abundance of information-related data. It is important that related data be kept together for easier manipulation. It is equally important, however, to abstract the generic (or common) data from specific details. A personnel system will be easier to implement if it uses "people," rather than specifics, such as "Tom," "Dick," and "Harriet."

Encapsulation is defined as hiding related data behind an interface of methods. These methods allow access to the data and manipulations to be performed on the data. An example would be the login screen that stops random users from accessing your computer. The login screen is an interface method provided by the operating system to hide the contents of your computer.

The premises behind data abstraction and encapsulation are as follows:

▶ The users do not know and should not know how an object is implemented.

▶ The users should not be aware how complex or simple the object really is.

▶ The users can only use the methods provided. These methods give them the necessary interface to perform tasks.

In essence, an object is nothing more than encapsulation and data abstraction, as shown in Figure 1-11.

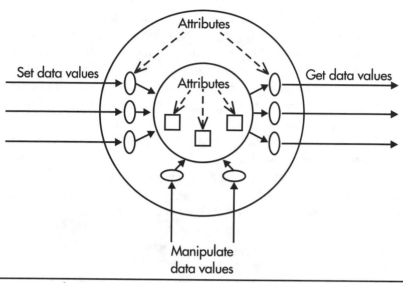

Figure 1-11 *Data abstraction and encapsulation*

Figure 1-11 shows how the attributes of an object are accessed through methods. There are different types of methods. These include methods that allow the attributes to be set (set methods), methods that allow these values to be obtained (get methods), and methods that manipulate the attributes in some way to return a complex result.

For instance, the attribute dateOfBirth in the object **ME:** can be accessed via a direct access method **ME:**getdateOfBirth() to return the date of birth.

The method **ME:**getAge() returns the age of **ME:** either by accessing the specific age attribute or using the attribute dateOfBirth in combination with the current date to determine the age (in years or years and months depending on the implementation of the method used). Age in this instance is a derivable element; it is something that can be calculated from another attribute. UML notation shows the attribute with a slash (/) preceding it.

Another example of how data abstraction and encapsulation works is shown in the following example. You go to the same store to buy your groceries every week. You know that if you go up aisle 1 and then back down aisle 2, you can get your groceries to fit neatly into your shopping basket.

In an unchanging world, object orientation offers no advantages. Instead of carrying the shopping basket and pacing the aisles to get to the goods directly, object orientation provides an intermediary. In the shopping example, the intermediary is a grocery clerk who will do the work for you. In programming terms, the intermediary is an interface, the set of methods that have been defined to allow the user to work with an object.

The real gain of object orientation is in a changing world. If the layout of the store changes, the grocery clerk can still get you your groceries; you do not have to know anything about the new layout of the store. In the same way, an interface can function despite any changes to the structure of the object. With a restructured object, all that needs to change is the way the interface carries out its function and not the way it is used, thus reducing the impact of changes to the system.

Another advantage of an intermediary is if the grocery clerk goes on vacation or is ill, another clerk can be used instead. In programming terms, one object can be replaced in the system by another of a similar type.

Existing systems would still be able to function, as all of the legacy features inherited from the old system would still be available, but new systems could be designed to make use of any new features that the new object may bring to the system. New grocery clerks are trained in the use of improved store facilities, receiving shoppers' orders over the telephone or by fax, but would still support the shoppers who come into the store to hand in their order.

In summary, object orientation provides an interface that remains constant, even though the object may be restructured or even replaced by an object of a similar type. This gives the system the ability to adapt to new situations and expand to include new features.

Inheritance

Inheritance as defined by object orientation brings properties that are common across several classes into one general class. This class then becomes the *parent* class to more specific or *child* classes.

Although the attributes and methods are actually implemented at different levels of an inheritance hierarchy, for any object whose class forms part of the hierarchy, the implementations will appear to be local. That is, there is no overhead when trying to use an inherited method as opposed to a local method. This in itself raises problems when trying to maintain code, because it is not apparent where methods are implemented. This topic is covered in the "Documentation" section later in this chapter.

The root class of the inheritance hierarchy is the class that is not derived from any other class. In Figure 1-12, the root class would be the **Person** class.

Inheritance I: Derived Inheritance

In the example shown in Figure 1-12, the **Person** class is defined as being the parent class for the **Employee** class. The **Employee** class is defined as being the parent class for the **Secretary** class and the **Manager** class.

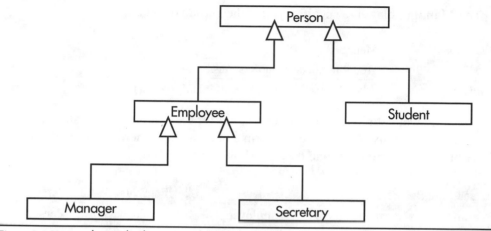

Figure 1-12   *A derived inheritance hierarchy*

The **Person** class contains the attributes and methods that are common across the hierarchy and are found at the highest level of the hierarchy.

ClassName	Person
Attributes	name, address, age
Methods	askName(), changeAddress(), askAddress(), askAge()

The **Employee** class contains attributes and methods associated with a more specific type of the **Person** class:

ClassName	Employee
Attributes	employeeNumber, jobTitle, phoneNumber
Methods	setEmployeeNumber(), promoteEmployee()

The **Secretary** class is a specific type of the **Employee** class:

ClassName	Secretary
Attributes	groupManager, secretarialAndAdministrativeSkills
Methods	askToBookTravel(), askToArrangeMeeting()

The **Manager** class is a specific type of the **Employee** class:

ClassName	Manager
Attributes	groupMembers, groupResponsibilities
Methods	askToAssessGroupMembers(), planProjects()

The graphical notation shown in Figure 1-12 for the example above shows an inheritance hierarchy. Any two levels form a relationship. There are several ways of describing this relationship, and they are shown in this table:

Person	Relationship	Employee	Relationship	Person
Person	is the parent class of	**Employee**	is the child class of	**Person**
Person	is inherited by	**Employee**	is derived from	**Person**
Person	is the superclass of	**Employee**	is the subclass of	**Person**

Inheritance II: Abstracted Inheritance

The previous section on inheritance discussed how classes could be made more specific, by deriving child classes from a parent class. This section discusses how parent classes can be identified from classes with similar attributes and methods.

As tables for attributes and methods are constructed, some classes will be seen to have features in common. These common features can be extracted and organized into a new class, a parent class. This has the advantage of reducing the effort in implementing the same methods across different classes. Start by using two separate classes, **Lecturer** and **Student**, and their properties as shown here:

Student
name, address, telephoneNumber
coursesAttended()

Lecturer
name, address, telephoneNumber
coursesGiven()

The attributes *name, telephoneNumber,* and *address* can be extracted and used to define a new class, the **Person** class:

Person
name, address, telephoneNumber

The new abstracted class **Person** forms the root of the inheritance hierarchy that links the class **Lecturer** and the class **Student**, as shown here:

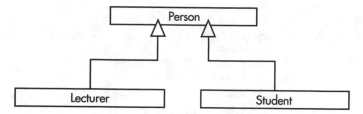

In this example, the **Person** class is said to be "inherited by," while the **Lecturer** and **Student** classes are said to be "derived from."

The next illustration shows how the **Lecturer** and **Student** classes inherit the attributes described in the **Person** class. As stated previously, from the user's point of view there is no distinction between inherited or local properties. Inherited properties require no more programming to use them than local properties.

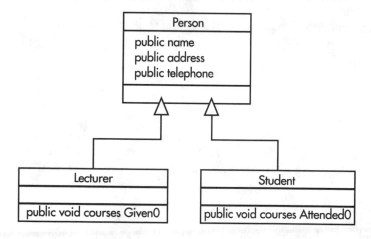

Polymorphism

There are two possible definitions for the term *polymorphism*. The typical definition of polymorphism concerns different classes supporting the same method. The classic example—or at least the example most often used—is that of a **Shape** class and two derived classes, **Square** and **Triangle**. The **Shape** class defines the method drawSelf(), which the **Circle** class (a derived class) re-implements, as shown here:

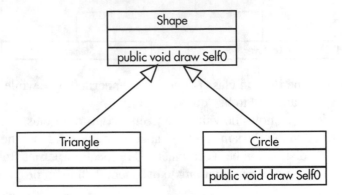

Using inheritance, when a **Shape** class pointer is defined, you know that it can also point to any class derived from **Shape**. This allows you to assign a **Circle** object to a **Shape** class pointer:

```
Shape *shape;
shape = new Circle ();

/*
** This will call the drawSelf () method of the Circle class as it
** re-implements the method described in the Shape class
*/
shape.drawSelf ();
```

Polymorphism states that even though the object associated with the **Shape** pointer is not a **Shape** object, it will call the appropriate drawSelf () method. In this instance, if the **Circle** class had re-implemented the drawSelf () method, it would be this re-implementation that would be used. This is facilitated by method overriding, which is covered in the next section.

The alternative definition of polymorphism is that an object supports multiple interfaces, as shown here and in the following example:

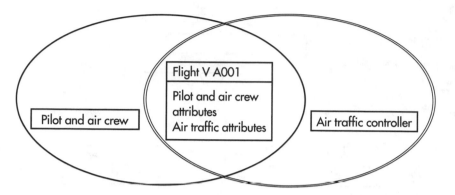

This definition of polymorphism allows the object **<u>Flight VA001:</u>** to exist in more than one domain. To the passengers, it is an object that allows them to travel. To the pilot, it is an object that needs to be flown. To the air traffic controller, it is an object that needs to be guided and given takeoff and landing rights at specific airports. Yet in every instance, the object being referenced is still **<u>Flight VA001:</u>**, it just means different things depending on the context in which it is viewed.

Overriding

Overriding is the mechanism by which a child class can provide an alternative implementation of a method currently provided by a parent class. An example of overriding is shown in Figure 1-13.

The example shows the parent class **Car** being inherited by three child classes: **Two_Seater**, **Four_Seater**, and **Seven_Seater**. The parent class **Car** supports the method *carryPassengers()*, however, the implementation of the method is very nonspecific. It is for this reason that two of the child classes re-implement or *override* the inherited method *carryPassengers()*.

When an instance of the class **<u>Sports Car:Two_Seater</u>** is asked how many passengers it can carry it will respond "One passenger," whereas an instance of the class **<u>Mini-van:Seven_Seater</u>** will respond "Six passengers." When an instance of the class **<u>Car:Four_Seater</u>** is asked how many passengers it can carry, it will defer to the inherited method of the base class **Car** and will respond "Two passengers."

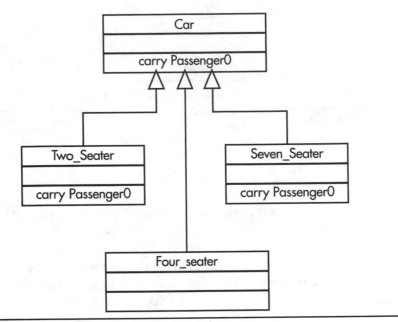

Figure 1-13   *Overriding the methods of a base class*

Documentation

The lack of documentation is the single biggest headache for anybody asked to maintain object-oriented code. The number of classes used in applications can vary from tens to hundreds, and without documentation, their relationships to each other is completely unknown. In fact, their reason for even being in the application at all can be questioned.

Class Descriptions

A class should be described in every detail. Use the questions below as guidelines for documenting your classes more fully.

Why Does this Class Exist?

There needs to be a description of the role this class plays in the overall design of the system. Describe whether this class came into existence as a result of analysis done, the design being used, or because of some special implementation needs.

What Is Its Relevance to Other Classes?

How does this class interact with other classes in the system? What are the tasks performed by this class that is necessary to the system? What is rational for putting these tasks together in this class? Does this class control other classes or is it controlled?

What Are the Attributes of this Class and What Do They Describe?

It is important to know why a class is described with certain attributes, what data type they are, and the role they play for the class. The way an attribute is declared also helps define the relationships between classes. For instance, a C++ pointer indicates a loose binding to another object, as the pointer could be set to nothing, meaning that no object has been assigned. A non-pointer indicates a tight binding; this object must contain at least one object of another class.

What Are the Methods of this Class?

Every class is defined with a set of methods. Some of these methods are used to assign values to the attributes; others are used to retrieve values. Some methods are for public use, while others are strictly for use by the class itself. What is important is that every method is documented, as follows:

- ▶ The documentation should include what the method does—what task the method performs on behalf of the class.

- ▶ Each method should be documented with what data types are to be expected as arguments—for example, do not try to pass a date to a method that is looking for a time, as it will fail.

- ▶ The return data type should also be documented, as well as what the value returned means—for example, a method could return an integer, but 0 could indicate success whereas -1 could indicate failure.

- ▶ Under what circumstances will the method fail? This assumes that testing the limits of the class was part of the acceptance criteria.

This last point cannot be emphasized enough. On many occasions, classes have been (and will be) written that will fail miserably when made public. The reason is the writer of the class will test it to what they consider generous constraints. Unfortunately, the user is never informed of these constraints and has a different interpretation of what is considered generous.

For example, a container class implemented to usually work for 10 items could be tested for as many as 20, but the user who tries to contain 100 items finds that the class fails with disastrous effects. The user should be informed of the tested limits, with a hint as to what might happen if the limits are exceeded. The class can also be implemented with safety checks to warn the user of possible misuse and prevent the object from failing.

Clear Diagrams

Another area of neglect is the use of diagrams. The use of clear diagrams must not be underestimated. Class hierarchies are so much easier to grasp when presented visually. Each aspect of object orientation can be presented on separate diagrams. This is mainly to reduce the clutter of trying to place too much information on the same diagram. Taken to the extreme, a class can be at the center of the diagram with related classes radiating out from it. This area is further explored in Chapter 2.

Inheritance

Unfortunately, class descriptions and diagrams rarely highlight inherited methods and data variables clearly. For this purpose, a graphical class browser is invaluable.

The example shown in Figure 1-12 shows a small inheritance diagram with three levels. Inheritance diagrams with too many levels start to become unusable and are rarely able to fit on a single page.

Coding Standards

Generally, coding standards are ignored as part of the documentation process. However, one of the major benefits of good coding standards is highlighting the differences in data variables and methods that are specific to a class or have been inherited when reading through source code.

Notation for Attributes and Methods

The following section introduces the notation used by UML v1.4 for attributes and methods. This section also includes the notation for temporary variables and inherited methods, something not currently covered by the standard.

- ▶ Instance attributes
- ▶ Class attributes

- ▶ Temporary variables
- ▶ Notation for methods
- ▶ Inherited methods

Instance Attributes   If you use as an example the color of the cars you drive, you can see that cars come in a variety of different colors. Therefore, when the class for a car is defined, it is necessary to allocate an attribute that allowed the color of the car to be unique. This attribute would be defined as an instance attribute, as the value can vary for every car modeled. The notation used to describe an instance attribute has the first character as lowercase, then each subsequent word is started with an uppercase character. For example, *colorOfMyCar* is a private instance attribute. Every car has its own unique value for this attribute.

Car
colorOfMyCar

Class Attributes   Conversely, when modeling a taxi company, you might want to define the class for the cars being used as having a common color attribute. In this way, you can guarantee that all of the cars belonging to the taxi company will return the same value for the color attribute. This type of attribute is called a *class attribute*. It exists outside of the instances of class. In fact, it can have a value without any instances of the class, in the same way that a new taxi company decides on its livery before buying its first car. The notation used to describe a class attribute is *colorOfCompanyCars*, a private attribute used to describe the collective color of the taxi company.

TaxiCo
colorOfCompanyCars

Temporary Variables   All other variables used in the notation are temporary. They are used to hold the results of method calls or calculations. The notation used to describe a temporary variable is *colorOfMyCar, which is similar to ordinary attributes except* that it is followed by an underscore.

Notation for Methods   During the design phase of the project, notation is required to show the difference between using methods that are local to the class (possibly overriding a parent) and using inherited methods.

Using the example of overriding in Figure 1-12 and the following notation, the method *carryPassengers()* could be written as follows:

Two_Seater
void carryPassenger()

Seven_Seater
void carryPassenger()

From this notation, the designers and developers can determine the number of methods that need to be coded and, from this information, the duration of the project.

Any Class methods are underlined in the same manner that class attributes are underlined.

Inherited Methods   Notation for inherited methods is not a part of UML. I have included this notation, as it is sometimes useful to fully document the class. Methods that have been inherited are prefixed with the name of the class in which they were initially defined. The notation used to describe an inherited method is

+ *Car_carryPassengers()*

This shows a public method that also denotes the class from which it was derived.

Four_Seater
void Car_carryPassenger()

Summary

In this chapter, objects have been introduced and ways of discovering them have been discussed. The characteristics of an object, its attributes, methods, and state have also been covered. A section discussed the class and the object blueprint or user manual.

This chapter also introduced the fundamentals of object-oriented techniques:

► Data abstraction and encapsulation
► Inheritance
► Overriding
► Polymorphism

The chapter concluded with a discussion on documentation.

Analysis

OBJECTIVES

► Learn how to gather information

► Describe the basic analysis document types
supported by UML v1.4

CHAPTER
2

Analysis

IN THIS CHAPTER:

Learn About Pre-Analysis, Information Gathering Tasks

Determine What Makes an Object

Learn About Use Cases

Learn How to Use Analysis Documents Defined by the UML v1.4 Standard

This chapter introduces the reader to the various stages of analysis. We start with a discussion of what it means to carry out analysis, followed by a discussion on how to limit the scope of the analysis by covering such aspects as the problem domain. The next area covered is in utilizing "use case" analysis to determine the high-level requirements of the system. Finally, all areas of recording the analysis are covered, including the static and dynamic aspects of both classes and the system.

Pre-Analysis

"Analysis is essentially about identifying and defining business problems that are worth solving within the resources likely to be available. Without analysis there is a real danger of designing and implementing systems that do not meet the user's needs—simply because the user's needs were not adequately identified and defined."

"If you do not know precisely what the user wants, the system is not going to deliver."

—*Basic Systems Analysis,* Alan Daniels and Don Yeates

So how does the analyst ensure that the user's needs are precisely understood? The following techniques can be applied to discover the user's needs.

Interviewing

Interviews are important in allowing the analyst to quickly discover facts. Everybody involved in the current or proposed process should be interviewed during the course of the analysis. This is to ensure that each nuance in the process is understood. It is very possible that the way people think the process works is not quite the way it actually works. For example, when you interview the manager, she may tell you the business process works in a particular way, but when you interview the person actually doing the job, he may tell you there is another step involved. It may not be much—it could simply be that he makes a copy of a document for safekeeping in a nearby filing cabinet, or it could be that he makes a copy of a document that is sent to another department for archiving. Whatever the step may be, it is completely transparent to the manager, so she couldn't give you that information, as she wasn't a party to the information in the first place.

Another important role of interviewing is to quickly check facts. It is often easier to have a brief meeting to clarify information than to search through a related document.

Questionnaires

Questionnaires are a useful way of collecting information from a large number of people or from a wide range of different sources. The information can be collected without having to schedule interviews with everyone involved. Questionnaires are also useful if they are distributed before a scheduled interview, as they allow the interviewee time to collect relevant data, thereby saving time during the interview.

Although questionnaires are a useful way of collecting an enormous amount of information from a variety of sources with the smallest amount of physical effort, care must be taken with the questions. They need to be carefully framed to obtain precise and pertinent information, as it is all too easy to elicit ambiguous information, such as the following:

> **Question:** *How long does it take to complete process A?*
> **Answer:** *Several hours, but it takes longer on Thursdays.*

This could lead to the conclusion that the workload is larger on Thursday, which seems strange, considering that other indicators do not back up this assumption. On closer inspection, it is revealed that the extra time spent has nothing to do with the workload: on Thursdays, an essential staff member arrives late to work. This person's late arrival consequently distorts the results of the original question.

Observation

In addition to interviewing and questionnaires, another good source of information is observation of any existing process in action. Operators can become so used to what they are doing that the process becomes second nature to them. They may neglect to mention key steps when asked to relate how the process operates.

Documentation and Notation

Although gathering information from any of the previous steps is immensely important, it will all be for nothing if the information is not recorded accurately, so this stage is by far the most important. Simply recording the information is not good enough. It must be recorded in a manner that maintains the maximum amount of information and the context in which it was gathered. Here's the previous example of the employee arriving late on Thursdays, including the context and expanded information:

> Process A ordinarily takes three hours; however, on Thursdays the reports are two hours late. The context is that the process is delayed waiting on an employee to report for work each Thursday. If it is important, reassignment of tasks could be considered.

The information you record is the only tangible thing produced during the investigation. It is important for the following reasons:

▶ **Analysis**   Formalized documents and notation enable the essential features of a system to be highlighted.

▶ **Communication**   Standardized documents and notation help the project team communicate with each other in an unambiguous way.

▶ **Clarity**   Providing a technical dictionary will ensure that all parties mean the same thing and that terms are not open for misinterpretation.

▶ **Training**   Using formalized documents and notation allows new entrants or transfers to become effective on a project in a shorter time.

▶ **Management**   Until a system is operational, the documents produced provide a means for all members of the project team to agree on progress.

▶ **Security**   Good documentation may be likened to blueprints. If anything is damaged or destroyed, the blueprints enable repair or reconstruction to be carried out as quickly as possible, with the likelihood of finishing with something as good as new. Likewise, accurate documentation of a computer system is invaluable for fast and effective problem resolution. The documentation used in this book for object-oriented analysis is discussed in later sections of this chapter. The notation used is primarily UML v1.4, with some additions.

When an Object Is Not an Object

One of the most difficult tasks in object-oriented analysis is identifying what is and what is not a class. In Chapter 1, the example was given of "money" identified as an object of a payroll application. Money in this context is more easily represented as a number. However, in a different context, money may become a class that needs to determine its currency rather than just being an amount. Does it need a specific class or is a number still adequate to represent it? The important thing is what an object is for you and for the problem you are trying to solve.

Another of the problems associated with identifying classes is identifying the *problem domain*. The problem domain is the scope of the problem that is under consideration. How much of the overall business or system needs to be considered to model the problem? When identifying objects, it is easy to stray outside of the problem domain and complicate the analysis unduly. The problem domain is best illustrated with some examples, which will include techniques that can be used to identify objects.

▶ The first example highlights the different needs of someone waiting for a bus at a bus stop and someone trying to drive a bus from stop to stop.

▶ The second example shows three different people's understanding of what a table means to them.

Bus Stop Problem Domain Example

This example examines three different views of how 'bus stops' and 'bus routes' interact.

Model of a Bus Route

The illustration below shows a model for a bus route. Each bus route is made from a collection of bus stops. The collection of bus stops is not random, as every new bus route determines in which order to place the bus stops.

If you are a prospective passenger waiting at a bus stop, this model is next to useless. Other than knowing that the bus stop you are standing at should be on at least one bus route, there is no indication which bus routes use the bus stop or when they are expected. This is because the relationship between the **:BusRoute** and the **:BusStop** is one-way. The **:BusRoute**s know about the **:BusStop**s, but not the other way around.

Model of a Bus Stop

The solution shown next is a better model for prospective passengers standing at a bus stop. There is information about the bus routes that happen to be using this bus stop. However, the relationship between the **:BusRoute** and the **:BusStop** is now reversed. The **:BusStop**s know about the **:BusRoute**s, but not the other way around. Consequently, there is no information about the route taken—where the bus route started and where it is going to finish, or how long the journey will take and when the next bus is due to arrive.

The downside is that the bus may still never get to a **:BusStop**. The reason for this is that although the prospective passengers know that they are on a **:BusRoute** (because each **:BusStop** knows about **:BusRoute**s), the bus driver for a **:BusRoute** has no knowledge of the **:BusStop**s that form part of a **:BusRoute**. Without this information, the bus driver does not know the correct route to take and therefore doesn't even leave the bus depot.

Model of Both

This solution shown below will benefit all parties. The class **TimeTable** has access to all the bus routes and all the bus stops, also the **BusRoute** class and the **BusStop** class have access to the **TimeTable** class.

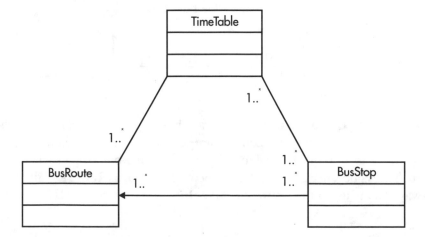

A **:TimeTable** could be a real instance in every class (such as a physical book at every bus stop), or it could be access to a single instance, for example, a central database. Each **:BusRoute** can access the **:TimeTable**, and using the **:TimeTable** can determine the **:BusStop**s to be traveled. Each **:BusStop** can access the **:TimeTable**, and using the **:TimeTable** can determine the **:BusRoute** and the schedule of the buses.

Table Problem Domain Example

You would have thought a table should not cause anyone any problems. After all, a table is just a collection of components. Unfortunately, different people will view a table in different ways, as described in the examples below.

The Cabinetmaker's View of the Table

The cabinetmaker spends many hours creating the components for a table. He may create and discard some components because they are flawed. Ultimately, however, he will settle on a collection of components, which he assembles into the finished product. Once assembled, the cabinetmaker describes the whole as a table. To the cabinetmaker, the table is nothing until the component parts have been assembled. It is the component parts that have importance.

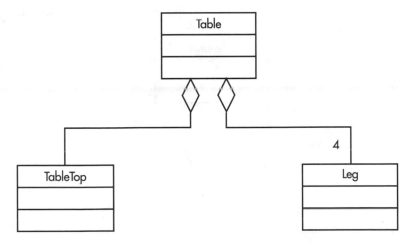

'Empty diamonds' are used in the notation to indicate a loose binding between the whole and the components. If the table is disassembled, the components survive for the cabinetmaker to reuse.

The Transportation Company's View of the Table

A representative from the transportation company arrives at the cabinetmaker's to arrange shipment of the table. Having exchanged comments about the workmanship of the table, the representative turns to things that are of real interest to him. To the representative, the table is one object that has height, width, length, and weight. The aesthetic value of the table does not enter into his consideration of what the object is nor do its component parts.

Table
width, height, length, weight

The Owner's View of the Table

When the package arrives, the owner unpacks it to reveal the table. The owner inspects the table and, when satisfied, moves the table to the desired location. Although the cabinetmaker may have built the table for one purpose, the owner makes the final decision. Everything about the table is important to the owner: its dimensions, its seating capacity, and its appearance. However, unlike the cabinetmaker who can replace or discard flawed components, the owner must accept any damage that happens or replace the table completely. Therefore, to the owner, the table is more than the sum of its components, and if any part of it gets damaged, the table is damaged.

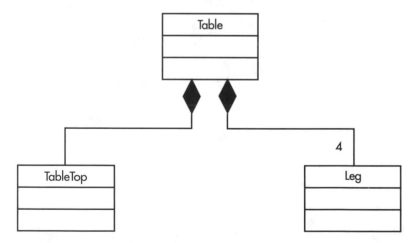

'Filled-in diamonds' are used in the notation to indicate the tight binding between the whole and the components.

Table Example Summary

Notice the difference between the notation used for the owner of the table and that used for the cabinetmaker. The owner sees the legs, but considers that they only exist as part of the table. A table is composed of parts, and a leg by itself is nothing. The cabinetmaker sees the legs as separate, independent objects and uses the name "table" as shorthand to describe the finished aggregate object.

Problem Domain Summary

In these examples, it is important to understand the problem domain. Who is the project trying to solve a problem for? What is their understanding of the objects in the system? If it is necessary to map an object through its lifetime, such as a table from a cabinetmaker, shipper, wholesaler, retailer, and on to purchaser, the designer will need to be able to morph the object from one perception to another seamlessly. A possible solution is described in the Chapter 5 section "Advanced API."

Using Use Case Analysis

Use cases are used to define the functionality of a system at a high level, not to describe in minute detail the classes and operations involved in making the system work. They allow users to describe the important requirements of the system.

Use cases are an integral part of the communication that takes place between clients and developers. They allow all parties to identify important external entities (such as users and databases), which are referred to as "actors." Knowing these actors, you can discuss their interaction with the system, including any variations or exceptions that may be possible. Finally, use cases let you create a shared technical dictionary and provide a valuable shared understanding of the problem domain.

A use case can be referred to from other use cases, so that nested use cases are possible.

Use Case Diagram

A use case diagram shows the relationships that exist between actors and use cases within a system. Use cases show the externally visible behaviors of the system.

Actors are used in use case diagrams to show the external entities interacting with the system, such as a user or a database.

A use case diagram can use any of the following symbols:

▶ Ellipses represent the use cases.

▶ Stick figures represent the actors.

▶ Boxes around the use cases represent the system under design.

▶ Solid lines between actors and uses cases represent associations.

▶ Dashed lines with open arrowheads between use cases represent associations, as shown next. <<include>> implies that the use case at the start of the line uses the use case at the arrowhead in order to complete its task. <<extend>> implies that the use case at the arrowhead can be extended by replacing a step with the actions contained in the extension use case.

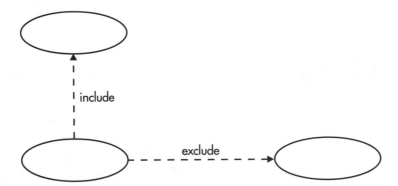

Example of a Simple Use Case

The simple example seen in Figure 2-1 shows how a client would register a student for a training course.

Although this graphical notation exists, it is preferable to keep a written record of a use case, as it allows additional information to be kept, including a full description of the use case.

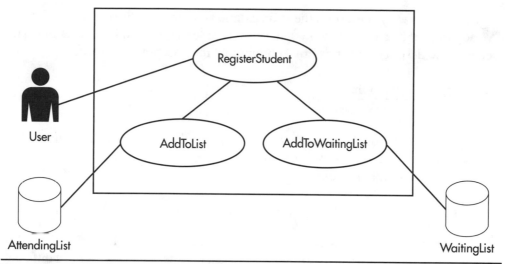

Figure 2-1   *A simple use case example*

A Use Case Template

The following is a description of each section of the use case template. Every use case is given a unique number and a reference name or short name, such as UC #1 registerStudent:

Use case number	<short name>
Description	Full explanation of the use case

These next four entries describe how the use case starts and finishes in terms of its external interactions:

Preconditions	For this use case to function, what condition does the system need to be in?
Trigger	What starts the use case?
Success	When the use case finishes, what condition should the system be in?
Abort	What happens if the use case is abandoned?

The actors section describes the main external entities involved in this use case. An actor could be a user of the system or a database that is used by the system. This section also describes other external entities that may become involved:

Actors	Primary	Who play the lead roles?
	Secondary	Who play the secondary roles?

The process section describes in detail every step that takes place for a normal, successful execution of this use case—for example, the client successfully registers the student in a training course:

Process	Step #	Short Name <action>	Description

The variations section describes alternative steps that may also lead to a successful conclusion of this use case—for example, the client may decide to register in a different course than the one originally stated:

Variations	Step #	<action>	Description

The exceptions section describes anything that could go wrong in the normal execution of this use case—for example, the student may not be known to the system and have to be entered:

Exceptions	Step #	<action> or UseCase	Description

Other Useful Information

The following lists supplemental information that provides a fuller description of a use case.

▶ **Priority**   What is the priority of this use case?

▶ **Duration**   How long is the use case expected to take?

▶ **Frequency**   How often does the use case happen?

▶ **Interface**   There are three possible interfaces with the actors:

  ▶ **Interactive**   Each client has a conversation with the system.

  ▶ **Static**   This use case relies on information that does not change, for example the syllabus and schedule of the training course.

▶ **Scheduled**   This use case relies on information that has a dynamic nature, for example the listing of movies being shown at a local cinema.

▶ **Open issues**   Is there anything that could affect this use case? For example, more students means more courses.

▶ **Delivery date**   When does the system have to be implemented?

▶ **Related use cases**   Are there any other use cases related to the current use case? For example, there may be a use case that handles the course confirmation.

A Use Case Example

Although a use case template is useful in keeping a use case model to the point, it is possible for it to be over-verbose and ambiguous. One of the reasons for this is that the techniques devised for use cases by Ivor Jacobson are not followed.

Here is a use case example that could be derived from the example shown in Figure 2-1; it is over-verbose and ambiguous:

Use Case #1		No room on course
Description		Mr. Smith tries to book Eric into a training course, but finds that it is fully booked.
Preconditions		The course must exist. Eric must be registered to be added to the course.
Trigger		Mr. Smith phones Tim and asks that Eric be admitted to a course being offered.
Success		Mr. Smith should be told that Eric is attending the course, or he should be informed of Eric's position on a waiting list.
Abort		Any additions made to either the AttendingList or the WaitingList should be removed.
Actors	Primary	Mr. Smith, Tim, the AttendingList
	Secondary	The WaitingList

Process	Step #	Short Name <action>	Description
	1	ClientContact	Mr. Smith phones Tim.
	2	QueryStudent	Is Eric registered as a student?
	3	RegisterStudent	Register Eric with the course.
	4	CheckTitle	Confirm the correct course has been requested.
	5	CheckDateTime	Confirm the date and time of the course.
	6	CheckLocation	Confirm the location of the course.
	7	CheckCapacity	Check the capacity of the AttendingList.
	8	PromptUser	The list is full, so ask Mr. Smith if he wants Eric to be added to the WaitingList.
	9	AddToList	Add Eric to the WaitingList.

Seven Tips for Writing Better Use Cases

The use case example given above is a bad example of how to write a use case template; it is not very generic, nor is it very specific. Here are seven tips for cleaning up a use case, based on a work written by Mark Ratjens and published at http://www.class.com.au/newsletr/97sep/usecases.htm.

Step 1: Give the Use Case an Appropriate Name

The guidelines state that a use case should document a basic case. A basic case for the example given is a course that describes a client phoning a system user, and the system user adding a student to a course. As such, the name for the use case would become "Registering for a course."

Step 2: Establish Easily Identifiable Styles

Identify the actors by their roles and use the names consistently throughout the use case model. Try to use a distinctive typeface or style (such as italics) to distinguish them from other parts of the use case—for example, Mr. Smith becomes *Client*, Tim becomes *User*, and Eric becomes *Student*.

Step 3: Remove Commentary

Remove commentary that describes events outside of the actors interaction with the system, such as the client asking if Eric is a registered as a student. The correct interaction is for the client to ask if a student is registered; the interaction should be specific.

Step 4: Create Both Essential and Elaborated Use Cases

At least one version of the use case must exist that deliberately excludes the specifics of the actor/system implementation interface. This version is called the essential use case. Larry Constantine, who coined the term 'essential use' case, says, "By representing the abstract, simplified structure of the user/system interaction, essential use case models help to capture better the underlying intent of users and the purpose of user interaction." Remove nonessential details from the use case to focus on essential requirements—for example, replace the confirmation of each course detail with one action.

Other versions of the use case may exist which specify interface specifics, one for each possible option. However, it is preferable to use working prototypes instead.

Step 5: Establish a Domain Model

Common use case modeling practice often glosses over or ignores the role of the domain model. According to Jacobson, the domain model's function is to support the use case model. The domain model describes objects that have a direct counterpart in the application environment and that the system must know about. Documenting domain objects as part of the requirements will help simplify use case models. Simplify the use case by referring to domain object definitions where possible. In the example, a client might be considered for a discount by registering several students for one course. This decision is outside the scope of this use case and should be deferred to a domain object.

Step 6: Step Wise

Employ a numbered systematic approach to describing the use case. The basic process defined in the use case template should be used to describe a successful execution of the process being defined. Should there be any variations in how an interaction can be carried out—for example, interaction with the client via fax or e-mail as opposed to receiving a telephone call—it should be noted in a separate section. Also, if at any point during the process an exception can occur, it should be described in a separate section; for example, if there is no room for the student in the course, the exception handles placing the student on the waiting list.

Step 7: Use Active Voice

To avoid any confusion and any possibility of misinterpretation, maximize the use of active voice in the use case model. Be explicit in describing what either an actor or the system is doing.

Using these suggested tips, here is the revised use case diagram, based on Figure 2-1:

Use Case #1	Registering for a course
Description	A system user books a client's student into a training course.
Preconditions	The course must exist. The student to be added to the course must exist.
Trigger	A client phones and asks that a student be admitted to a course being offered.
Success	The client should be told whether the student is attending the course or advised of the student's position on a waiting list.
Abort	Any additions made to either the AttendingList or the WaitingList should be removed.

Actors	Primary	The system user and the AttendingList
	Secondary	The WaitingList

Process	Step #	Short Name <action>	Description
	1	ClientContact	The client phones.
	2	RegisterStudent	Register the student in the course.
	3	ConfirmCourse	Confirm the course details with the client: date, time, and location. Depending on the complexity of the operation, this could become its own use case.
	4	CheckCapacity	Check the capacity of the AttendingList.
	5	AddToList	Add the student to the AttendingList.
	6	CheckDiscount	If the client has booked several students into a course, they might be considered for a discount.

Variations	Step #	\<action>	Description
	1	ClientContact	Fax
	1	ClientContact	E-mail

Exceptions	Step #	\<action> or UseCase	Description
	4a	ListIsFull	Prompt the user to ask the client if they want to be put on a waiting list.
	4b	AddToList	Add the student to the WaitingList only if the client agrees to be on the list.
	4c	"AnotherCourse" (This is the name of another use case.)	Interface with another UseCase to offer another course if there are enough people on the waiting list.

Recording Analysis

The purpose of analysis is to gather information about a system and present it in a useful format. This section will concentrate on the documents used when undertaking analysis. There are four areas that need to be covered, each with its own documents:

► Analyzing the static aspects of classes

► Analyzing the dynamic aspects of classes

► Analyzing the static aspects of the system

► Analyzing the dynamic aspects of the system

Analysis Documents: Static Aspects of Classes

The documents discussed in this section provide information about the static aspects of classes, the details that define each class. This section also discusses the interactions between the classes. The documents are as follows:

► Class diagrams document just the class.

► CRC cards start to define the role of each class.

► Scripts document the class-to-class interactions.

Class Diagrams

Class diagrams fully describe the attributes and methods that exist for a class, as shown in the tables below for Loan and CashAccount. As a class description matures during analysis, these documents will have numerous changes made to them.

The notation used in class diagrams is as follows:

+	Public attribute/method
#	Protected attribute/method
-	Private attribute/method
/	Derived attribute/method
$	Class-based attribute/method

The following two class diagrams are taken from Appendix 1—Case Study #1—SimCo.

Class Name	Loan	Description
Attributes	-duration, -repayment	Two private attributes.
Operations	+Loan (amount:double, duration:integer) : Loan	A public method with the name of the class that returns a object of the class is called a constructor. A constructor is called whenever a new object is required. Most constructors do not require arguments; in this example, a loan is meaningless without knowing the amount of the loan and its duration.
	+showRepayment (void) : double	A public method that takes no arguments, but returns a double datatype.
	+adjustDuration (void) : void	A public method that takes no arguments and returns no value.

Class Name	CashAccount	Description
Attributes	-balance	One private attribute.
Operations	+CashAccount (void) : CashAccount	A public typical constructor method that takes no arguments.
	+credit (double) : void +balance (void) : double +debit (double) : void +setBalance (double) : void +adjustMonth (void) : void	

CRC (Class:Responsibilities:Collaborators) Cards (Non-UML)

CRC cards are used in conjunction with class diagrams to document classes as they are identified during analysis. A CRC card is designed around a standard postcard and is set out as shown in the tables below. Opposite Class: is the name of the class. In the Responsibilities: section a note is made of the tasks or responsibilities the class will be asked to support. The Collaborators: section covers classes that make use of or are used by this class.

The following are examples of CRC card usage from Appendix 1— Case Study #1—SimCo:

Class:	Loan
Responsibilities:	Manage the details of a loan
Collaborators:	Display, CompanyDetails, CashAccount

Class:	CashAccount
Responsibilities:	Manage the cash for the company
Collaborators:	Loan, CompanyDetails, Machine, Display

All of the information should fit on a single CRC card. If this is not the case, it is generally because the class is overly complex and should be divided into less complex classes.

A useful side effect of using CRC cards is in resolving deadlocks during the analysis phase. A group of people can each take a CRC card and role-play each class's responsibility within the system, resolving the interactions that take place between classes. At this point in the process, the CRC cards are used as memory aids. That is to say, the CRC cards are used to document the existence of a class and no more.

Caller	Method	Called	Result	Use Case #
:User	*requestLoan()*	**:Display**	Select loan option	1
:User	*PurchaseMachine()*	**:Display**	Select new machine option	2
:User	*nextTurn()*	**:Display**	Select next turn	3
:User	*displayDetails()*	**:Display**	Select display details option	5

Table 2-1   *Interaction :User*

Scripts (Non-UML)

Scripts are used to show all possible interactions between classes in preparation for other documents. Scripts are broken into tables and are written so that each table shows the interactions that take place between two classes. Table 2-1 shows how the **:User** interacts with other classes in the application.

Analysis Documents: Dynamic Aspects of Classes

The documents that are used to show the dynamic aspects of classes are statechart diagrams. The dynamic aspects of classes show how an object of a class responds to stimuli of the course of its lifetime.

Statechart Diagrams

A statechart diagram is used to document how an object responds internally to various methods. The notation used by statechart diagrams is shown next.

Start and Stopping a Statechart:

start   stop

State Symbols   Here's a simple state symbol:

State Symbol with Actions

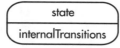 list of internal actions or activities that are performed while the object is in this state

Here's a state symbol example:

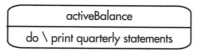

Simple Transition   A simple transition shows the relationship between two states. For the transition to occur, the event labeling the transition needs to have occurred. The notation for the transition event is

<event name> (parameter list) [guard condition] / action

For example, debit (amount : double) [balance < -10000] / finish, as shown here:

An example of a statechart diagram, taken from Case Study #1—SimCo, is shown in Figure 2-2.

The **CashAccount** class defines five basic operations:

CashAccount
CashAccount(void) : CashAccount setBalance (double) : void credit (double) : void debit (double) : void balance (void) : double

A **:CashAccount** object starts with a balance of zero. The statechart diagram shown in Figure 2-2 documents the state changes that are expected to take place for the life span of any **:CashAccount** object.

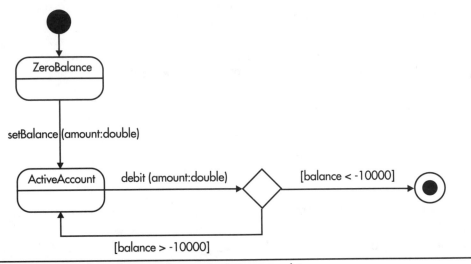

Figure 2-2   *A statechart diagram for a* **_:CashAccount_** *object*

Additional useful notation allows there to be separate branches or threads of execution. The notation for this is

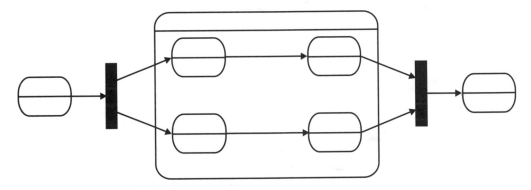

Analysis Documents: Static Aspects of the System

The documents in this section provide information about the system, showing how the classes interact. Class relationship diagrams are used to document the relationships between the classes. Collaboration diagrams show the interactions between objects of a system.

Class Relationship Diagrams

Having discovered and documented the classes of the system using CRC cards and class diagrams, the next step is to document the many relationships that exist between the classes. The class diagrams that are used show the following:

▶ **Simple association**   Shows the typical association

▶ **Directed association**   Shows one-sided relationships

▶ **Association class**   Shows a class that is derived from an association

▶ **N-ary association**   Shows associations between more than two classes

▶ **Aggregate association**   Shows a class as an aggregate of other classes

▶ **Composite association**   Shows a class as being composed of other classes

▶ **Inheritance**   Shows classes that are inherited/derived from other classes

All association diagrams share a common notation; inheritance diagram notation will be covered in the "Inheritance" section later in this chapter. The association notation is explained here:

▶ Qualifiers are placed at either end of the association line and are used to indicate the role played by each class in the association. A qualifier is shown as a small rectangle placed between the class and the end of the association line. For an example, a company can have many employees. If the qualifier is employee-number, the relationship becomes exactly one.

▶ Multiplicity is used to show the complexity of the relationship, such as 1-to-0..1, 1 to 1, 1-to-many or any other combination.

▶ Association name is the name given to the association, so that it may be referenced by name.

▶ Navigation arrowheads are used to show the direction of the association. The default is that neither end is labeled.

Simple Association   The first of the association diagrams is used to document how classes are connected to allow them to interact and perform their roles within the system. Using the bus route example described earlier in this chapter, here is a fully documented diagram.

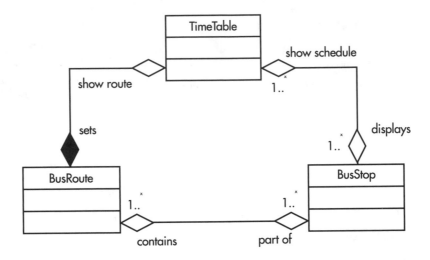

Directed Association   This is a unidirectional relationship between objects. Only the source of the directed association (client user) knows about the target (the server). The target of the relation can receive messages without knowing their source. In the example shown next, a **:Polygon** object knows about **:Point** objects, but not the other way around.

Association Class   This is a model element that has both association and class properties. An association class can be seen as an association that also has class properties or as a class that also has association properties.

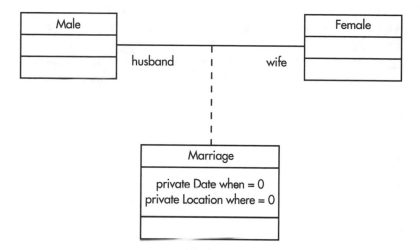

N-ary Association   This is an association that exists between three or more classes. Each instance of the association is an n-tuple of values from the respective classes.

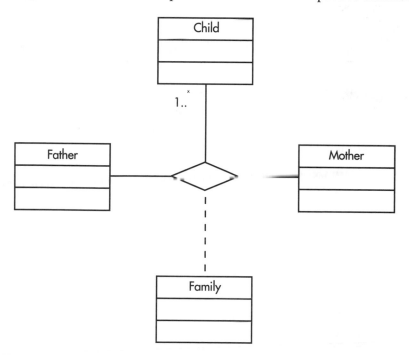

Aggregate Association A special form of association that specifies that one class contains references to the other class. This association is known as a whole/part relationship between the aggregate (whole) and a component (part). This form of association allows a class to share its component parts with other classes. The problem domain example from the section "The Cabinetmaker's View of the Table," earlier in this chapter, is shown again here:

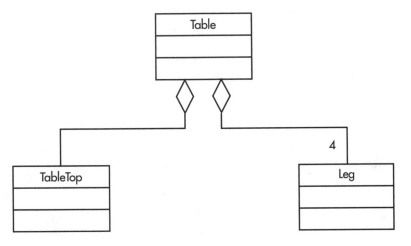

Composite Association Composition is a form of aggregation association with strong ownership. Composition is a form of aggregation association in which the lifetime of the whole determines that of its parts. The problem domain example from "The Owner's View of the Table" is shown again here:

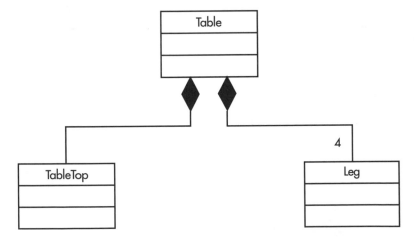

There are two possible UML notation alternatives to the above diagram described in the UML v1.4 specification. The first is a class diagram, and the second a graphical class diagram:

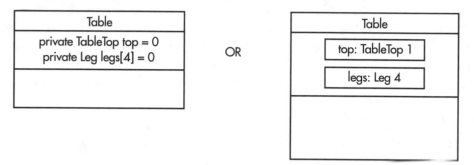

Inheritance   As described in Chapter 1, inheritance has two forms. The first derived inheritance concerns deriving child classes from a single parent class. The second abstracted inheritance is concerned with creating the parent class to bring together common attributes and methods. The notation is shown again here:

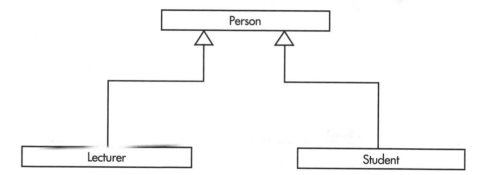

An alternative UML notation exists and is shown here:

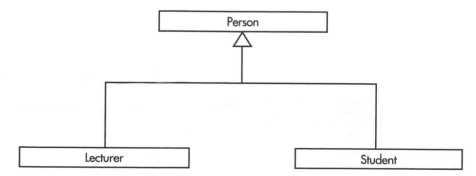

Collaboration Diagram

A collaboration diagram is used to show the objects, as well as their relationships given a particular situation. For example, there will be a collaboration diagram for each use case diagram. A collaboration diagram can exist on two levels.

The first level is called the *instance level*. It shows objects, the links between them, and the methods used to execute the required collaboration. An example is shown in Figure 2-3.

The following are characteristics of an instance-level collaboration diagram:

▶ Objects are stick figures or boxes.

▶ Objects are typically labeled like this:
  <instance_name>:<class_name>.

▶ A '/role' is allowed, as it is just specifying the class.

▶ Methods are labeled 1:<method_name> (arguments).

▶ Method repetition can be achieved by 1.1*[i:=1..n]:<method> (i).

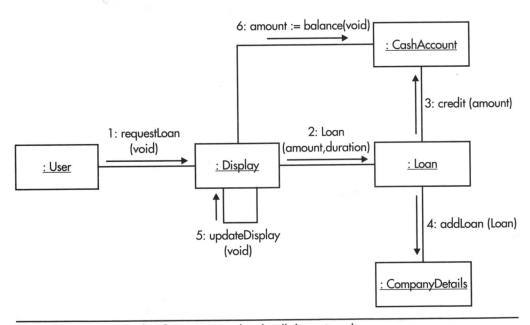

Figure 2-3   *An example of an instance-level collaboration diagram*

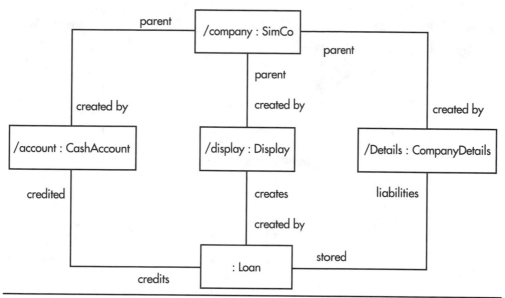

Figure 2-4   *An example of a specification-level collaboration diagram*

The second level is called the *specification level*. It shows the roles played by the objects and the associations that exist between them. An example is shown in Figure 2-4.

With specification-level notation:

▶ Each line is an association and should be labeled as such.

▶ Each box contains a role played by a specific class, noted as /role:class.

Analysis Documents: Dynamic Aspects of the System

The documents discussed in this section are activity diagrams and sequence scripts and diagrams.

Activity Diagrams

In contrast to the statechart diagrams that were used to document the internal states of an object, activity diagrams are used to document the states of the system. An activity diagram, as shown in Figure 2-5, shows the steps involved in completing a task.

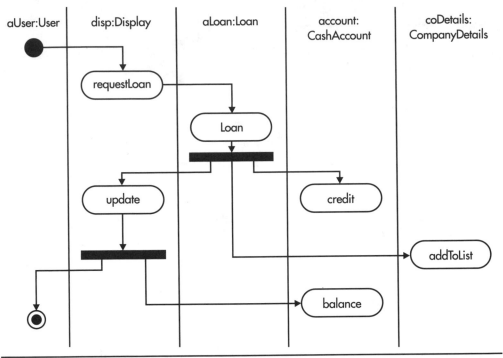

Figure 2-5 *An example of an activity diagram*

The notation used is described here:

▶ The diagram is divided into logical columns or "swim lanes." Each swim lane denotes some responsibility for carrying out the actions assigned to it. The actions may be carried out by one object or a group of objects working together as a unit.

▶ A filled-in circle indicates the start of overall activity.

▶ An action state represents an executable computation that cannot be interrupted. It appears on an activity diagram as a "lozenge" that contains the name of the action.

▶ A transition represents a change from one action state or activity state to another. A transition appears on an activity diagram as a solid line with an open arrowhead pointing to the new action state or activity state for the given object.

▶ A branch shows decision points at which one path may become two or more new paths. Decisions are shown as diamonds. On each of the outputs is a guard condition, shown in square brackets, indicating the criterion that would lead the application to follow that path.

▶ A filled-in circle contained within a larger open circle indicates the end of overall activity.

Additional notation is explained here:

▶ Thick synchronization bars show how flows of control split (fork) and come together (join), as shown here:

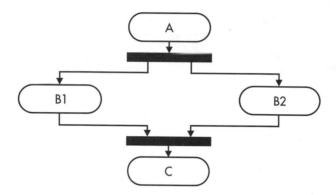

▶ Signals can be used to allow resource sharing. If a resource is in use, a process can wait until it is signalled that the resource has become free, as shown in Figure 2-6. Signals are sent from a symbol shown as a convex pentagon that looks like a rectangle with a triangular point on one side. The signals are received by a symbol shown as a concave pentagon that looks like a rectangle with a triangular notch in its side.

Sequence Scripts/Diagrams

Sequence scripts and diagrams are used to show object interactions arranged in the order in which they occur. In particular, they show the objects participating in the interaction and the sequence of messages exchanged between them.

Sequence Script Notation   Sequence scripts are an alternative to using sequence diagrams. When documenting the state aspects of a system, scripts were generated to ensure every interaction between classes was recorded. Sequence scripts grow that notation and are used to show sequence diagrams in table form.

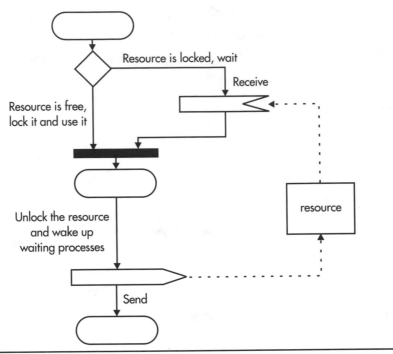

Figure 2-6   *Signals used to allow resource sharing*

Static scripts are shown as:

Source	Method	Destination

Dynamic sequence scripts are shown as:

Ref #	Source	Method	Destination	Next Ref #

The 'Ref #' and 'Next Ref #' fields show the flow of the system. The sequence of actions is indicated by a trailing character, such as 1 to 1.a to 1.b to 1.c., shown here in table form as:

Ref #	Source	Method	Destination	Next Ref #
1				1.a
1.a				1.b
1.b				1.c

To show the internal behavior of a process, put it in curly braces, such as {return void} or {performAction}:

Ref #	Source	Method	Destination	Next Ref #
1	User	Save	Display	1.a
1.a	Display	saveData (data:datatype)	Database	1.b
1.b	Database	{doSomething}	Database	1.c
1.c	Database	{return}	Display	1.d
1.d	Display	{end}	-	-

The flow of the system is never as simple as "step *a* followed by step *b* followed by step *c*," so additional notation is used in these instances.

The first addition includes user-directed decision-making. The user is prompted to provide some input:

2.a	Display	"enter amount"	User	2.b

Every possible input shares the same 'Ref #'; in the example, it would be '2.b'. However, each input causes a different outcome, so the reference numbering is modified to reflect this:

2.b		<amount <= 0>	2.1
2.b		<amount > 0>	2.2

The second addition allows for application directed decision making—for example, a method is called to return a specific object from a database:

3.a	User	Find (void)	Database	3.b
3.b		[!found]		3.1
3.b		[found]		3.2

In summary, the notation used is:

{}	Used to describe the internal behavior of the process at this point
""	Prompt the user to make a decision, such as "Accept" or "Reject" changes
<>	Indicates a user-directed branch based on the response to a user prompt
[]	Indicates an application-directed branch based on the return result of an operation

This example sequence script is taken from Case Study #1—SimCo. The sequence diagram is seen in Figure 2-7.

Ref #	Source	Method	Destination	Next Ref #
1	User	RequestLoan	Display	1.a
1.a	Display	"Enter amount"	User	1.b
1.b		<amount <= 0>		1.1
1.b		<amount > 0>		1.2
1.1	Display	{end}		
1.2	Display	"Enter duration of loan"	User	1.2.a
1.2.a		<duration <= 0>		1.2.1
1.2.a		<duration > 0>		1.2.2
1.2.1	Display	{end}		
1.2.2	Display	"Confirm Loan"	User	1.2.2.a
1.2.2.a		<Reject>		1.2.2.1
1.2.2.a		<Accept>		1.2.2.2
1.2.2.1	Display	{end}		
1.2.2.2	Display	Loan (amount, duration)	Loan	1.2.2.2.a
1.2.2.2.a	Loan	Credit (amount)	CashAccount	1.2.2.2.b
1.2.2.2.b	CashAccount	{return}	Loan	1.2.2.2.c
1.2.2.2.c	Loan	AddLoan (self)	Company Details	1.2.2.2.d
1.2.2.2.d	Company Details	{return}	Loan	1.2.2.2.e
1.2.2.2.e	Loan	{return}	Display	1.2.2.2.f
1.2.2.2.f	Display	UpdateCash (void)	Display	1.2.2.2.g
1.2.2.2.g	Display	balance (void)	CashAccount	1.2.2.2.h
1.2.2.2.h	CashAccount	{return}	Display	1.2.2.2.i
1.2.2.2.i	Display	{end}		

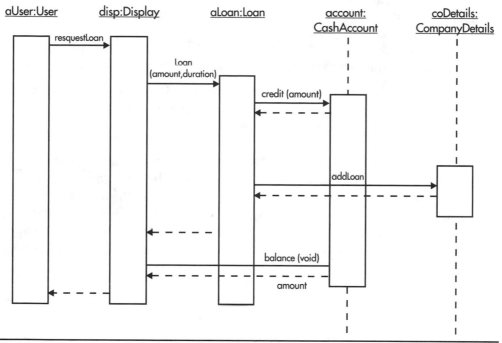

Figure 2-7   *The sequence diagram for the SimCo example*

Sequence Diagrams   The notation used consists of four main elements:

▶ The objects involved in the given interaction are arranged horizontally across the top of the diagram.

▶ Each object has an associated lifeline. If the object is in existence prior to the interactions shown on this diagram, its lifeline is a dashed vertical line. As soon as the object becomes an active part of the interactions, its lifeline changes to a tall thin rectangle.

▶ If an object is created within an interaction, its lifeline starts at the point of creation—that is, it does not start at the top of the diagram. Similarly if an object is destroyed within an interaction, its tall thin lifeline has a large X through it at the point of its destruction.

▶ The messages that pass between pairs of objects are connected to the edges of the relevant active rectangles. These messages are arranged from top to bottom according to when they are sent over time, with the first message at the top of the diagram and the last at the bottom. The outgoing messages are drawn with solid lines, with their return shown as dashed lines.

Additional notation can be added to show the following:

► **Self referencing**   Shown as a small attached rectangle with curved arrows leaving and returning to the same lifeline.

► **Branching**   Shown as several lines leaving from the same point on a lifeline, each with a guard condition shown in square brackets that determine which path is chosen.

The diagram shown in Figure 2-7 shows a user requesting a loan through a **disp:Display** object. A conversation (not shown) ensues between the user and the **disp:Display** object regarding the amount and duration of the loan. When the details have been confirmed, a **:Loan** object is created. This **:Loan** object credits the **account:CashAccount** object and gets itself added to the list of loans held by the **coDetails:CompanyDetails** object. Control is then returned to the **disp:Display** object, which asks for an update of the balance from the **account:CashAccount** object and then returns control to the user for the next interaction.

Summary

This chapter has offered a comprehensive guide to the UML 1.4 notation that is required to perform the analysis of a system. Not every aspect of every notation has been documented, but enough has been documented to make good use of the notation.

Armed with the knowledge and understanding of the notation, the next few chapters on various design criteria can be explored.

Design

OBJECTIVES

► Learn the basics of good design

► Understand why measuring design is important

► Learn how to measure design

► Highlight classic bad design and provide alternatives

► Introduce some advanced design constructs

# CHAPTER 3

Design Do's

IN THIS CHAPTER:

Learn About Design Abstraction and Interfaces

Learn the Difference Between Templates and Inheritance

Learn About Design Principles

Understand the Metrics of Good Design

Understand How Implementation Decisions Can Affect the Design

Understand the Different Types of Copy Constructor

The task for any software designer is to create a design that is functional and easy to maintain. With that design in hand, the implementation team must carry it through the initial development phase and into the final application, without making any modifications.

When compromises in that initial design begin—whether or not they are intended to fix a problem or just enhance the product—each modification is a cancer. As with most cancers, if they are caught early enough, the patient, or in this case the design, can be saved. Surgery is not radical; it just requires that each modification maintain the purity of the original design.

If left unchecked, a cancer in the design becomes inoperable. Eventually, it takes so much effort to make even the simplest of changes that everybody thinks that a new design is necessary. The ideal solution is to avoid the start of the cancer in the first place.

Abstract Class

An abstract class is a design construct that allows designers to create a class that can never have instances created. Under normal circumstances, every class can have instances. To prevent this from occurring, the difference between a normal class and an abstract class is defined in their implementation. An abstract class has some methods that do not have a corresponding implementation: these are known as abstract methods. This means that the definition for the abstract class is incomplete, and therefore can never have instances created.

There are several reasons for using an abstract class. One reason is that it helps to create a logical inheritance hierarchy, by occupying a place in the hierarchy that does not have objects generated from it, but nonetheless needs to be described. An example of an abstract class as part of an inheritance hierarchy is shown next. Although an object is never created from, for example, the **Shape** class, it still has a place in the hierarchy. The UML 1.4 notation for an abstract class has the name in italics, and the abstract methods are also shown in italics.

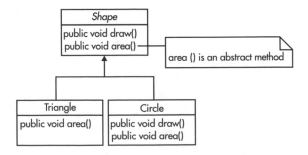

The advantage of having a placeholder class in the inheritance hierarchy is when using collections. Instead of having a collection of **:Triangle** objects and another collection of **:Circle** objects. The design can include a collection of **:Shape** objects that can include both **:Triangle** objects and **:Circle** objects. This is advantageous, as it requires no additional changes to the source code if the collection is now to include objects created from the **Square** class, another class derived from the **Shape** class.

Another reason is explored in the next section on the Application Programming Interface. To ensure that a class never has objects created from it, most object-oriented languages provide keywords to indicate that the class is abstract.

In Java, an abstract class is defined by using the keyword 'abstract' as shown here:

```
public abstract class <classname>
{
    public abstract <returnType> <methodName> (<arguments>);
}
```

In C++, a class is described as being abstract if any of its methods are declared as 'pure virtual'. A pure virtual method uses the pure specifier '= 0' as shown here:

```
public class <className>
{
    virtual <returnType> <methodName> (<arguments>) = 0;
}
```

Application Programming Interface

In Chapter 1, when methods were first introduced, they were described collectively as the interface of the class. With normal inheritance, not only does the interface of the class get inherited, but also the methods that implement them. An application-programming interface (API) is defined here as a class that only allows its interface to be inherited. An API class is typically used to bring together in one class the interfaces of several other classes. It is important to note that the API class only contains the interface and should never have objects created directly from it. The API class is therefore an abstract class. The methods that are declared as abstract are inherited as interface-only methods by derived classes.

To associate the API class with the other classes, they must form a hierarchy with the API class forming the 'root' class. However, unlike an inheritance hierarchy, the subclasses do not inherit attributes and methods. Instead, they promise to provide an implementation of the methods contained in the interface. All of the interface methods are defined in the API class, with each subclass implementing the methods in its own terms.

Without the API Construct

Prior to the API construct, if an object **_X:_** wanted to interact with objects of different classes that provided the same interface, the object **_X:_** would be required to have a specific reference to each of the differing classes.

In this example, an air traffic controller for a small airport would know details about most of the aircraft that would use the airport:

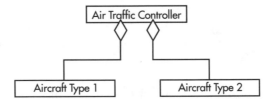

In fact, he may be able to recognize each of them, know the pilot, and refer to each of them by name. The Air Traffic controller knows that Eric has an aircraft with a call-sign of "XY123Z", and he wants to know his current altitude:

```
Eric = new TwinJet (callsign = "XY123Z");
altitude = Eric.altitude ();
```

Obviously, the more aircraft types that want to use the airport, the more difficult the task of air traffic control becomes. It is very unlikely that the air traffic controller knows every type of aircraft, so what happens when a new type of aircraft arrives unannounced? Does the air traffic controller refuse to let it land just because he has never seen it before?

Why Use the API Construct?

What happens in the preceding example when the new aircraft arrives is that the air traffic controller assumes that the aircraft conforms to some basic criteria, it has a basic interface, and labels it 'plane', a default generic classification for an aircraft.

The air traffic controller would not be overly concerned if all aircraft were labeled 'plane', if it did not prevent them from doing their job. After all, the dot on the radar screen remains the same size, no matter what type of aircraft it really is. So 'plane' became the API class for all aircraft. As long as every type of aircraft had a response for every 'plane' interaction, the 'plane' API class would suffice.

Deriving the API Class

As mentioned at the beginning of this chapter, an API class is the 'root' of a hierarchy. The hierarchy for the aircraft is shown next. The different classes **AircraftType1** and **AircraftType2** inherit all of the attributes and methods defined in the class **AirTrafficControllerAircraft**.

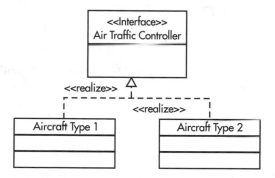

Using the API Class

The UML 1.4 notation for associating a class with the API class is shown next, where the hierarchy is replaced by a class to API class notation. Instead of showing the class **AircraftType1** as being derived from the class **AirTrafficControllerAircraft**, it is shown connected to a circle that represents the API class.

A usage diagram is shown next. This diagram shows the addition of the class **AirTrafficController**; this class uses the methods and attributes defined in the API class in its interactions with the derived classes.

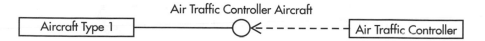

A 'jet plane' that equates to the class **AircraftType1** implements the interface described by 'plane' that equates to the class **AirTrafficControllerAircraft** and used by the air traffic controller. A fully annotated usage diagram is shown here:

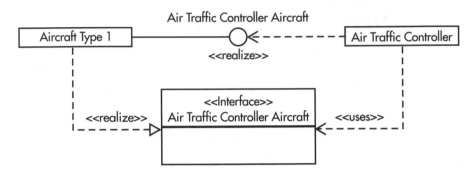

Notice that in every case the user, the Air Traffic Controller, is designed to interface with the Air Traffic Controller Aircraft and not individual aircraft types. This is to ensure that they do not stray from the agreed interface.

Java Native Interface

The API class can also be used if a user is to use native features of the system directly from Java. This is called a Java Native Interface (JNI). It allows the user to have access to the system using what appears to be Java, but is in fact implemented in a native language, such as C++. The Java interface class is compiled and then processed to produce a header file for use in the C++ program. The C++ classes can then be written to implement the required feature, compiled and then built into a shared library for use by the Java program.

This model fits perfectly with the API model, as the Java class provides the interface but does not provide the implementation hidden in the C++ library. It is important to note that the Java program does not have to be rebuilt should the implementation in the C++ library change. The program only needs to be rebuilt if the interface changes, as it would if any of the other Java classes were to change.

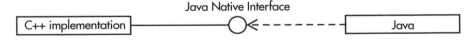

An example of how this is done is described in the following.

Dinner.java

```
..
public class Dinner
{
    static
    {
        System.loadLibrary("phil_java");
    }


..
    public native void StartUp();
}
```

Having created the Dinner.java file, the next step is to compile it by using 'javac'. 'javac' is the java compiler that is available with the java developer kit:

```
javac Dinner.java
```

Now that we have compiled the file called Dinner.class, the header file can be obtained by using 'javah'. 'javah' generates C language header files that describe the specified classes. These C files provide the information necessary to implementing the native methods:

```
javah -jni Dinner
```

The header file produced is shown next.

Dinner.h

```
/* DO NOT EDIT THIS FILE - it is machine generated */
#include <jni.h>
/* Header for class Dinner */

#ifndef _Included_Dinner
#define _Included_Dinner
#ifdef __cplusplus
extern "C" {
#endif
/* Inaccessible static: threadGroup */
/*
 * Class:     Dinner
```

```
 * Method:     StartUp
 * Signature: ()V
 */
JNIEXPORT void JNICALL Java_Dinner_StartUp
  (JNIEnv *, jobject);

#ifdef __cplusplus
}
#endif
#endif
```

The native code can now be written using the generated header file, an excerpt of which is shown next.

phils.cpp

```
# include "Dinner.h"
..
JNIEXPORT void JNICALL
Java_Dinner_StartUp( JNIEnv *env, jobject obj )
{
..
}
```

This native code should now be compiled and built into a shared library with the named explain that was originally specified in the Dinner.java file. In this example, the name of the shared library would be 'libphil_java.so' on Solaris and 'phil_java.dll' if Microsoft is used.

Templates

Templates are a mechanism for generating generic classes. A generic class defines a set of methods that operate on a data type that is specified when objects of that class are created. A generic class specifies the logic for handling an abstract data type.

A good example would be collection classes. The only thing that differentiates the collection classes are the objects they collect. A generic collection class would use the same methods as the other collection classes. However, the generic collection would be defined to collect objects of a type to be defined later. When an object is created from a generic class, the data type is specified. In C++, a term such as a generic class is known as a template.

The definition of a template collection class is the same as for a normal collection class, with a few exceptions:

▶ The object to be collected is defined by 'T'.

▶ The class definition is prefixed by 'template <class T>'; this is an instruction to the compiler.

The UML 1.4 notation for a template is shown next. A template class called **Set** is used to create another class called **Students** based on a data type class **Student**.

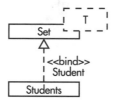

In C++ a template is created and given an object type to use, as follows:

```
RealCollection    < collectStudents>        myCollectionOfStudents;
```

When to Use a Template Instead of Inheritance?

Making the choice between using a template rather than using inheritance is illustrated by these two examples:

▶ **Example 1**   There is a need to provide a collection of different students attending school. However, each collection will only contain students from a specific course subject, such as a collection of physics students and another for history students. The only methods to be supported are those of creation, destruction, addition, and deletion.

▶ **Example 2**   There is a need to provide a collection of the different students attending school. However, unlike the previous example, the collections will be designed to contain the students from the various distinct age groups, such as 11-12, 12-13, 13-14, and so on The methods to be supported are those of creation, deletion and the subjects being taught, and how they are being taught.

These two examples sound fairly similar in their descriptions, but they result in two totally different designs.

The relationship between the behavior of the classes and the type of the object being stored in the collection is related, such as if methods of the implementation in the collection require a different implementation for each of the classes. For example, in the first example, the collection has methods that are not affected by the different classes; however, in the second example, at least one of the methods is different: in particular, how the classes are taught.

So for the first example, the design would be implemented as a collection based on templates, while the second design is implemented using inheritance.

Sample Template Implemented in C++

The following are the two files required for any class, a header file and the implementation file. They show how a 'set' can be written as a template.

Class Header

```
#ifndef SET_H_
#define SET_H_

enum Status { OK, FULL, EMPTY, ERROR };

template <class T>
class Set
{
    public:
        // Constructor
        Set ( int numElements );

        // Destructor
        ~Set ();

        // Container Methods
        Status add ( T *value );
        Status read ( int index, T ** value );
        Status removeIndex ( int index );
        Status removeValue ( T *value );
        Status resizeSet ( int newSize );

        // Information methods
        Status getTotalSize ( int *size );
        Status getCurrentSize ( int *size );

    private:
        // The container
```

```
        T    **base_;

        int    totalSize_;
        int    currentSize_;
};
#endif // SET_H_
```

Class Implementation

```
#include <stdlib.h>
#include "Set.h"

template <class T>
Set<T>::Set ( int numElements )
{
    // create a container whose size is given as a parameter
    // to this method
}

template <class T>
Set<T>::~Set ()
{
    // delete the elements created by the constructor
}

template <class T>
Status Set<T>::add ( T *value )
{
    // check that there is still space in the container for the new item
    // if there is enough room, add the value
    // if there is not enough room, call resetSet to increase the size
}

template <class T>
Status Set<T>::read ( int index, T **value )
{
    // check that the required index is within the current range
    // if the index is within range, return the value
}

template <class T>
Status Set<T>::removeIndex ( int index )
{
    // check that the required index is within the current range
    // if the index is within range, delete the value
    // then reset the container to eliminate the deleted value
```

```
}

template <class T>
Status Set<T>::removeValue ( T *value )
{
    // try to determine if the value is in the set
    // if the value is not in the set return an error
    // if the value is in the set, delete the value
    // then reset the container to eliminate the deleted value
}

template <class T>
Status Set<T>::resizeSet ( int newSize )
{
    // increase the size of the allocated space
}

template <class T>
Status Set<T>::getTotalSize ( int *size )
{
    *size = totalSize_;
    return OK;
}

template <class T>
Status Set<T>::getCurrentSize ( int *size )
{
    *size = currentSize_;
    return OK;
}
```

Create a Set of Integers

```
Set <int>     setOfInt;
```

Good Design—Principles and Metrics

The subject of design principles and metrics is based on several works by Robert C. Martin from ObjectMentor, Dr. Linda Rosenburg from NASA's Software Assurance Technology Center, and the results of a study[1].

---

[1] References: Robert C Martin, Design principles and design patterns, http:www.objectmentor.com; Dr. Linda Rosenburg, Software Quality Metrics for Object Oriented System Environments, satc.gsfc.nasa.gov

Identifying the Causes of Design Cancer

This section discusses the different aspects of design cancer. The four recognized symptoms of design cancer are described as follows: rigidity, fragility, immobility, and viscosity.

► **Rigidity**   The term rigidity is applied to software that has a tendency to be difficult to modify, including simple modifications. The problem is the result of the modules being too closely related, such that any change causes a ripple of other changes in the dependent modules.

► **Fragility**   A closely related symptom to rigidity is fragility. Fragility is a term that is applied to software with the tendency to break in many places every time it is changed. Another aspect of fragility is that the application can break in areas that do not appear to have any conceptual relationship with the area that was changed.

► **Immobility**   The term immobility relates to an application's inability to reuse classes from other projects or from parts of the same project. The problem arises from engineers trying to save time and extra work. An engineer discovers that there is a class that is similar in functionality and abilities to one that they now require. However, as often happens, the original class also has more functionality than is required, or does things slightly differently. After some investigation the engineer discovers that trying to separate the required functionality from the existing class requires so much work that the work is not a viable proposition. The unfortunate result is that the class is simply rewritten instead of reused.

► **Viscosity**   Viscosity is a term used to describe the difficulty or ease with which design-preserving modifications can be made. If it is more difficult to implement methods that preserve the design, than it is to implement hacks, then the viscosity of the design is high. It is easy to do the wrong thing, but hard to do the right thing.

Any of these four symptoms is a telltale sign of poor design architecture, and any application that exhibits them is suffering from a design that is dying from cancer. The big question is, What causes the rot to take place?

Changing Requirements

As every designer and developer will appreciate, the normal causes for design cancer stem from new requirements that the initial design did not anticipate. Another problem occurs when new developers make changes, developers who were not in the original development team. These new developers are not appreciative of the original design, so their modifications may be violating the original design without even knowing it. So if the design is failing under the pressure of changing requirements, the problem is with the design. Somehow a way needs to be found to make the design resilient to change and protect it from design cancer.

Principles of Object-Oriented Class Design

Whenever the dependencies that exist between classes change, these changes are directly or indirectly responsible for each of the four symptoms mentioned above. To help manage the effects of change to the class dependencies, here are a few basic design principles that prove useful. The principles discussed here are the Open Closed Principle, the Liskov Substitution Principle, and the Dependency Inversion Principle. These and other principles are covered in depth in works by Robert C.Martin.

Open Closed Principle

The definition of the open closed principle (OCP) states that a module should be open for extension but closed for modification.

Of all the principles of object-oriented design, this is the most important. Put simply, classes should be written so that they can be extended, so that functionality can be changed, without the need to change the source code of the classes.

There are several techniques for achieving open closed principle (OCP); all of these techniques are based upon abstraction. Several of these techniques are described in this section.

Dynamic Polymorphism   The next example shows that the LogOn function must be changed whenever new functionality is required to support a new modem. To make matters worse, each new type of modem will cause a modification to be made to the Modem::Type enumeration, forcing the existing code, which has a dependency on the enumeration to be recompiled.

```
Listing for LogOn (which must be modified to be extended)
struct Modem
{
    enum Type {hayes, courrier, newModem) type;
};
struct Hayes
{
    Modem::Type type;
    // Hayes related stuff
```

```
};
struct Courrier
{
    Modem::Type type;
    // Courrier related stuff
};
struct NewModem
{
    Modem::Type type;
    // NewModem related stuff
};
void LogOn(Modem& m, string& pno, string& user, string& pw)
{
    if (m.type == Modem::hayes)
    {
        DialHayes((Hayes&)m, pno);
    }
    else if (m.type == Modem::courrier)
    {
        DialCourrier((Courrier&)m, pno);
    }
    else if (m.type == Modem::newModem)
    {
        DialNewModem ((NewModem&)m, pno)
    }
}
```

As this simple example code shows, the problem comes from the use of if/else or switch statements. The problem with these statements is that whenever a modification needs to be made, an if/else or switch statement will need to be updated to choose the correct function to use. When an addition needs to be made, every selection statement must be found and modified.

A real problem exists if a programmer tries to be clever and make assumptions to optimize the code. In this next example, the function is exactly the same for Hayes and Courrier modems, so an optimization may look like this:

```
if (modem.type == Modem::newModem)
{
    SendNewModem((NewModem&)modem, c);
}
else
{
    SendHayes((Hayes&)modem, c);
}
```

If the problems with the if/else or switch statements were not enough to deal with, this optimization will lead to all kinds of complications if the Hayes and Courrier modems ever diverge in their 'Send' functions. Developers will spend a considerable amount of time trying to determine why the application is not working correctly. They will be laboring under the assumption that the correct function is being called, never realizing that the code had been 'optimized'.

An example of how to implement the OCP is shown in Figure 3-1, using the interface construct. The LogOn function now depends upon the Modem interface. As such, additional modems can be added without causing the LogOn function to change. This example now shows a class can be extended, with new modems, without requiring modification.

The code for the new Modem interface class is shown here:

```
LogOn has been closed for modification
class Modem
{
    public:
        virtual void Dial(const string& pno) = 0;
        virtual void Send(char) = 0;
        virtual char Recv() = 0;
        virtual void Hangup() = 0;
};
void LogOn(Modem& m, string& pno, string& user, string& pw)
{
    m.Dial(pno);
    // etc.
}
```

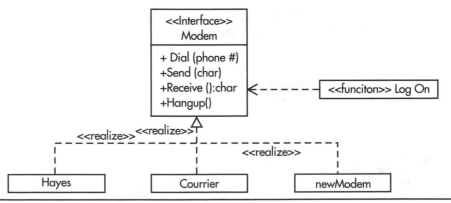

Figure 3-1   *Using an interface to implement OCP*

Static Polymorphism   Templates are another technique for conforming to the OCP. The following code shows how this is done. The LogOn function can be extended with many different types of modems without requiring modification.

```
LogOn is closed for modification through static polymorphism
template <typename MODEM>
void LogOn(MODEM& m, string& pno, string& user, string& pw)
{
    m.Dial(pno);
    // you get the idea.
}
```

Summary of the OCP: Even if the OCP cannot be fully achieved, even partial OCP compliance can make dramatic improvements in the structure of an application.

Dependency Inversion Principle

The definition for the dependency inversion principle (DIP) states that a design should depend upon Abstractions; do not depend upon concretions. Abstractions define the interfaces of the system; an example of an abstraction is the application programming interface discussed earlier in this chapter.

Depending upon Abstractions   The implication of this principle is quite simple. Every dependency in the design should target an interface, or an abstract class as shown in Figure 3-1, where every method is referred to the interface class Modem and not directly to a specific modem class.

No dependency should target a concrete class. This may sound like a draconian restriction, but the principle should be adhered to as much as possible. A reason for this is that the interfaces are agreed upon early in the design process and are therefore less likely to change than the concrete classes.

Also, as has been discussed in the description of OCP, the design is very flexible around the interface and abstraction classes.

Mitigating Forces   A driving force behind the DIP is trying to prevent dependencies upon volatile classes. An assumption is made by the DIP that anything concrete is volatile. While the design and application are in the early stages, this assumption is frequently true. There are of course exceptions to any assumptions. For example, the header files that are apart of the standard C library are very concrete, but they are not at all volatile. So having dependencies on these header files are not harmful. A similar exception can be made for classes and packages of classes from other projects or

> Unicode is a 16-bit character encoding and has been designed to support aspects such as the display and other aspects of the written texts of the diverse languages of the modern world.

external companies, since they are not likely to change; they are not likely to inject volatility into your design.

However, just because something is deemed non-volatile is no substitute for not using an abstract interface. For example, an application that uses standard strings will face problems if it forces you to use Unicode characters.

Object Creation A problem with this approach is when an application is required to create instances, instances can only be created from concrete classes. So, to create an instance depends upon having a concrete class, something the design was trying to avoid.

As the creation of instances can happen anywhere in the architecture of the design, it seems that it is almost impossible to escape from concrete classes and the dependencies on them. However, there is a solution to this problem: implement a 'factory'. This solution is too advanced for this book and will left as further reading.

Design Metrics

Discussed here are six metrics for validating the quality of a design. Each metric relates specifically to object-oriented systems. Shown in Table 3-1, each metric is presented with the object-oriented construct applicable.

Metric Name	Description	Object-Oriented Construct
WMC	Weighted methods per class	Class/Method
RFC	Response for a class	Class/Message
LCOM	Lack of cohesion of methods	Class/Cohesion
CBO	Coupling between objects	Coupling
DIT	Depth of inheritance tree	Inheritance
NOC	Number of children	Inheritance

Table 3-1 *Six Design Metrics for Validating Quality*

Metric Evaluation Criteria

The difference between metrics for the traditional design approaches deals with the design structure and/or data structure independently. The metrics for object-oriented design must deal with objects, where each object is a combination of attributes and methods. The following areas should therefore be evaluated by object-oriented metric criteria:

- ▶ **Efficiency** Has the design been implemented efficiently?
- ▶ **Complexity** How complex is the architecture within the design?
- ▶ **Clarity/Usability** Is the design easy to understand and is it easy to use?
- ▶ **Reusable/Specific** Is the design reusable or is it application specific?
- ▶ **Testable/Maintainable** Does the design enhance testing?

As with any metric, it must be effective in measuring one of these areas. Each metric will be presented with a description, an example of its use, and an interpretation of the results obtained. The metrics measure the principal structures that, if they are improperly designed, negatively affect the design and code quality attributes.

Example Design

Object-oriented design requires a different way of thinking. The example shown in Figure 3-2 was developed in order to demonstrate the concepts of object-orientation and how the suggested metrics could be applied. Shape, the set of all geometric figures, is a superclass.

Shape has a method to draw the specified figures and a method that calculates the perimeter. From this, we can develop two subclasses, triangle and quadrilateral; these become classes since they have children objects that are subclasses.

A triangle has three sides, three angles, a base, and a height. A triangle also has a constraint when it is created that all of the angles add up to 180 degrees. A new method is added to calculate its area: the calculation is ½ × (base × height). The triangle class has three subclasses: scalene, equilateral, and isosceles.

A scalene triangle introduces no new attributes or methods. However, it does add a constraint to the creation method that no two sides are equal.

An isosceles triangle introduces no new attributes or methods. However, it does add a constraint to the creation method that two sides are set to the same value. Base is set to ½ × remaining side. Height is set to square root of [$(\text{side } 1)^2 - (\text{base})^2$].

An equilateral triangle introduces no new attributes or methods. However, it does add a constraint to the creation method that all sides are equal and that the angles all equal 60 degrees. Base is set to ½ × one side. Height is set to (sin (60) × one side).

A quadrilateral has four sides and four angles. A quadrilateral also has a constraint when it is created that all of the angles add up to 360 degrees. The quadrilateral class has two subclasses: trapezium and rectangle.

A trapezium introduces one new attribute, 'height', which it uses in a new method, 'area'. The method 'area' uses the lengths of the parallel sides multiplied by the height. The creation method has a constraint that two sides are parallel.

A rectangle introduces no new attributes or methods. The creation method has a constraint that sides 1 and 3 are equal, sides 2 and 4 are equal, and finally all of the angles are equal (90 degrees). The method 'area' is modified so that sides 1 and 2 are multiplied together. The rectangle class has a single subclass, square.

A square introduces no new attributes or methods. The creation method has a constraint that all sides are equal. The method 'area' is modified so that side 1 is multiplied with itself.

A full hierarchy of classes is shown in Figure 3-2.

Class Based Metrics

The first three metrics described next measure the complexity of a class using the classes' methods: messages and cohesion.

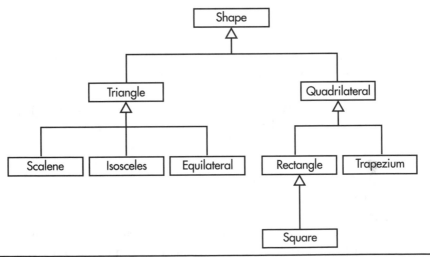

Figure 3-2   *A shape inheritance hierarchy*

Weighted Methods per Class   Two possible interpretations for the weighted methods per class (WMC) metric exist. The first is called method complexity and will not be discussed in this book. The second is a count of the methods implemented within a class. The table shown next gleans information from the hierarchy shown in Figure 3-2 and shows the respective WMC values for each class.

Shape	2
Triangle	2
Scalene triangle	1
Equilateral triangle	1
Isosceles triangle	1
Quadrilateral	1
Trapezium	2
Rectangle	2
Square	2

Empirical evidence leads to the conclusion that the larger the number of methods there are in a class, the greater its impact. The impact of a class with a large number of methods ranges from the amount of testing required to the increased probability of it being application specific, limiting the possibility of reuse.

This metric measures usability and reusability.

Response for a Class   The response for a class (RFC) metric is simply the number of methods that can be invoked in response to a message sent to an object of the class. This includes all methods accessible within the class hierarchy. The table shown next again uses information from the hierarchy shown in Figure 3-2 and shows the respective RFC values for each class.

Shape	2
Triangle	4
Scalene triangle	5
Equilateral triangle	5
Isosceles triangle	5
Quadrilateral	3
Trapezium	5
Rectangle	5
Square	7

The larger the number of methods that can be invoked from a class through messages, the greater the complexity of the class. If a large number of methods can be invoked in response to a message, the testing and debugging of the class becomes complicated since it requires a greater level of understanding on the part of the tester.

This metric evaluates system design as well as usability and testability.

Lack of Cohesion of Methods   The lack of cohesion of methods (LCOM) metric measures the degree of similarity of methods by instance variable or attributes. Any measure of separateness of methods helps identify flaws in the design of classes.

Cohesion is the degree to which methods within a class are related to one another and work together to provide well-rounded behavior. Cohesion refers to the internal consistency within the parts of the design. Cohesion is centered on data that is encapsulated within an object and on how methods interact with data to provide well-bounded behavior. The degree of similarity of methods is a major aspect of object class cohesiveness. The objective is to achieve maximum cohesion. Programs that are adaptable and reusable are low in coupling and high in cohesion.

Effective object-oriented designs maximize cohesion since it promotes encapsulation. This metric investigates cohesion.

There are at least two different ways of measuring cohesion:

▶ Calculate for each data field in a class what percentage of the methods use that data field. Average the percentages, then subtract from 100 percent. Lower percentages mean greater cohesion of data and methods in the class.

▶ Methods are more similar if they operate on the same attributes. Count the number of disjoint sets produced from the intersection of the sets of attributes used by the methods.

The following table also gleans information from the hierarchy shown in Figure 3-2 and shows the respective LCOM values for each class.

Shape	100%
Triangle	37.5%
Scalene triangle	37.5%
Equilateral triangle	37.5%
Isosceles triangle	37.5%
Quadrilateral	22 1/3%
Trapezium	43.75%
Rectangle	43.75%
Square	43.75%

High cohesion indicates good class subdivision. Lack of cohesion or low cohesion increases complexity, thereby increasing the likelihood of errors during the development process. Classes with low cohesion could be subdivided into two or more subclasses with increased cohesion. This metric evaluates the design implementation as well as reusability.

Coupling Between Object Classes   The coupling between object classes (CBO) metric is a count of the number of other classes to which a class is coupled. It is measured by counting the number of distinct non-inheritance related class hierarchies on which a class depends.

Coupling is a measure of the strength of association established by a connection from one entity to another. Classes (objects) are coupled three ways:

▶ When a message is passed between objects, the objects are coupled.

▶ Classes are coupled when they interact. That is, a method declared in one class uses a method in another classes.

▶ Inheritance introduces significant tight coupling between superclasses and their subclasses.

No results can be entered here based on the inheritance hierarchy itself. This metric is calculated on the interactions that occur between classes and not on inheritance.

Excessive coupling is detrimental to modular design and prevents reuse. The more independent a class is, the easier it is to reuse in another application. The larger the number of couples, the higher the sensitivity to changes in other parts of the design, and therefore maintenance is more difficult. Strong coupling complicates a system since a module is harder to understand, change, or correct by itself if it is interrelated with other modules. Complexity can be reduced by designing systems with the weakest possible coupling between modules. This improves modularity and promotes encapsulation.

CBO evaluates design implementation and reusability.

Depth of Inheritance Tree   The depth of inheritance tree (DIT) shows that the depth of a class within the inheritance hierarchy is the maximum length from the class node to the root of the tree and is measured by the number of ancestor classes.

Another design abstraction in object-oriented systems is the use of inheritance. Inheritance is a type of relationship among classes that enables programmers to reuse previously defined objects including variables and operators. Inheritance decreases complexity by reducing the number of operations and operators, but this abstraction of objects can make maintenance and design difficult. The two metrics used to measure the amount of inheritance are the depth and breadth of the inheritance hierarchy.

The following table also gleans information from the hierarchy shown in Figure 3-2 and shows the respective DIT values for each class.

Shape	0
Triangle	1
Scalene triangle	2
Equilateral triangle	2
Isosceles triangle	2
Quadrilateral	1
Trapezium	2
Rectangle	2
Square	3

The deeper a class is within the hierarchy, the greater the number methods it is likely to inherit, making it more complex to predict its behavior. Deeper trees constitute greater design complexity, since more methods and classes are involved, but the greater the potential for reuse of inherited methods. A support metric for DIT is the number of methods inherited (NMI).

This metric primarily evaluates reuse but also relates to understandability and testability.

Number of Children   The number of children (NOC) is the number of immediate subclasses subordinate to a class in the hierarchy. (See the following table.) It is an indicator of the potential influence a class can have on the design and on the system.

Shape	2
Triangle	3
Scalene triangle	0
Equilateral triangle	0
Isosceles triangle	0
Quadrilateral	2
Trapezium	1
Rectangle	1
Square	0

This table also gleans information from the hierarchy shown in Figure 3-2 and shows the respective NOC values for each class.

The greater the number of children, the greater the likelihood of improper abstraction of the parent and maybe a case of misuse of subclassing. But the greater the number of children, the greater the reuse since inheritance is a form of reuse. If a class has a large number of children, it may require more testing of the methods of that class, thus increasing the testing time. NOC, therefore, primarily evaluates testability and design.

Metrics Summary

In addition to assessing the software attributes related to software quality, software metrics should meet certain theoretical criteria. These criteria are specified in terms of the object-oriented structures to which the metrics are to be applied.

▶ **Noncoarseness**   Not every class can have the same value for a metric, otherwise it has lost its value as a measurement.

▶ **Nonuniqueness (notion of equivalence)**   Two classes can have the same metric value (that is, two classes are equally complex).

▶ **Design details are important**   Even though two class designs perform the same function, the details of the design matter in determining the metric for the class.

▶ **Monotonicity**   The metric for the combination of two classes can never be less than the metric for either of the component classes.

▶ **Nonequivalence of interaction**   The interaction between two classes can be different between two other classes, resulting in different complexity values for the combination.

▶ **Interaction increases complexity**   When two classes are combined, the interaction between classes can increase the complexity metric value.

Table 3-2 summarizes the metrics by showing the key concepts for object-oriented designs: methods, classes (cohesion), coupling, and inheritance. Although some numeric thresholds are suggested, there is little (if any) application data to justify them. Table 3-2 instead gives a general interpretation for the metrics (such as, larger numbers denote application specificity).

Metric	Object-oriented Feature	Concept	Measurement Method	Interpretation
WMC Weighted methods per class	Class / Method	Complexity Usability Reusability	1. # methods implemented within a class 2. Sum of complexity of methods	Larger => greater potential impact on children through inheritance; application specific
RFC Response for a class	Class / Method	Design Usability Testability	# methods invoked in response to a message	Larger => greater complexity and decreased understandability; testing and debugging more complicated
LCOM Lack of cohesion of methods	Class / Cohesion	Design Reusability	Similarity of methods within a class by attributes	Low => good class cohesion. High => low cohesion - subdivide
CBO Coupling between objects	Coupling	Design Reusability	# distinct non-inherited related classes inherited	High => poor design; difficult to understand; decreased reuse; increase maintenance
DIT Depth of inheritance tree	Inheritance	Reusability Understandability Testability	Maximum length from class node to root	Higher => more complex; more reuse
NOC Number of children	Inheritance	Design	# immediate subclass	Higher => more reuse; poor design increasing testing. Overly concentrated in one class

Table 3-2   *Object-Oriented Metrics Summary*

Global Objects

A global object is an instance of a class that has application scope, that is an object that can be accessed by another object anywhere in the system. There are many times when a single or a controlled number of instances of a class are required, for instance a single CEO of a company or a single referee of a soccer game or two referees of an ice hockey game.

It is very easy to create a class called CEO or referee; the problem comes in limiting the number of instances created. The solution seems obvious, let the class keep track of the number of instances in existence and not allow more than the pre-determined number to exist.

If just a single instance of a class was the only purpose of a global object, then class methods might be considered. Class methods do indeed allow access to an object from anywhere in the system; however, they do not provide the flexibility of using instances. Some advantages are as follows:

▶ Class methods can not be overridden by subclasses, whereas instance methods can be overridden.

▶ Instance methods can be overridden by subclasses and can therefore provide flexibility in functionality.

▶ Having a class that can control the number of available instances provides greater flexibility over class methods, which do not.

Implementation

In Smalltalk 80 shared pools are used. Any object wishing to be given a wider audience is placed in a shared pool. Other objects can then access the pool to find the object they want. This example sets the 'MyObject' up to be apart of the shared pool 'Smalltalk':

For example, Smalltalk at: #MyObject put: nil

Unlike most other objects in the system, a global object need not be created until it is first required. A class definition for the global object defines a single class method, which is used to gain access to the object.

The first time the class method is used it creates the global object and returns a handle to it. On subsequent calls to the class method, the handle of the global object is returned.

The notation for a global object is shown here:

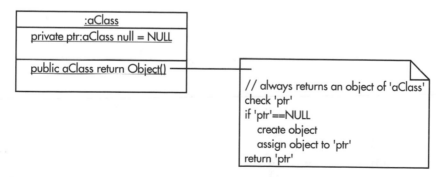

To access any of the non-class methods within the global object, use the access method:

```
answer = GlobalObjectClassDefinition::ReturnObject ().question();
```

The following is example code showing how to implement a global object in Java.

GlobalObj.java

```java
public class GlobalObj
{
    /*
    ** This is the reference to the single instance of this class
    */
    private static GlobalObj          globalObj;

    public GlobalObj ()
    {
    /*
        ** Assign this object to the variable
        */
        globalObj = this;
        :
    }

    public static void main (String[] args)
    {
        /*
        ** Create the main application object
        */
        GlobalObj go = new GlobalObj ();
    }

    public static GlobalObj GetThis ()
    {
        /*
        ** When requested, return the reference to the object
        */
        return globalObj;
    }
}
```

The following shows how Java global objects are used:

```
SimCo    parent;
parent = (SimCo)SimCo.GetThis();
```

The following is example code showing how to implement a global object in C++.

Global.h

```
#ifndef GLOBAL_H_
#define GLOBAL_H_

class Global
{
    public:
        // static / class method that returns a handle to the global
        // object
        static   Global    &GetGlobal ();
        char*     name();

    private:
        // the global variable used to hold the handle to the global
        // object
        static   Global    *myGlobal_;
};
#endif // GLOBAL_H_
```

Global.cpp

```
#include "Global.h"
// initialisation of the global variable
Global    *Global::myGlobal_ = 0;

// the static / class method that will return a handle to the global
// object
Global&
GetGlobal ()
{
    // if this is the first time that this method has been used then
    // the value
    // of the global variable will be NULL
    if (myGlobal_ == NULL)
    {
        // if this is the case, then create the global object and set
```

```
        // the global
        // variable to hold the handle to the global object
        myGlobal_ = new Global;
    }

    // return the value of the global variable,
    // i.e. the handle of the global object
    return myGlobal_;
    }
```

The following shows how C++ global objects are used:

```
name = Global::GetGlobal().name();
```

Implementation Decision

This example highlights the different customer requirements (choice of implementation language) that have to be taken into consideration during design. For example, here are three designs that essentially achieve the same functionality but by very different means.

Using a Collection of Student Objects

In the design shown here, a **Course** class is designed to contain a collection of **Student**s:

This design gives the **:Course** object immediate access to **:Student** objects via one method call, as all **:Student** objects are contained locally within the **:Course** object. This design has the advantage of allowing immediate access to any **:Student** object.

The problem with this design, especially if implemented in C++, is that the **:Course** object contains a collection of copies of the **:Student** objects. This means that if any **:Student** object is updated, the **:Course** object will need to update its copy of the **:Student** object. Languages such as Java do not have this problem since they allow immediate access to objects from different locations within a program without the need for objects to exist as copies.

Using a Collection of Student Identifiers

In the design shown next, the **Course** class contains a collection of student identifiers (*StudentID*s). Each *StudentId* is unique.

The **:Course** object only has immediate access to the identities of the students via the **:StudentID** objects.

The problem with this design is that retrieving additional information places a noticeable overhead on the system:

1. The appropriate **:StudentID** needs to be found.

2. The corresponding **:Student** object needs to be found using the **:StudentId** object.

3. The **:Student** object is asked to return the required information.

This design has the advantage of only keeping minimal information locally about any one **:Student** object. This allows **:Student** objects to be updated independently of the **:Course** object. The previously mentioned disadvantage is the overhead involved in getting any information from a specific **:Student** object.

Using a Collection of Student Object References

C++ supports the use of pointers as shown next, where the object itself can be replaced by a reference. It has a lot of advantages.

▶ Offers all of the advantages offered in the first design solution, immediate access via the reference to the object

▶ Any changes made to the object do not require an update of the **:Course** object

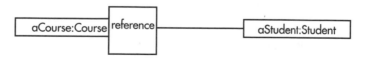

The main disadvantage is that not all languages support it.

Virtual Methods

This is a particular feature of C++ that can cause problems if not properly understood. When using inheritance within a design, it is important to know when to use the keyword **virtual**. The keyword **virtual** in C++ allows derived classes to override the methods of their parent. As not every method needs to be overridden, not every class needs to be associated with this keyword. The example that follows illustrates what happens when a particular method, the **destructor** method, is not defined as being **virtual**.

A class definition for a wine monitoring application looks like the following:

```
class WineBottle
{
    public:
        WineBottle ( void ) { numWineBottles++; }
        ~WineBottle ( void ) { numWineBottles--; }
        int getNumWineBottles ( void ) { return numWineBottles; }

    private:
        static int    numWineBottles;
};
```

The class variable needs to be initialized as required by C++:

```
int WineBottle::numWineBottles = 0;
```

This class will suffice for the most basic applications, but the designer would now like to keep track of the varieties of wine available. A new class can be derived from the first WineBottle class so that the number of WhiteWineBottles can be kept as well as the total number of WineBottles.

```
class WhiteWineBottle
{
    public:
        WhiteWineBottle ( void ) { numWhiteWineBottles++; }
        ~WhiteWineBottle ( void ) { numWhiteWineBottles--; }
        int getNumWhiteWineBottles ( void )
        { return numWhiteWineBottles; }

    private:
        static int    numWhiteWineBottles;
};
```

Again the class variable needs to be initialized:

```
int WhiteWineBottle::numWhiteWineBottles = 0;
```

It can be assumed that somewhere in the application, a WhiteWineBottle object is created using the new method, which is later destroyed when the delete method is invoked.

```
WineBottle *bottlePtr = new WhiteWineBottle;
...
delete bottlePtr;
```

According to the class definitions, the destructors of the two classes will reverse the effects of the appropriate constructors. However, there is something wrong: when delete is invoked on the bottlePtr, it will not call the WhiteWineBottle destructor. The problem is the manner in which the destructor was defined. When the delete method is invoked, the compiler has a choice: should it call the destructor method for the WineBottle class or the destructor method for the WhiteWineBottle? As it cannot make a decision, it decides to use the destructor of the pointer, the WineBottle destructor.

The solution to this problem is to define the destructor as a virtual method. By declaring the destructor as a virtual method, the compiler will treat the call to the destructor as it does with any other virtual method, so the destructor will be invoked on the object being pointed to, that is, the WhiteWineBottle object.

Copy Constructor

A copy constructor is designed to produce a copy of the object being passed to it. For instance, the following would be used to create a copy of a String from an existing String object.

```
String (const String &object);
```

There are two forms of copy constructor, shallow copy and deep copy.

Shallow Copy Constructor

The shallow copy constructor, as shown next, will copy the object but will not copy anything pointed to.

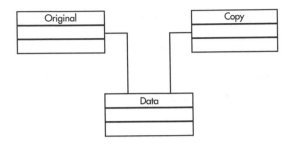

There is a problem with this approach, and that is when either the original object or the copy is deleted, as shown next. How does either of them know that the other exists? A solution to this is discussed in the "Reference Counting" section of Chapter 5.

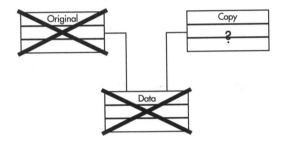

Deep Copy Constructor

The deep copy constructor, as shown next, will not only copy the object but will copy everything being pointed to.

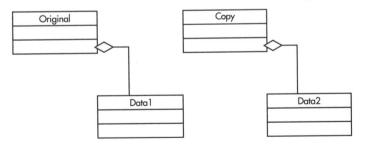

Unfortunately, a problem exists with this deep copy constructor if a large number of objects are generated as copies. The problem is memory usage. The solution to this problem is the same as the solution for the shallow copy constructor and will be discussed in the "Reference Counting" section of Chapter 5.

Implementing Associations

There are two forms of association: the first is bi-directional and the other is one way.

Bi-directional Association

Using the example shown next, it can be seen that there are two distinct associations: the first is from the company to the employee, the company 'employs' the employee, the second is from the employee to the company, the employee is 'employed by' the company.

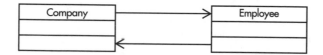

These associations exist as an attribute for the company in the employee and an attribute for the employee in the company. With the associations being in two places, it is important that when a change occurs both sides be kept up-to-date.

As an alternative to having attributes that correspond to the association, an association class is defined that now holds the associations; this new class is shown in context here:

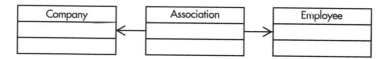

One-way Associations

A one-way association is shown next, with each employee performing a task for the company, while each task does not belong to just one employee.

Summary

This chapter provides an introduction to the most common design decisions, which are

► Abstract classes

► Application Programming Interface

► Templates

► Good design—principles and metrics

► Global objects

► Implementation decision

► Virtual Methods

► Copy Constructor

► Implementing Associations

The next chapter discusses the design decisions that should be avoided.

CHAPTER

4

Design Don'ts

This chapter covers some of the design constructs (or schemes) that I consider to be inappropriate design. By inappropriate design, I mean those constructs that do not fit the object-oriented paradigm and are used whenever the design is not fully thought through, or a shortcut is taken. The inappropriate constructs that I discuss in this chapter are process objects, delegating responsibility, method responsibility, the *friend* construct, multiple inheritance, and misused inheritance. Each design construct will be fully discussed with examples and alternatives.

Process Objects

In Chapter 1, I gave an example of how to convert a structured system into an object-oriented system. The initial structured system is shown here:

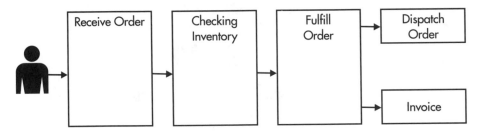

While the desired object-oriented system would look like this:

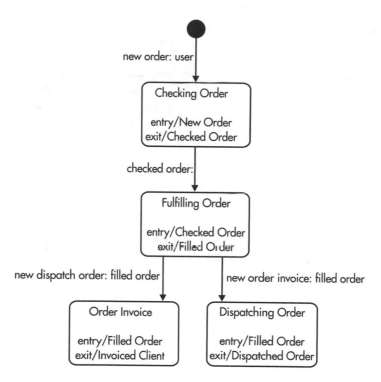

Unfortunately, the typical response to the initial system is to create process objects. Process objects are objects that embody all of the previous system, but do so in the name of object orientation. The major difference between a process object design and an object-oriented design is process objects are designed to push the data through the system in the same manner that the old processes used to. Whereas in an object-oriented design, the objects respond to messages and move themselves through the system following a pre-defined path. The process object diagram for the system is shown here:

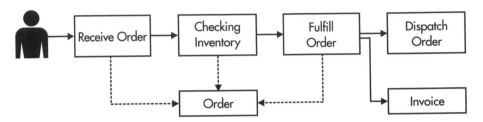

The embodiment of the structured system also brings with it the embodiment of all that initial system's problems:

▶ A change in the process forces major re-coding.

▶ Using different methods for processing of orders based on some pre-defined criteria, which is also known as differential processing, is less efficient.

▶ The addition of a new order type requires a major recoding effort, which results in almost a complete rewrite.

▶ The order objects are under external control by the 'process' objects.

The question is, "Can these problems be avoided?" The answer simply stated is YES. It is readily acknowledged that objects have both attributes and methods. Chapter 1 introduced the notion of an object having a state. In fact, UML v1.4 provides a notation for this state in the form of statechart diagrams, as described in Chapter 2.

The trick is to turn innocent looking objects into objects with a purpose by empowering them to make discussions for themselves. The initial system followed a step-by-step approach. Each transition from one process to another was preceded by a signal. For example, to transition from 'Check Order' to 'Fulfilling Order' required a signal that all of the items required by the order were in stock.

To determine if the items ordered were in stock required the 'Check Order' process object to inquire of the warehouse object if the required items were available. Once all of the required items have been successfully located in the warehouse, a signal can be generated that this order can be fulfilled, as shown here.

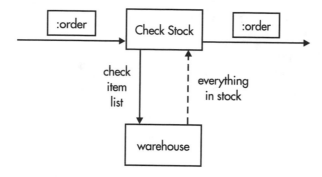

The solutions are as follows:

1. To turn the step-by-step approach into a statechart diagram.
2. Have the order object check its requirements with the warehouse object itself.
3. Internalize the statechart diagram so that the order object transitions through process states and not process objects.

Using these solution steps changes 'Check Order' from the original system design into a segment of a statechart diagram and a segment of a collaboration diagram, as shown in Figure 4-1.

Having decided that the order object will use a statechart to drive its own destiny, how does this then solve the problems with the previous designs?

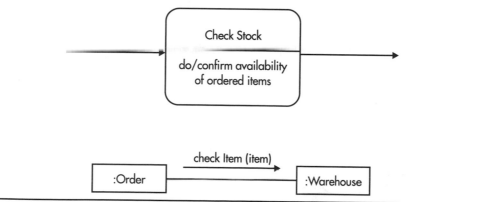

Figure 4-1   *'Check Order' as statechart and collaboration diagram segments*

A Change in the Process

Unfortunately, to support any process changes, there is a need for some re-coding. The good news is that the re-coding is restricted to the statechart diagram with the object, as shown in Figure 4-2. Any other changes are restricted to the objects required to support the change.

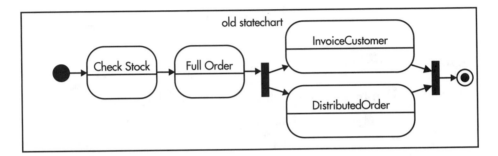

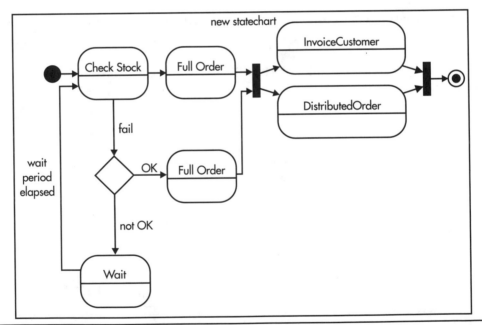

Figure 4-2   *Changes in the process are reflected in the statechart diagram*

Differential Processing

Using statechart diagrams allows different objects to follow different paths without making major changes. The only coding changes required are those necessary to support the design changes. A statechart diagram showing the statechart for the new object 'invoice preferred customer' instead of the generic 'invoice customer' is shown here:

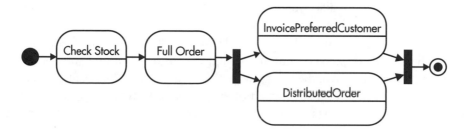

Addition of a New Order Type

Any new order type can be added to the system with a minimum of effort. The new order type needs to be derived from an existing order type and added to the order creation method so that the objects can be created using the order type.

Internalizing the Control Process

With the full internalization of the statechart diagram an order diagram, is shown here:

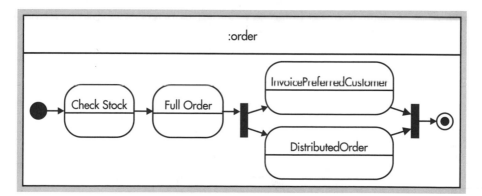

Delegation of Responsibility

In performing the analysis on a system, the objects that are needed to support the system are discovered. From these objects, you can write the classes to document the attributes and methods that the object is to support. Unfortunately just discovering the methods to be supported by an object is not enough.

A classic mistake made during object-oriented design is to design a system using the objects as they were discovered. Simply replacing a data item with an object as shown in Figure 4-3 is not good design.

This section discusses how the use of delegation can improve the design of a system. The first example shows an inefficient way of determining someone's age. The second example shows the wrong way of filtering data. This example starts by showing how a poor object-oriented filter system is designed followed by an efficient object- oriented design. The filter example adds a final design that is the most flexible object-oriented design.

Example 1—Determining Someone's Age

As previously mentioned, the classic mistake is to replace data with a data object. Having done this, another mistake is to treat the data object as if it were data.

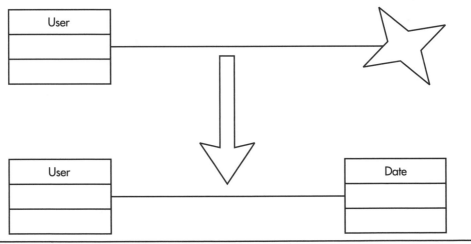

Figure 4-3   *Diagram showing how data is turned into data objects*

What I mean by this is shown in the following diagram. The **:User** object asks the **:Person** object for their 'date of birth', having obtained the date of birth, the **:User** object then asks the **:Calendar** object for the current date. With these two pieces of information the **:User** object can determine the age of the **:Person** object.

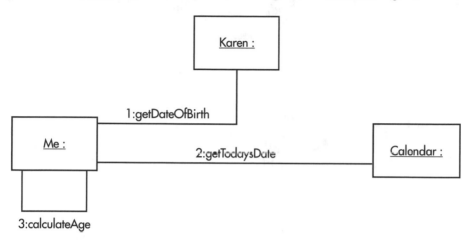

A real problem with not asking the person to do the work is that you have to know how to handle the result of asking the date of birth:

- ▶ 20 March 1963
- ▶ March 20 1963
- ▶ 20/03/63
- ▶ 20-03-63
- ▶ 03/20/63
- ▶ 03-20-63

All mean the same, but are different. In addition, the response from the person may be different to the format of the argument required by the calendar.

The real solution to this problem is to avoid all of the work involved with handling date-of-birth formats, especially when all that is required is to determine the age of the person. To implement the solution, get the **:User** object to ask the **:Person** object to return their age, then get the **:Person** object to ask the **:Calendar** object for the current date so that they can calculate their age, as shown in the diagram here:

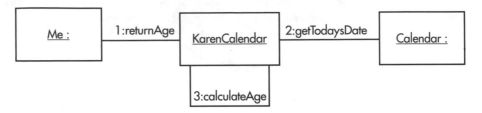

Example 2—Filtering Data

The first design example shows the data object passed for filtering, the second shows the data object invoking the filter, and the third shows the data object with a changeable filter.

Passing the Data Object

This design illustrates an understanding of object-oriented design in the sense that everything is an object; unfortunately, that is where the understanding finishes. The point of object orientation is not to convert everything into objects, but to provide a design that is both flexible and maintainable.

The design shows a **:Process** object passing a **:Data** object to a **:Filter** object. In object orientation, objects are not passed to other objects for processing. Having the design pass a **:Process** object to a **:Data** object is indicative of pre–object-oriented designs.

Data Object Invokes the Filter

In object orientation, objects are sent messages. So instead of a **:User** object passing a **:Data** object to a **:Filter** object, the **:Data** object is sent a message by the **:User** object to perform filtering of its data. When this message arrives at the **:Data** object, the **:Data** object decides what needs to be filtered and performs the filtering by using the internal **:Filter** object to perform the function:

The Most Flexible Filter System Design

The previous example showed the **:Data** object invoking the **:Filter** object to perform the task required. In the design shown next, the **:Data** object has the opportunity to use a **:Filter** object that is determined at runtime. This is achieved by designing the **:Data** object to use a filter interface and then writing the **:Filter** object to implement this interface. In this way filter objects can be made interchangeable to allow for different filtering functions.

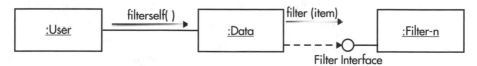

Method Responsibility

The previous section discussed how delegation could be used to improve the design of a system. This section takes the subject of delegation further by now focusing on where it is best for the methods to be executed.

In this section, we design a typical system so that an object asks for the information and then uses it to compute the result. Here is an equivalent real-world example of why this design is absurd.

Example 1—Buying a Toaster

You go into a department store and ask to view the toasters that they have for sale. You then decide on the toaster you want, and ask to purchase it. The clerk disappears for a few moments, and returns with a box containing the toaster, which you purchase and take home.

When you get home, you find to your horror that the box contains only the parts of a toaster, along with the instructions on how to assemble it. If you build the toaster and do not complain about it, then you have just helped condone in the real world something that is bad design in the programming world.

But you would likely complain. You would take the box of parts back to the store and demand that they assemble it for you. However, unlike the toaster, you find it acceptable in your software for a design to have objects that give you basic information and make you perform additional tasks. Why?

The store clerk is now in a position where instead of just selling the product, they are now expected to assemble it. In fact, they are expected to be able to assemble all models of toasters that the store sells. Additionally, the store is now required to provide assurances that the toaster not only works, but also is safe. The store clerk and the store now both complain. So a committee is formed to decide who should assemble the toaster.

The eventual decision of the committee is that the company that designed and manufactured the toaster should assemble it. The reason for the decision is that having designed the toaster they would know how to assemble it. Not only that, but they would be responsible for testing the toasters and providing assurances of quality to the end user. This would leave the shop assistant free to return to selling the toasters, and you could go home and have a fully assembled, tested, and guaranteed quality toaster.

The examples that follow help to illustrate this point further.

Example 2—Displaying Information About a Sports Team

This example works through various designs associated with a **:League** object obtaining information from a **:Team** object sent to a display. A discussion of the three designs follows the three descriptions.

Design 1

The following diagram shows a **:League** object making a series of requests of a **:Team** object to collect all of the information it needs before sending the information to a display.

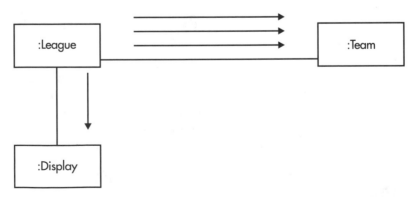

Design 2

The next diagram shows a **:League** object making a single request for information from a **:Team** object, leaving the responsibility for collecting the information to the **:Team** object. The **:Team** object is still required to return the collected information to the **:League** object so that it can be passed to a display.

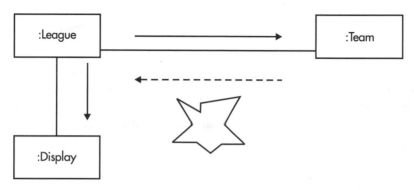

Design 3

This final variation, shown next, is based on Design 2. Instead of returning the information from the **:Team** object to the **:League** object, the **:Team** object sends the information directly to the display.

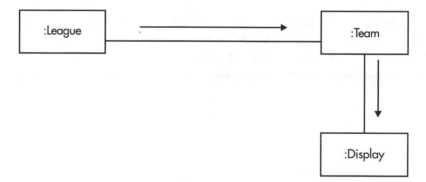

Design 1 employs a design that is little better than the original nonobject-oriented design. The choice between Designs 2 or 3 is a little less clear-cut.

Questions come up, such as:

▶ Does the **:League** object want to intersperse information from teams with some of its own information, such as labels and comments?

▶ Is it sensible to have each team using the same display?

Other issues then arise from these questions:

▶ Using Design 1, the **:League** object has to know what attributes are available in the **:Team** object to be able to request them.

▶ If the number or type of the **:Team** object attributes changes, then the **:League** object needs to be modified.

▶ Design 3 enables multi-processing, as the **:League** object can broadcast a Display message to all of the team objects, and then move on to other things.

▶ Design 3 also allows the type of team to be changed without the **:League** object needing to be modified. For example, the **:League** object may be implemented using a generic **Team** class. This allows it to use objects from classes that are derived from the **Team** class. In this way, the **:League** object can support different team types.

Example 3—Updating a League Table

A similar set of problems to that of the preceding example arises when the **:League** object wishes to update the individual team objects. The **:League** object is required to update each team object with new information as it becomes available.

Design 1

The **:League** object updates each individual attribute of each team, as shown next. The **:League** object needs to know which attributes are available for updating, as it may have been given more information than currently supported by the **:Team** object.

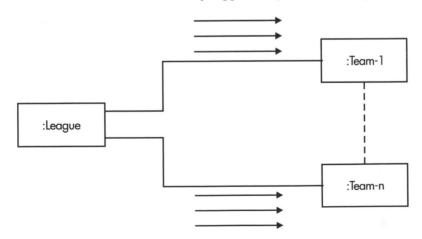

Design 2

The **:League** object packages the information and sends it to each team in one message, as shown next. If there is too much information, each **:Team** object will ignore the excess.

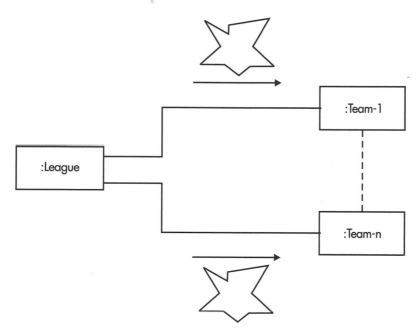

Example 4—Sorting a League Table

Using the previous configuration the **:League** object has access to a collection of **:Team** objects. This next problem discusses how the **:League** object can be sorted based on the values of certain attributes within each **:Team** object.

A typical response to this problem is to use the first design described next; however, it would be wrong to do so.

Design 1

The **:League** object makes a series of requests for information from team objects that are currently adjacent in the league table, as shown next. The **:League** object then compares the information and determines by some internal criteria the relative positions of the two team objects, making any changes to their positions in the league table by itself.

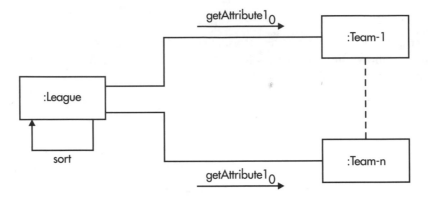

However, any change in the number or type of the attributes in the **Team** class and the **League** class would need to be modified to reflect changes. These changes would not be restricted to the information gathered, but also in the tests made to differentiate between two team objects.

Design 2

The problem with the previous design is the possible number of modifications that could arise. Not only that, but the **:League** object has lost the ability to support multiple team types, as each team type will require to be sorted using differentteam attributes.

For example:

▶   A soccer team would want to be sorted on points gained from games won and drawn.

▶   A baseball team would also want their record of points gained from games won only, as baseball games are never tied.

When it comes down to it, a sort procedure does two things:

1.   Determines, using some criteria, how to sort two objects, such as which team has won the most games.

2.   If the result of the comparison shows that the teams are in the wrong order, repositions them.

The solution to the problem is shown in the next illustration. The first **:Team** object is passed a second **:Team** object. This first **:Team** object then undertakes a comparison of attributes to determine which of the two teams sorts higher. Having decided which of the two teams sorts higher, the first **:Team** object can return the result that the **:League** object can use to order the two teams within the league.

For example, the first **:Team** object could return a value of TRUE if the result of a comparison yields the fact that it should be placed first in the table, and FALSE if the positions should be reversed. Based on the returned value, the **:League** object can then carry out any repositioning of the teams.

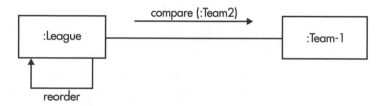

The advantages of passing responsibility for undertaking the comparison are

▶   The **:League** object does not have to gather information about the teams.

▶   The team objects can determine for themselves what is a valid test criterion.

▶   The **:League** object can be used to support different team types that support the compare-me-against-another facility.

Review of Methods

This section illustrates that it is not only important to determine by analysis which methods are needed and where the attributes reside, but it is equally important to determine where the responsibility for the work is to be carried out.

The examples have shown that a class may define a method such as 'UpdateEntries' for a **:League** object, but the actual updating of the attributes is left to the individual **:Team** objects. The **:Team** objects are given the responsibility for doing the work on behalf of the **:League** object.

The main consequence of this approach is that the **:League** object is required to know very little about the team objects. This in turn allows the **:League** object to support a wide variety of different team types. This approach not only puts the responsibility for the work where it is best suited, but also gives rise to flexible objects.

Friend Construct in C++

This section discusses the visibility levels associated with any object-oriented programming language, of both the attributes and the methods. Following this discussion is an introduction to the *friend* construct, with a discussion of how the *friend* construct affects these visibility levels.

Levels of Access

Every object-oriented programming language offers three levels of access to an object's attributes and methods. The three levels are as follows:

private	Any attributes and methods declared at this level can only be used by member functions.
protected	Any attributes and methods declared at this level can only be used by member functions and by member functions in derived classes.
public	Any attributes and methods declared at this level can be used by any function.

How Does the Friend Construct Affect the Access

The *friend* construct breaks these access rules by allowing unlimited access to another object. By using the *friend* construct, the three levels of access become as follows:

private	Any attributes and methods declared at this level can only be used by member functions and *friend*s of the class in which it is declared.
protected	Any attributes and methods declared at this level can only be used by member functions and *friend*s of the class in which it is declared; and by member functions and *friend*s of classes derived from this class.
public	Any attributes and methods declared at this level can be used by any function.

For example, class **A** grants friendship rights to class **B**, then any **:B** object is allowed unlimited access to attributes and methods of any **:A** object.

The implications of allowing special access become apparent if in the example above Class **A** is the definition of a secret agent and Class **B** is the class definition of an agent controller.

A public use of 'askName' would only reveal the agent's cover name, while the agent controller object would be able to use the 'realName' method. A solution that does not require the *friend* construct is discussed in Chapter 5.

The negative side in C++ is that it allows access beyond the protected interface to such an extent that nothing within the class being befriended is secure.

The new rules that apply for friends are shown here:

```
class A
{
    friend class B;
    private:
        int a;
};

class B
{
    friend class C;
    void function (A* aPtr)
    {
        aPtr->a++; // this will work as B is a friend of A
    }
};

class C
{
    void function (A* aPtr)
    {
        aPtr->a++; // error: C is not a friend of A
        //despite being a friend of a friend
    }
};

class D : public B
{
    void function (A* aPtr)
    {
        p->aPtr++; // error: D is not a friend of A
        // despite being derived from a friend
```

```
    }
};
```

The above set of classes is illustrated here:

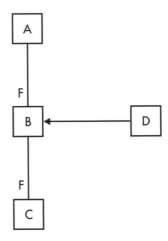

As the **B** Class is a direct *friend* of the **A** Class, its function can access the private attribute 'a' of the **A** Class.

The **C** Class is a *friend* of the **B** Class and so is an indirect *friend* of the **A** Class however being an indirect *friend* does not allow it access to the private attribute 'a' of the **A** Class.

The **D** Class is derived from the **B** Class and so is a derived *friend* of the **A** Class however being a derived *friend* does not allow it access to the private attribute 'a' of the **A** Class.

Using the Friend Construct

The following shows three ways of using the *friend* construct. Inside an objects class definition, the *friend* construct can be used as follows:

Access from a C Language Routine

The notation for this construct is

> friend   <return type>   methodName

Any class definition that includes this construct allows access to any attributes or methods by the named method. The method is class-less as it is typically a standard

C routine that needs to have access to the internals of several classes at the same time. It is used to reduce the need for data encapsulation routines, thus improving performance, but breaking the principles of object orientation.

> e.g. friend   void   accessNoProblem ()

This declaration would appear in several class declarations. The method *accessNoProblem* has access to everything within this class.

Access from a Class Method

The notation for this construct is

> friend   <return type>   className::methodName()

Any class definition that includes this construct allows access to any attributes or methods by the named method of the class specified.

> e.g. friend   void   seemsOk::limitedAccess ()

Any **:seemsOk** object can gain access via the *limitedAccess* method to any attributes or methods contained in this class definition.

Access from a Class

The notation for this construct is

> friend   class   className

Any class definition that includes this construct allows access to any attributes or methods by any method of any object created from the named class definition.

> e.g. friend   class   realCloseFriend

Any **:realCloseFriend** object can gain access via any method to any attributes or methods contained in the class definition, as they have all now been granted unlimited access.

Review of Friend Construct

In summary, the *friend* construct is used to grant additional or exceptional access to the attributes and methods of objects created from consenting class definitions. If the level of access granted to a *friend* equated to that granted to a derived or child class, then I think that the construct has some merit. However, the level of access granted goes beyond access to the protected parts of an object and allows access to the private parts of an object. I believe this level of access should be reserved for very special friends or spouses.

Multiple Inheritance

Multiple inheritance is, as the name suggests, defining a class with more than one parent class definition. Multiple inheritance is used to combine the features of several classes into one. Several object-oriented programming languages do not support multiple inheritance, and as such, are not deemed by purists to be a true object-oriented construct.

Discussion in this section includes the following:

▶   Why designers think they need to use multiple inheritance

▶   The problems associated with multiple inheritance, in terms of how memory is mapped and how conflicts arise when the compiler tries to determine which method to use

▶   Design alternatives to multiple inheritance: what is the designer trying to model?

A typical use for multiple inheritance is shown here:

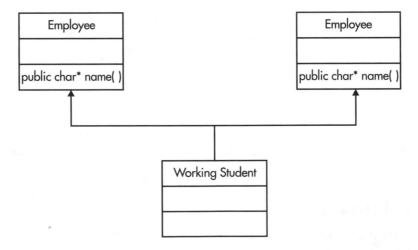

This example shows three classes, two parent classes and one child class, which is derived from the two parent classes. The code for the three classes is shown here:

```
class Employee
{
    public:
        virtual char* name ();
    private:
        char* name;
};

class Student
{
    public:
        virtual char* name ();
};

class WorkingStudent : public Employee,
                       public Student
{
    // this class does not declare it's own name method
};
```

Using the multiple inheritance example described previously, the code can now be put to work:

```
WorkingStudent*    wsPtr = new WorkingStudent;

wsPtr->name ();    // error!
```

This creates an error because each of the two parent classes has been declared with a *name* method. So when a derived **:WorkingStudent** object tries to use the derived method *name,* the system does not know which one to choose.

The solution is to be explicit in the choice of *name* method to use, as shown here:

```
wsPtr->Employee::name ();
wsPtr->Student::name ();
```

Deriving a Class from WorkingStudent

As an extra twist derive a class from the **WorkingStudent** class called **DayReleaseStudent**. This **DayReleaseStudent** class has been declared to override the *name* method. The new hierarchy is shown here:

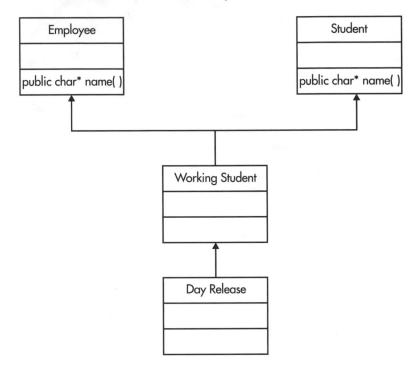

with the code for the new class as shown here:

```
class DayRelease
{
    public:
        virtual char* name ();
};
```

Use this new class and the overridden method as shown here:

```
DayRelease*    drPtr = new DayRelease;
```

However, there are still problems:

```
drPtr->Employee::name ();        // works as before
drPtr->Student::name ();         // works as before
drPtr->name ();                  // error! this is still ambiguous
```

The only way to invoke the local method is to do the following:

```
drPtr->DayRelease::name ();
```

Redefining the Inherited Name Method

It is possible that the designer would like the derived **WorkingStudent** class to redefine both of the inherited versions of the *name* method. Unfortunately this is not possible, basically this is because a class is only allowed to have a single method called *name*. The solution to this problem is shown here:

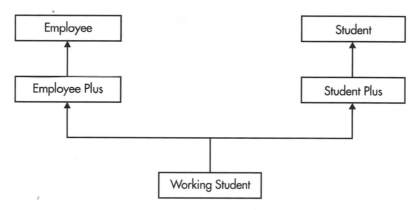

The solution involves adding two intermediary classes and then deriving the **WorkingStudent** class from these two new classes.

```
class EmployeePlus : public Employee
{
    public:
        virtual char* employeeName () = 0;
        virtual char* name () { return employeeName (); }
};

class StudentPlus : public Student
{
    public:
        virtual char* studentName () = 0;
        virtual char* name () { return studentName (); }
```

```
};

class WorkingStudent : public EmployeePlus,
                       public StudentPlus
{
    public:
        virtual char* employeeName ();
        virtual char* studentName ();
};
```

Each of the two new derived classes rename the *name* method that they inherit. The new name is defined as a pure virtual method; this is so that the derived class **WorkingStudent** is forced to provide implementations, thus achieving the required redefinition.

The last thing to do is to tie the name of the original method to the new method's names. This is achieved by getting the original method to invoke the new method, which has been implemented in the derived class.

An example of its usage is shown here:

```
WorkingStudent*    wsPtr = new WorkingStudent;

Employee*          ePtr = wsPtr;
Student*           sPtr = wsPtr;

ePtr->name ();
// rather than calling the original Employee::name method
// the following will call the redefined method WorkingStudent::employeeName

sPtr->name ();
// rather than calling then original Student::name method
// the following will call the redefined method WorkingStudent::studentName
```

Multiple Inheritance Diamond

A multiple inheritance diamond is shown in Figure 4-4. The diamond configuration comes about when the two classes that are multiply inherited are derived from one class. In the diagram, both the **Employee** class and the **Student** class are inherited from the **Person** class.

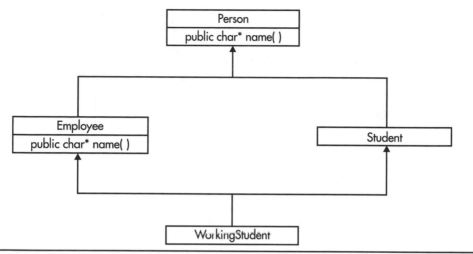

Figure 4-4 *A basic multiple inheritance diamond configuration*

There are some special attributes of this configuration that will be discussed now. The first is related to memory usage, while the second is again related to derived methods.

Mapping Memory

When a class is derived from another, the two class definitions exist in memory together. This poses a problem for the diamond configuration because it would appear that the **Person** class exists in memory twice. Unfortunately, this is true:

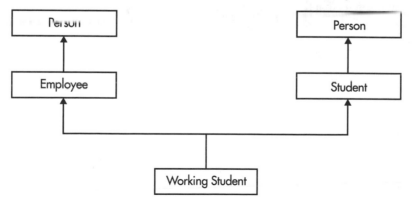

There is, however, a solution to this memory problem, and that is for both the **Employee** class and the **Student** class to inherit the **Person** class as a virtual base class:

```
class Person
{
    public:
        virtual char* name ();
    private:
        char* name;
}

class Employee : virtual public Person
{
...
}

class Student : virtual public Person
{
...
}

class WorkingStudent : public Employee,
                       public Student
{
...
}
```

This virtual base class arrangement now means that only one copy of the Person class exists in memory for each **:WorkingStudent** object, rather than the two copies that previously existed.

The down side is that this configuration is slower to use, because to avoid duplication of the memory, the memory associated with the Person class is referenced via a pointer, as shown here:

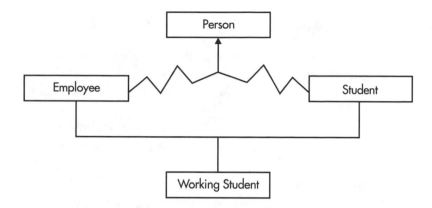

Derived Methods

In the diamond configuration shown in Figure 4-4, suppose that the **Person** class declares the *name* method. Now suppose that the **Employee** class overrides this method and the **Student** class does not. As before, the **WorkingStudent** class is derived from both the **Employee** class and the **Student** class.

So what happens when the *name* method is invoked? Is the *name* method inherited directly from the **Employee** class or via the **Student** class from the base class **Person**?

At first glance it would seem that, just like the previous derived method examples, the answer would be 'ambiguity', but you would be wrong.

The answer is worse than the question; it all depends on how the **Person** class is inherited by the **Employee** class and the **Student** class:

▶ If the **Person** class is the non-virtual base class of the **Employee** class OR the **Student** class, then the answer is ambiguous

▶ However, if the **Person** class is the virtual base class of BOTH the **Employee** class AND the **Student** class, then the answer is unambiguous and the *name* method inherited from the **Employee** class will be used. The *name* method from the **Employee** class is given preference over the original *name* method in the **Person** class.

Alternatives to Multiple Inheritance

So now that you are totally disillusioned with the idea of using multiple inheritance, is there an alternative? Fortunately there is an alternative to multiple inheritance that will not only resolve the issue of ambiguity, but may also make the intentions of the system clearer.

The following examples are based on the previous WorkingStudent problem. The first is a Student that goes to work, while the second is an Employee that returns to study.

Schema 1—Student Who Works

The **Working Student** Class is derived from the **Student** Class, as shown here:

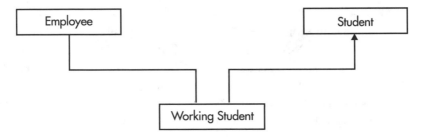

In addition to being able to fulfill student tasks, a **:WorkingStudent** object needs to fulfill employee tasks. The **WorkingStudent** class contains a reference to an **:Employee** object that the **:Student** object will need when it starts work. The **WorkingStudent** class will define methods that will use the **:Employee** object reference to invoke the methods.

Example: **:WorkingStudent**.*WhenIsPayDay()* is implemented to forward the request to the **:Employee** object to resolve.

Analysis will determine the number of **Employee** class methods that need to be supported in the **WorkingStudent** class, that is, it is unlikely that a **:WorkingStudent** object will be asked about pension arrangements or their choice of company car.

Schema 2—Studying Employee

The StudyingEmployee Class is derived from the Employee Class:

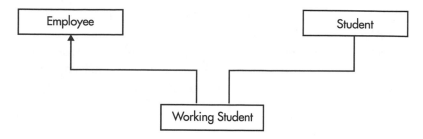

In addition to being able to fulfill employee tasks, a **:StudyingEmployee** object needs to fulfill students tasks. The **StudyingEmployee** class contains a reference to a **:Student** object that that **:StudyingEmployee** object will need when it starts to study. The **StudyingEmployee** class defines methods that will use the **:Student** object reference to invoke methods.

Example: **:StudyingEmployee**.*WhenDoesSchoolStart( )* is implemented to forward the request to the **:Student** object to resolve.

Misused Inheritance

The example shown next is of an inheritance hierarchy that has some logic behind it, as both of the derived types are numeric.

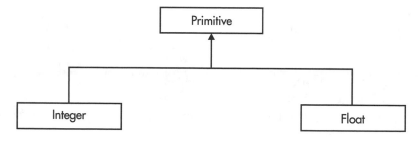

Wherever an instance of a **Primitive** class can be used, by virtue of inheritance, so can instances of the derived classes. In fact there exists in these derived classes a logical ability to be interchangeable with each other.

However, there is also a problem with this that some highly paid consultants have even fallen into.

As previously mentioned, having an inheritance hierarchy of interchangeable components reduces the cost of code development as they share common code. For instance, interfaces can be designed to have just one method to perform each task. These methods take as an argument an object created from the **Primitive** class or any of its derived classes. The code for the interface is

```
class Interface
{
    public:
        void method1 (Primitive p);
        void method2 (Primitive p1, Primitive p2);
}
```

Now watch what happens when the hierarchy is extended:

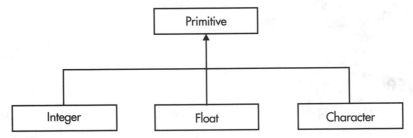

This hierarchy does not lend itself to having interchangeable components in quite the same way as the previous example. The question that you should ask is "What happens when method1 is invoked with a **:character** object as a parameter?"

The answer should be simple. Unfortunately, the problem is with how the consultant had made the project's infrastructure team implement support for the new derived type. The development team had not been allowed to implement a correct design. Instead, the consultant told them to make adjustments to the interfaces that they had already defined.

The changes they were forced to implement were in the form of run-time checks:

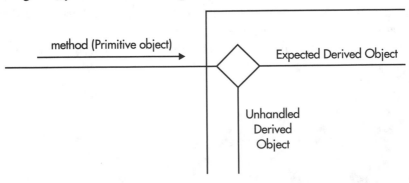

Feeling vindicated by this seemingly easy directive, the consultant extended the hierarchy to include many diverse types:

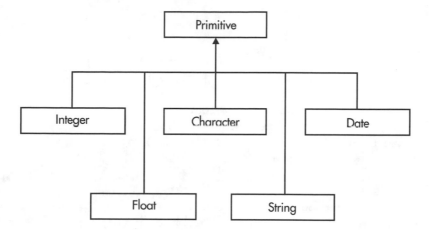

Although the infrastructure team did their best, mistakes were made. At one point, having spent several days trying to implement a feature using these infrastructure classes and making no progress, we humbled ourselves and asked for help. After some investigation, we were told that the problem was the fault of our own programming. The exact phrase used was "You are not using the classes correctly."

After several minutes of being in shock, one of us recovered enough to ask the simple question, "If this is the published interface and our usage of it compiles, how can we be using it incorrectly?"

The immediate response was, "You should only pass supported types to the methods."

It was at this point that we realized that although the infrastructure team were C++ experts, this was not a team blessed with object orientation skills. We tried several times to reason with them with no success. Within a month, most of us had left the project, as we could all see that the problems with the project would only be getting worse.

The Real Solution

Although arguments can be made against the inheritance hierarchy, the real problem was with the interfaces and the consultant's quest for maximum code reuse. Hence, the methods were as generic as possible and used arguments based on the **Primitive** class.

However, with a little thought and a minimum of effort, the interfaces could have been made to work correctly. The solution is to move the run-time checking of the argument types to the compiler. After all, the compiler is very good at determining if a method is being called with the correct argument types. The interface could have been coded as follows:

```
class Interface
{
    public:
        void method1 (Integer i) { oldMethod1 (i); }
        void method1 (Character c) { oldMethod1 (c); }

        void method2 (Integer i, Float f)
                    { oldMethod2 (i, f); }
        void method2 (Integer i, String str)
                    { oldMethod2 (i, str); }

    private:
        void oldMethod1 (Primitive p);
        void oldMethod2 (Primitive p1, Primitive p2);
};
```

Using this new interface, it can never be used incorrectly, as the published methods support specific types and not the generic **Primitive** class, as shown here:

```
Integer i = 0;
Character c = 'a';
Float fl = 2.1;
Interface* If = new Interface;

If->method1 (i)       // this will compile
If->method1 (fl)      // this will not compile

If->method2 (i, fl)   // this will compile
If->method2 (c, fl)   // this will not compile
```

The compiler now does the job of deciding whether the type of an argument can be used in conjunction with a particular method, rather than waiting to see if it is checked correctly at run-time.

In addition, any further extensions to the **Primitive** class hierarchy will have no effect on the interface, unlike before, unless appropriate methods are added.

Summary

This chapter has discussed the following design constructs:

- ► Process objects
- ► Delegating responsibility
- ► Method responsibility
- ► Friend
- ► Multiple inheritance
- ► Misused inheritance

The next chapter discusses advanced design topics.

Advanced Design

This chapter takes design constructs to the next phase. The constructs discussed are not used in every project, but they will be invaluable for more complex projects. The design constructs discussed are, as follows:

▶ Advanced Application Programming Interface (API), providing an extension to the standard API construct.

▶ Threading, designing applications that do more than one thing at a time.

▶ Model / View / Controller, the model is the engine of the application, the controller directs it, and the views register to watch the changes in the model.

▶ Exposing the interface; this construct allows the designer to expose the interface of a class in discrete steps.

▶ Reference counting; this construct is used to avoid memory problems encountered with shallow copy constructors, when the copies are shared between multiple tasks. Chapter 4 has introduced the definition of the shallow copy constructor.

Advanced API Construct

The API construct allows a class to be written against a specific interface that several, essentially similar, classes will be written to support. As a recap, this illustration shows the notation used by the API construct discussed in Chapter 3.

This construct works well, unless objects based on the interface classes are interchanged. For example, Illustration 2 shows an object that is created representing a person as a baby. As the baby grows up, it is replaced with the object of an infant, followed by a teenager, and finally by adult. At each transition, a new object needs to be created to replace the existing one. Any references to the previous object now need to be updated to use the new object. It would be useful if the transitions between the ages of a person could be made without updating references to the objects.

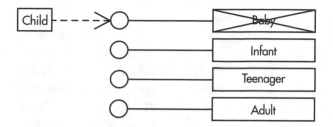

What Is the Advanced API Construct?

What is different with the Advanced API construct is that it provides a central reference that hides the underlying changes. The following illustration shows the notation for this new construct.

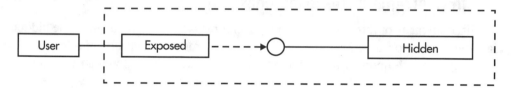

Although the API construct allows similar objects to be interchanged with one another, it imposes an overhead. In the following API example, the **:User** object will do the work if one variant object is replaced with another. The reference held by the **:User** object needs to be set to use the new variant object. It would be useful if the transitions between the ages of a person could be made without involving outside objects. You can achieve this by adding another layer of abstraction. The diagram for this example is shown here:

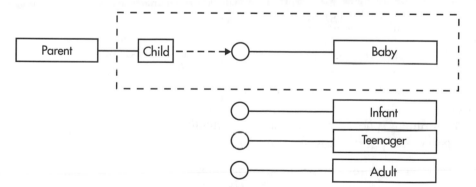

This new layer isolates the changes without involving outside objects. This is particularly important if the **:User** object was joined by other **:User** objects. Using the API construct, each outside object would need to be involved if the object underwent a transition from Baby to Infant. Every reference to the object would have to be changed.

Using the Advanced API construct, every outside object maintains its reference to the object, while the object associated with the interface changes. The advantage of this construct is that it enables the system to grow while reducing the impact of change.

The disadvantage of this construct is that all of the hidden class definitions have different interfaces. The **Baby** class definition defines a more limited set of methods than either the **Child** or **Adult** class definitions. This means that the interface cannot be implemented to support them all.

How to Overcome Its Disadvantages

The disadvantages of this construct can be overcome when you write all of the hidden class definitions to support the specific interface. To resolve the problem of the derived class definitions defining different interfaces, apply one of the following two solutions:

▶ Cater for every method in both the exposed class and the interface class definitions. Obviously not a viable solution as both the front and interface class definitions will need to be updated to keep track of new methods. Not only that, but every hidden class definition needs to provide an implementation of a method if it is supported by another derived class definition.

```
baby:changeNappy ()
adult:changeNappy ()

baby:whereDoYouWork ()
adult:whereDoYouWork ()
```

▶ The alternative is to provide a limited subset of methods that are supported by most or every derived class definition. These can then also be supported by the front and interface class definitions.

The problem is now how to support the remaining methods. The solution is to add a method that supports a keyword and some arguments:

```
answer = aPerson:question ( "changeNappy" );
answer = aPerson:question ( "whereDoYouWork" );
```

The **aPerson:** object (**PersonEnvelope** class definition) passes the question through to the enclosed derived class object (Baby, Child, or Adult), which have all overridden the *question* method defined in the **PersonLetter** class definition. If the question is not supported by the derived class object, then a "NotSupported" response can be given; otherwise, the appropriate response is returned.

Threading

Threading allows an application to execute a secondary task while continuing to execute the main task. An advantage of using threads is that applications can better utilize machines that provide multiple CPUs, since each thread of an application could execute on its own CPU.

An example of a software application that uses threads is Philosophers. The basic description of how the philosopher's application works is as follows:

> "There are 10 philosophers who spend their lives either eating or thinking. Each philosopher has his own place at a circular table, in the center of which is a large bowl of rice. To eat rice requires two chopsticks, but only 10 chopsticks are provided, one between each pair of philosophers. The only chopsticks a philosopher can pick up are those on his immediate right and left. Each philosopher is identical in structure, alternately eating, then thinking."

A solution to the above problem is to write the code for one philosopher. Having written this code, the next step is to create a number of threads each running the philosopher code. Problems associated with sharing the chopsticks between the philosophers are discussed in the next section.

Threads essentially come in two forms:

▶ **Detached**   A thread that runs independently of the main program. The main program could exit before this thread finishes. Notation for this form of thread is:

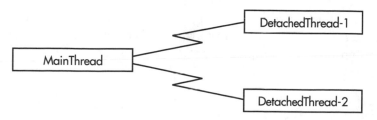

► **Joinable**   Use this style of thread if you want the main program to wait for it to finish. Notation for this form of thread is shown here:

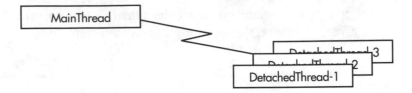

Synchronizing Resources

It is likely that threads will share resources, and therefore there is the possibility that they will also try to use these resources at the same time. This is a called a race condition, as each thread tries to access the resource before another. To prevent this, the code can be synchronized to allow only one thread to access the resource at a time.

In C++, this synchronization is achieved by using a mutually exclusive lock, or *mutex*. Only one thread can hold the mutex, thus preventing other threads from doing so. In Java, this synchronization is achieved by using the keyword 'synchronized.' Both implementations are shown here.

Synchronizing in C++

```
lock_mutex (named_mutex)
    synchronized code
unlock_mutex (named_mutex)
```

Synchronizing in Java

```
synchronized (lock variable)
{
    synchronized code
}
```

Sometimes, however, it is important to be able to take control of a resource and keep it for a prolonged period. In this instance, the location in the code where the mutex is acquired could be remote from where it is to be unlocked. The C++ supports this prolonged controlling of a resource, and in fact, the implementation is similar to before.

```
// inside first method
lock_mutex (named_mutex)
```

```
// inside second method
unlock_mutex (named_mutex)
```

Unfortunately, Java does not support this, as the 'synchronize' construct is limited to working within a single method.

Problem with Java Synchronization

In the C++ implementation, if the lock of the mutex fails because it is already locked, the calling thread stops processing waiting for the *mutex* to become free. To provide full synchronization of resources in Java, there is a need to provide a blocking mechanism, similar to the mutex construct in C++. Here are two sets of example utility methods. The first set uses a single Boolean for each mutex, while the second set uses a list for the mutex.

First Set of Utility Methods—Single Boolean per Mutex

The chopsticks are implemented as an array of Booleans:

```
private static Boolean    chopsticks = new Boolean [<number of philosophers>];
```

This method is the request method:

```
public void Psem (int pos)
{
    boolean    flag;

    System.out.println (threadName + " RequestLock");
```

The code is synchronized (one thread at a time):

```
    synchronized (Dinner.chopstickLock [pos])
    {
```

A snapshot is taken of the current value of the mutex:

```
        flag = Dinner.chopstickLock [pos].booleanValue ();
```

If the result is 'false' (mutex is free), set the value to true (acquire it) and then return

```
        if (flag == false)
        {
            Dinner.chopstickLock [pos] = new Boolean (true);
            System.out.println (threadName + " AcquiredLock");
            return;
```

```
        }
    }
```

else, while the flag remains true (acquired by someone else):

```
    while (flag == true)
    {
```

synchronize the code,

```
        synchronized (Dinner.chopstickLock [pos])
        {
```

and take a snapshot of the value of the mutex:

```
            flag = Dinner.chopstickLock [pos].booleanValue ();
```

If the result is 'false' (mutex is free), set the value to true (acquire it) and then return

```
            if (flag == false)
            {
                Dinner.chopstickLock [pos] = new Boolean (true);
                System.out.println (threadName + " AcquiredLock");
                return;
            }
        }
```

else, wait for 0.2 of a second and repeat

```
        try {wait (200);}
        catch (InterruptedException e) {}
    }
}
```

This method is the release method:

```
public void Vsem (int pos)
{
    System.out.println (threadName + " Vsem " + pos);
```

The code is synchronized (one thread at a time):

```
    synchronized (Dinner.chopstickLock [pos])
    {
```

The boolean is set to false (released):

```
        Dinner.chopstickLock [pos] = new Boolean (false);
    }
}
```

Second Set of Utility Methods—A List per Mutex

The lockList is implemented as a Vector. A Vector is an array of objects that provide indexing facilities and dynamically resizes when appropriate.

```
private static Vector     lockList = new Vector ();
```

This method requests the lock, and if it fails, the method causes the thread to block until the thread acquires the lock or is unblocked.

```
public void RequestLock ()
{
    Boolean     empty;
```

First, synchronize usage of the lockList so that only one thread has access, then set a flag to show the emptiness of the list. Finally, add self to the list—this is important.

```
    synchronized (lockList)
    {
        empty = lockList.isEmpty ();
        lockList.addElement (this);
    }
```

The empty flag reflects the number of threads waiting for the lock:

▶ If 'empty == false', there is a thread already using the mutex, so this thread must wait

▶ If 'empty != false', then the mutex is free to use, so the routine returns immediately.

▶ If this thread had not added itself to the list when it acquired the mutex, a second thread would see an empty list and would not wait. A second flag could be used to indicate a locked mutex, but adding the thread to the list works equally well.

```
    if (empty == false)
    {
```

```
        try {this.wait ();}
        catch (InterruptedException e) {}
    }
```

This method exits if the list is empty or this thread has been woken up (unblocked). The thread is woken up by the ReleaseLock method:

```
}
```

This method is called when the active thread wants to release the lock. It finds the first waiting thread (if any) then wakes it up.

```
public void ReleaseLock ()
{
    Thread    peek;
```

Synchronize usage of the lockList so that only one thread has access:

```
    synchronized (lockList)
    {
```

Remove self from the list, leaving only waiting threads on the list:

```
        lockList.removeElement (this);
```

If the list is not empty, there is another waiting to use this lock:

```
        if (lockList.isEmpty () == false)
        {
            try
            {
```

Get the first element on the list:

```
                peek = (Thread)lockList.firstElement ();
```

Synchronize the thread, so that nothing else is trying to use it:

```
                synchronized (peek)
                {
```

Wake up the thread:

```
                peek.notify ();
            }
        }
        catch (NoSuchElementException e) {}
    }
}
```

These methods can now be used to provide locking to resources and to provide the blocking capabilities provided in C++. They are used, as follows:

```
public void run()
{
    System.out.println ("Starting " + threadName);
    RequestLock ();
    System.out.println ("Doing something " + threadName);
    ReleaseLock ();
}
```

Deadlock on Resources

Deadlock is a condition that occurs when two more threads have taken out locks on resources that other threads require for continuous use. For example, there are two threads that each requires two locks to complete the action they want to perform. If the first thread obtains the first lock and the second thread obtains the second lock, the system reaches a deadlock as neither thread can continue, as it can never obtain the second lock.

The classic threading example Philosophers is used not only to demonstrate how threading works, but also to provide an example of deadlock. The premise behind the Philosophers' program is that several philosophers reach a table and sit down to eat.

In order to eat, each philosopher must pick up two chopsticks; one chopstick is shared with the philosopher on the left and the other chopstick is shared with the philosopher on the right. Having taken one mouthful, to stop the other philosophers from starving, the philosopher puts down both chopsticks and does some thinking before trying to pick up the chopsticks for another mouthful. Deadlock occurs when every philosopher picks up his right-hand chopstick, thus depriving his right-hand neighbor of a left-hand chopstick.

The typical implementation of Philosophers relies on the philosophers sitting down to the table and starting their sequence sequentially, as in philosopher number 1 always gets to the table before the last philosopher.

This theory works well until a random element is introduced. Philosophers could take differing lengths of time to think between eating their food, or if they failed to pick up a chopstick they could take differing lengths of time again.

Try to Lock a Mutex

So how can this issue be fixed? C++ has a mechanism that allows a thread to try and lock a mutex, or in the example to try and pick a chopstick. This is fine, but how does it help? If the philosopher manages to pick up the right-hand chopstick, they then try to pick up the left-hand chopstick. If they fail to pick up the left-hand chopstick, control is returned to the philosopher thread, which being of a generous nature, could release the right-hand chopstick, thereby allowing the philosopher on his right-hand side the opportunity to eat if able.

```
// The argument passed in, is the position of the philosopher at the table
public int Psem_try (int pos)
{
```

First, synchronize usage of the chopstick at the position specified. If the chopstick is on the table (booleanValue is false), then pick it up, change the booleanValue to true, and return the value 0—chopstick acquired. Otherwise, return the value 1—chopstick in use; philosopher must wait:

```
    synchronized (Dinner.chopstickLock [pos])
    {
        if (Dinner.chopstickLock [pos].booleanValue () == false)
        {
            Dinner.chopstickLock [pos] = new Boolean (true);
            System.out.println (threadName + " AcquiredLock");
            return 0;
        }
        else
```

```
            {
                System.out.println (threadName + " WaitingForLock");
                return 1;
            }
        }
    }
}
```

These methods can now be used to provide locking to resources while providing protection from deadlock. They are used as follows:

```
// Each philosopher is tasked taking 5 bites from the food in front
of them for (int i = 0; i < 5; i++)
{
```

Acquire the chopstick to the philosopher's right:

```
    Psem (rightChopstick);
```

While the request to acquire the left-hand chopstick using the method 'Psem_try' is denied, release the right-hand chopstick. Contemplate for 20 milliseconds. Re-acquire the right-hand chopstick:

```
    while (Psem_try (leftChopstick) == 1)
    {
        Vsem (rightChopstick);
        try {sleep (20);}
        catch (InterruptedException e) {}
        Psem (rightChopstick);
    }
```

With both chopsticks acquired, take a bite of the food. Take 20 milliseconds to digest the food. Release both chopsticks:

```
    System.out.println ("All chopsticks acquired " + threadName);
    try {sleep (20);}
    catch (InterruptedException e) {}
    Vsem (leftChopstick);
    Vsem (rightChopstick);
```

Contemplate for 100 milliseconds before trying to eat again:

```
    try {sleep (100);}
    catch (InterruptedException e) {}
}
```

Deadlock can also occur using the other set of utility methods. while testing the Java code I had written for Case Study #2, the multi-threading airport in Chapter 11, I noticed that although an aircraft had just left the airport and had released the runway mutex, one waiting aircraft did not land, nor did another waiting aircraft take off. The reason was another form of deadlock where neither aircraft knew the runway was free. On careful examination of the code is was possible for both aircraft to snapshot the list and determine it was not empty. The departing aircraft released the runway mutex and tried to wake up the waiting aircraft. The problem was that neither requesting aircraft had added itself to the list yet, so the release 'notify' was missed. So both requesting aircraft put themselves to sleep, never to be woken up.

This is the modifications needed to the 'RequestLock' code:

```
while (empty == false)
{
```

Previously the thread would have waited indefinitely; now make it wait 2 seconds:

```
try {plane.sleep (2000);}
catch (InterruptedException e) {}
```

When the thread wakes up, check the first element in the list:

```
try
{
    peek = (Plane)lockList.firstElement ();
```

If the first element is the thread itself, set the flag to true and exit the while loop:

```
if (peek == plane)
    empty = true;
}
catch (NoSuchElementException e) {}
}
```

Model / View / Controller

Model/View/Controller (MVC) is a mechanism by which the **:Model** object can change its state and have other **:View** objects watch this state change, and perform an action. The state change happens independently of the **:View** objects. Also, the **:Model** object need not know that it is being viewed. A quick example of an MVC model is a radio station as shown in Figure 5-1. The radio station is the **:Model** object, while the listeners are

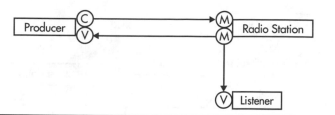

Figure 5-1   *Notation used by MVC diagrams*

the **:View** objects. The radio station does not know who is listening, which is how the **:Model** object works. The **:Controller** object would be the producer who schedules the music, news, and weather reports. The only criteria for the **:Model** object is that it should generate event messages when the changes of state occur. It is these events that the **:View** objects register an interest in.

In the diagram in Figure 5-2, the **:MyStreet** object is designed to simulate my local street. The simulation plays through from 00:01 to 23:59. Some significant events that occur are 'SunRise' and 'SunSet'. The **:MyStreet** object broadcasts an event message whenever these events occur.

The **:StreetLight** object and **:PostalWorker** object have registered an interest in specific event messages, as shown below. The **:StreetLight** object switches itself off when it receives the 'SunRise' event message and switches itself on when it receives the 'SunSet' event message. The **:PostalWorker** object delivers the mail when it receives the 'SunRise' event message.

In the example shown in Figure 5-2, there could be another **:View** object, for instance a **:HomeOwner** object. Instead of viewing the **:MyStreet** object for event messages it could be viewing the **:PostalWorker** object for a MailDelivered event message to collect the newly delivered mail. In this instance, the **:PostalWorker** object would be fulfilling two roles, a view for the **:MyStreet** object and a model for the **:HomeOwner** view object.

A **:Controller** object would send control messages to the **:Model** object; in the simulation of my local street, typical control messages could be, as follows:

▶   StopSimulation

▶   StartSimulation

▶   SunRise

▶   SunSet

▶   ResetSimulation

▶   StartSimulationFromTime

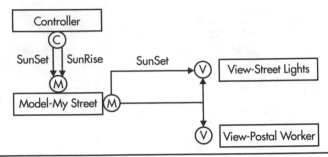

Figure 5-2   *An MVC model of MyStreet*

As a result, the model **:MyStreet** object may generate new event messages, Reset and TimeNow, which can be used by **:View** objects to adjust their state.

Start the simulation from midday would mean that the **:StreetLight** object would need to start in the off state, so it would need to register the TimeNow event.

In the same way that the **:PostalWorker** object could be asked to play two roles, the controller could register as a view of **:MyStreet**. In this way, the controller could ensure that the model is functioning correctly.

Central MVC Controller Approach

This first approach is based around a central MVC controller. This central controller keeps several lists of relevant information. The lists kept by the central MVC controller are

▶   A list of control messages to model methods

▶   A list of model event messages

▶   A list of view objects and model event messages

List 1—Control Messages

This list contains entries that associate a control object message with a model object and the model method that will respond to that message, as shown here:

The model object registers to respond to a control object message. To add to and delete from the list, the methods supported by the central MVC controller are, as follows:

```
ControlRegister (self, controlMessage, model, model_method)
ControlUnregister (self, controlMessage, model)
```

When the control object wants to action the method in the model object, it raises the specified event. To raise the event, a method is called on the central MVC controller, which determines if there are any models registered, and then invokes the specified model methods. The central MVC controller's method is as follows:

```
ControlRaise (self, controlMessage)
```

List 2—Model Event Messages

This list contains entries that record the events that the model object can generate, as shown here:

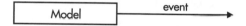

To add to and delete from the list, the methods supported by the central MVC controller are as follows:

```
ModelRegister (self, event)
ModelUnregister (self, event)
```

When the model object wants to generate an event in response to an action, a method is called on the central controller. The central MVC controller's method is as follows.

```
MethodRaise (self, event)
```

List 3—View Objects

This list contains entries that record how a view object reacts to an event raised by a model object, as shown here:

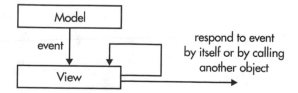

To add to and delete from the list, the methods supported by the central MVC controller are as follows:

```
ViewRegister (self, self_method, model, event)
ViewUnregister (self, model, event)
```

When a specified model raises the specified event, the central MVC controller checks the list of interested view objects and calls the appropriate method.

Possible Problems

A couple of problems can arise when trying to manipulate the event lists; they are

▶ Be careful when adding, searching, or deleting from the list, as other objects may be trying to access the list at the same time. It is important to lock the resource so that only one user can do this at any one time.

▶ Be careful to avoid circular dependencies in the control/model list, as shown here:

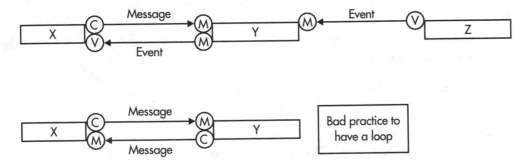

Threaded Approach

Each model object creates a list to accept views interested in a particular event. The nature of MVC is that the model events are asynchronous. To help the system support this, each view creates a thread that then registers with a model. This thread then handles the raised event, as shown here:

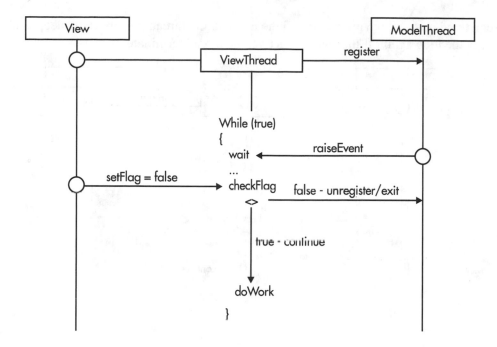

Register for an Event

The **:View** object creates a thread that is used to view any events raised by the **:Model** object. This thread invokes a register method on the **:Model** object, which adds the thread to a list of interested event viewers:

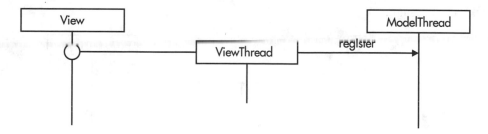

Wait for an Event

The viewer thread has a program loop it will follow. The loop starts by putting the thread to sleep. When the thread is woken up, it checks a flag to see if it has been unregistered while it was asleep. If the flag is still active, the thread processes the registered method; having processed the method, the thread goes back to sleep, and starts the loop again. If the flag is inactive, the thread terminates.

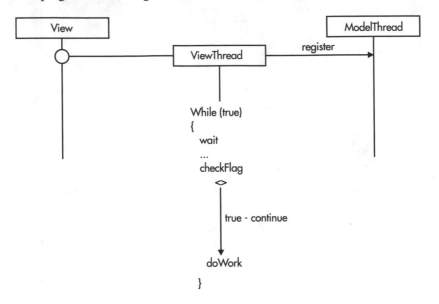

Raise the Event

When the **:Model** object wishes to raise an event, it finds the appropriate event list and takes a copy of it; this is to avoid problems with modifications made to the list while it is being processed. Using the copy of the list, each thread on the list is sent a wake-up message:

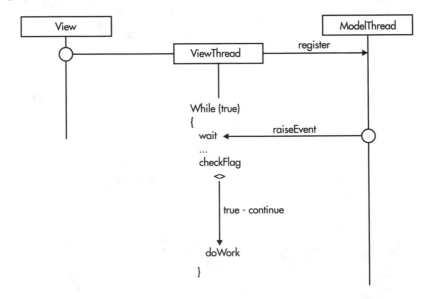

Unregister from Viewing Event

When the main **:View** object thread no longer wishes to be notified by model changes, it sets the threads flag to false, so that the next time the event thread is woken up, it checks the flag, exits the loop, unregisters from the **:Model** object, and then terminates.

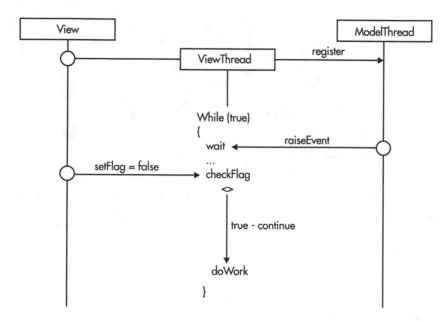

Reactive Approach

The reactive approach does not use separate threads to manage the **:View** objects. Unlike the previous approach, the **:View** object in this example does not perform work other than to react to raised model events.

Java Approach

This approach makes use of the Observer interface and **Observable** class provided by the Java programming language.

The Observer interface provides the ability for any object to become a **:View** object. The **Observable** class is used to create objects that are **:Model** objects. These two classes automatically handle the notification functions of the MVC design. They provide the mechanism by which the views can be automatically notified of changes in the model.

The example shown next has two windows, one with a text field and the other with a scrollbar. The model is a class derived from the **Observable** class and is created by the main application class. The example shows how when the scrollbar is moved, the value in the text field changes, or if the value in the text field changes, the scrollbar changes position.

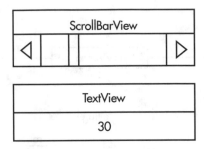

Model

Part of the code for the **Model** class is shown next. The class defines one attribute for storing the viewable information. The **:Model** object does not modify the value of this information itself, it provides a method. The method is passed a new value that is assigned to the attribute. When the attribute has its value changed, the **:Model** object invokes the *setChanged( )* method on itself to indicate that a change has occurred, it then invokes the *notifyObservers( )* method to notify the **:View** objects of the change.

```
import java.util.Observable;

public class Model extends Observable
{
    // set a default value
    private int value = 0;

    public Model (int newValue)
    {
        // set an initial value
        this.value = newValue;
    }

    public void setValue (int newValue)
    {
        // change the value
        this.value = newValue;

        // set the value changed flag
```

```
        // then notify all view objects
        setChanged();
        notifyObservers();
    }
}
```

Observers

Implementing the Observer interface creates the objects that view the changes in another object. The Observer interface requires that an *update( )* method is provided in the new class. The *update( )* method is called whenever the **:Model** changes state and informs the **:View** objects by calling its *notifyObservers( )* method. The **:View** object should then determine the new value and adjust its view appropriately.

Part of the code for a **View** class is shown here:

```java
import java.util.Observer;
import java.util.Observable;

public class View implements Observer
{
    private Model model;

    public View(Model model)
    {
        this.model = model;
    }

    public void update (Observable obs, Object obj)
    {
        // if the object sending the notifyObservers is the
        // expected model
        if (obs == model)
        {
            // display the new value of the model attribute
            System.out.println (model.getCurrentValue());
        }
    }
}
```

Registering a View

Having created a **:Model** object and several **:View** objects, the next step is to register the views with the model. The **Observable** class uses the *addObserver( )*

method to add a viewer to its internal list of **:View** objects to be informed of changes. The following code shows how the *addObserver()* method is used to add the **:View** objects TextView and ScrollBarView.

```
import java.util.Observer;
import java.util.Observable;

public class MVC
{
    public MVC()
    {
        // this model is created with an initial value
        // and minimum and maximum values
        Model model = new ObservableValue (50, 0, 100);
        TextView tv = new TextView (model);
        ScrollBarView sbv = new ScrollBarView (model);

        // add the view objects to the model
        model.addObserver(tv);
        model.addObserver(sbv);
    }

    public static void main(String [] args)
    {
        MVC m = new MVC();
    }
}
```

Implementing Control

This diagram shows the current example.

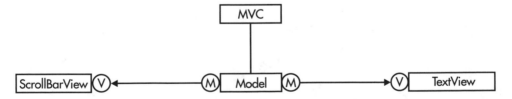

This example moves the scrollbar to the appropriate position and displays the appropriate text value depending on the value within the **:Model** object. The **:Model** object already has a *setValue()* method, it just needs to be utilized.

Each of the existing **:View** objects can be converted into controllers when changes in a **:View** object are reflected in the **:Model** object. When the user moves the scrollbar, the new position is set in the model. This new value is reflected in the text field. When the user changes the value in the text field, the new value is set in the model; this new value is reflected by moving the scrollbar to an appropriate position.

Conclusion

This diagram shows the full example and is followed by the code for the **Model** class, the **ScrollBarView** class, and the **TextView** class.

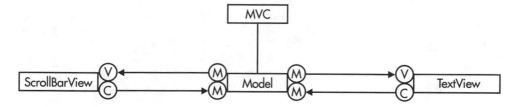

Model

```
import java.util.Observable;

public class Model extends Observable
{
    private int modelValue = 0;
    private int minValue = 0;
    private int maxValue = 0;

    public Model(int value, int min, int max)
    {
        this.modelValue = value;
        this.minValue = min;
        this.maxValue = max;
    }

    // this method sets the model value
    // and then notifies viewing objects
    public void setValue(int value)
    {
        this.modelValue = value;
        setChanged();
```

```
            notifyObservers();
      }

      // this method is used by the view objects to update themselves
      public int getCurrentValue()
      {
            return modelValue;
      }

      // this method returns the minimum value
      public int getMinimumValue()
      {
            return minValue;
      }

      // this method returns the maximum value
      public int getMaximumValue()
      {
            return maxValue;
      }
}
```

ScrollBarView

```
import java.awt.*;
import java.util.Observer;
import java.util.Observable;

public class ScrollBarView extends Frame implements Observer
{
      private Model model;

      private Scrollbar sb = null;

      public ScrollObserver(Model model)
      {
            super("Scroll Observer Tool");

            this.model = model;

            setLayout(new GridLayout(0, 1));
```

```java
        sb = new Scrollbar(Scrollbar.HORIZONTAL,
                        model.getCurrentValue(), 10,
                        model.getMinimumValue(),
                        model.getMaximumValue());

        add(sb);
        pack();
        show();
    }

    public boolean handleEvent(Event evt)
    {
        // if the window is being destroyed,
        // unregister the view object then return
        if (evt.id -- Event.WINDOW_DESTROY)
        {
            model.deleteObserver(this);
            dispose();
            return true;
        }
        else
        {
            if ((evt.id == Event.SCROLL_LINE_UP)
              || (evt.id == Event.SCROLL_LINE_DOWN)
              || (evt.id == Event.SCROLL_PAGE_UP)
              || (evt.id == Event.SCROLL_PAGE_DOWN)
              || (evt.id == Event.SCROLL_ABSOLUTE))
            {
                // change the value in the model to reflect
                // the position of the scrollbar
                model.setValue(sb.getCurrentValue());
                return true;
            }
        }

        return super.handleEvent(evt);
    }

    // this method uses the current value of the model
    // to position the scrollbar
    public void update(Observable obs, Object obj)
    {
        if (obs == model)
        {
```

```
                        sb.setValue(model.getCurrentValue());
                }
        }
}
```

TextViewr

```java
import java.awt.*;
import java.util.Observer;
import java.util.Observable;

public class TextView extends Frame implements Observer
{
    private Model model;
    private TextField txtf;

    private int minimum = 0;
    private int maximum = 0;

    public TextObserver (Model model)
    {
        super("Text Observer Tool");

        this.model = model;

        setLayout(new GridLayout(0, 1));

        minimum = model.getMinimumValue();
        maximum = model.getMaximumValue();

        txtf = new TextField(
                String.valueOf(model.getCurrentValue()));
        add(txtf);
        pack();
        show();
    }

    public boolean action(Event evt, Object obj)
    {
        if (evt.target == txtf)
        {
            int num = 0;
```

```java
        try
        {
            num = Integer.parseInt(tf.getText());
        }
        catch (NumberFormatException nfe)
        {
            num = 0;
        }

        // if the num is less than the minimum
        // set it to minimum
        if (num < minimum)
            num = minimum;

        // if the num is greater than the maximum
        // set it to maximum
        if (num > maximum)
            num = maximum;

        model.setValue(num);
        return true;
    }

    return false;
}

public boolean handleEvent(Event evt)
{
    // if the window is being destroyed,
    // unregister the view object then return
    if (evt.id == Event.WINDOW_DESTROY)
    {
        model.deleteObserver(this);
        dispose();
        return true;
    }

    return super.handleEvent(evt);
}

// this method uses the current value of the model
// to set the text in the text field
public void update(Observable obs, Object obj)
```

```
    {
        if (obs == model)
        {
            txtf.setText(String.valueOf(model.getCurrentValue()));
        }
    }
}
```

Exposing the Interface

The premise behind this construct is that the derived class exposes more of the interface of the inherited class. The notation for this is shown here.

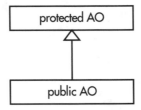

Here is an example of how to use this notation:

```
class Parent
{
    public:
        virtual void method1 ();

    protected:
        virtual void method2 ();
}

class Child : public Parent
{
    public:
        virtual void method2 ();
}
```

An example of how exposing the interface can be used as a replacement to the C++ friend construct. The original design, shown next, is using the friend construct to show a **SecretAgent** class that manages to hide the real name of a **:SecretAgent** instance, by providing a fake *name* method, while hiding the *realName* method as a private method. The **SecretAgent** class makes the **Controller** class a friend, allowing a **:Controller** instance access to the hidden *realName* method.

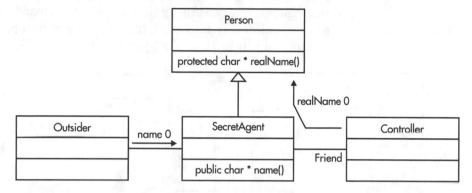

The new design, shown next, is using the exposing interface construct to show a **SecretAgent** class. However this time, because the construct uses inheritance, the *realName* method is declared as a protected method. To provide access to this method, a new class is derived from the **SecretAgent** class. This **AgencyEmployee** class is a special class used by the controller to access the appropriate method.

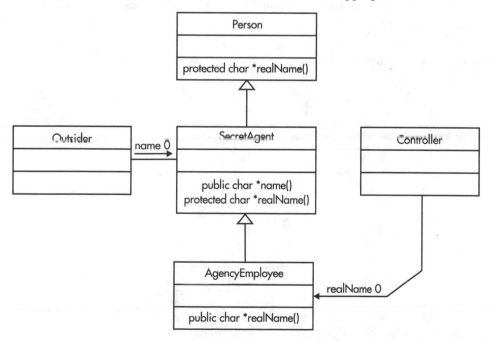

The only problem with this approach is the approach is too realistic; an enemy agency can also derive a class from the **SecretAgent** class to access the *realName* method. However, as with a real secret agent, they have to be suspected first.

Reference Counting

In the previous section on the shallow copy constructor, it was mentioned that there would be a problem if the original object was destructed, then the copy of the object would no longer have data associated with it, as shown here:

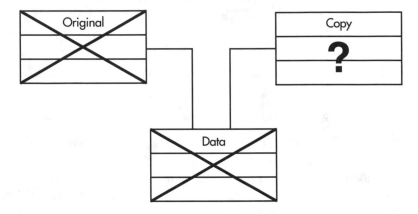

The solution to this problem is to count the number of objects referencing the data, as shown next. This is called reference counting. The idea behind reference counting is for each new reference, such as when the object is copied, to be incremented. When this reference is removed, the count is decremented. If this count reaches zero, the data object is released.

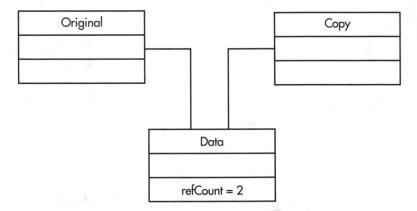

There are two ways to implement reference counting. The first implementation is via inheritance, while the second is via association.

Reference Counting via Inheritance

In this implementation, a class is defined to manage the reference counting. This means that each class that wants to have reference counting facilities should be derived from it. The class declares one attribute, the count, and two methods. The first method increments the count. The second method decrements the count. However, if the count equals zero, then the object can be destroyed.

```
class RefCount
{
    public:
        incRef() { count++; }
        decRef() { --count; if (count == 0) delete this; }
    private:
        int count;
};
```

The RefCount Class can be used as follows:

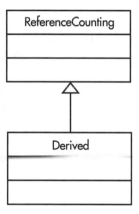

```
class A: public RefCount
{
    // A is now able to support reference counting.
};
```

Reference Counting via Association

In this implementation, there is still a class that manages the reference counting; however, this time, the class is used via association and not via inheritance, as shown next. There is also a difference in the decrement method of the class: it no longer controls the destruction of the data object, it must do that itself.

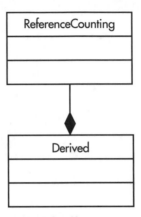

An example of the new reference class and how to associate with it is shown here:

```
class RefCount
{
    public:
        incRef() { count++; }
        decRef() { --count; }

    private:
        int count;
};
class String
{
    public:
        void incRef() { refCount.increment(); }
        void decRef()
            { if (refCount.decrement() == 0) { delete (this); } }

    private:
        char    *buffer;
        RefCount refCount;    // reference count
};
```

An example of an implementation of a copy constructor using a reference counted object is shown here:

```
String::operator = (const String& str)
{
    char *temp = buffer;
    // if the incoming string buffer is not empty, increment the count
    if (str.buffer)
        str.incRef();

    // overwrite the existing buffer with the incoming string buffer
    buffer = str.buffer;

    // if the old string buffer was not empty decrement the count
    if (temp)
        temp.decRef();

    // return a pointer to this object
    return *this;
}
```

Multiple Threaded Applications

There is no correct answer as to which implementation to choose. However, reference counting by association does allow for operating systems that provide a native data type called an atomic integer. This data type is especially important if the application is designed to be multiple threaded. The problem is that any thread can try to access the reference counter at any time, even if there is already a thread accessing it. To avoid such collisions, the atomic integer provides a lock, so that only one thread can modify its value at any given time. Also notice that in the code for the copy constructor above, the incoming **:String** object was incremented before anything else happened; this avoids the object being destroyed while it is being copied.

For operating systems that do not provide a native atomic integer data type, the following code shows how one can be created using mutexes.

```
# include <pthread.h>

class RefCount
{
    public:
        RefCount ();
        ~RefCount ();
```

```
        // lock the mutex, save the incremented value,
        // then unlock the mutex and return the saved value
        int incRef()
        {
            pthread_mutex_lock (&m_mutex);
            int rval = ++m_value;
            pthread_mutex_unlock (&m_mutex);
            return rval;
        }

        // lock the mutex, save the decremented value,
        // then unlock the mutex and return the saved value
        int decRef()
        {
            pthread_mutex_lock (&m_mutex);
            int rval = --m_value;
            pthread_mutex_unlock (&m_mutex);
            return rval;
        }

    private:
        pthread_mutex_t      refMutex;
        int                  count;
};
```

Conclusion

This chapter is the last chapter devoted purely to object-oriented design. The next chapter discusses what happens after the application has been implemented. Subsequent chapters cover testing and debugging, among other topics.

Programming

OBJECTIVES

► Understand the levels involved in testing

► Understand the techniques used when debugging an application

► Learn the basic commands for the three most widely available debugging tools (DBX, GDB, and JDB)

► Learn about porting—multiple operating system support and multiple language support

► Understand the life cycle of an application

# CHAPTER 6

Testing

IN THIS CHAPTER:

Learn the Importance Testing Each Method

Understand How to Test Integrated Classes

Appreciate the Differences Between Stress and Scalability Testing

Understand the Importance of Regression Testing

T he importance of testing cannot be overstated. Testing is used to ensure the quality of the product. It is also used to ensure that the product has not regressed (such as, breaking a feature that previously worked). Finally, testing can help porting teams ensure that the version of the product they have created is every bit as good as the original.

Testing has many different levels, with each level having a particular place in the life cycle of the product. The testing discussed in this chapter covers the whole gamut from testing each line of code to full system testing.

All testing must be planned. If the testing is not planned, as in ad hoc testing, the testing that does take place may not cover significant portions of the application.

Java code from the SimCo case study is used in the test examples that follow.

Test Harness

A test harness is an environment into which software components can be placed and tested. If the class under test does not interact with any other classes, then the test harness consists of a main program and the class under test. If, however, the class under test does interact with other classes, then the test harness consists of a main program, the class under test, and dummy classes to replace the other classes. For each new class or subsystem under test, there will probably be a need for a new main program.

The idea of the test harness is to create an instance of a class or classes, and then via a series of method calls, exercise these classes. With each test, it is important that it is written to be reproducible, self-contained, and very specific.

The reproducible aspect is very important if using a random number generator to mimic unpredictable behavior. When testing the logical flow of the unit under test, do not, for instance, set the random number generator to have a seed (starting point for generating the numbers) based on a truly random event such as the current time. This gives truly unpredictable behavior and makes it impossible to reproduce the test if a problem is detected. For this purpose, load the random number generator with a fixed seed. When this test works, change the seed for the random number generator. Do this several times to build confidence that the test is successful.

The tests need to be self-contained so that they can be run in isolation by anybody. This feature is important when asking someone to fix a problem, as they will need to rerun the test several times to isolate the problem. Finally, when the problem is fixed, the test needs to be rerun to confirm that the problem has indeed been fixed.

A test needs to be very specific so as to achieve its goal of testing specific pieces of functionality. If a test is too broad and a problem is discovered, it will then be necessary to write more tests that are specific enough to identify the problem.

To help in making sure that every line of code is run, use print or output statements at key points during the program. It is important that the output statements are left in place, but can be switched off when no longer required. This may seem unnecessary, but problems can be introduced when the output statements are incorrectly removed. The switch is provided as a system environment variable and is accompanied with the name of a log file. The system environment variable will be introduced when 'Class Testing' is discussed.

What follows is a description of each of the levels of testing that are needed.

Testing the Create and Destroy Methods

Before anything can be tested in a class, it is important to know whether or not instances can be created from the class. Then, having created an instance, test to make sure that when destroyed, it does not leave a residue in the system (known as memory leaks).

Example of a Test

The java code tested comes from CashAccount.java.

TestHarness.java

```
/*
** Name: TestHarness
** This class is the main class in the test harness
*/
import java.util.*;

public class TestHarness
{
    /*
    ** define a variable of the desired class
    */
    public       CashAccount      cash;

    public TestHarness ()
    {
        System.out.println ("Pre-new CashAccount");

        /* Create an object of class 'CashAccount' */
        cash = new CashAccount ();
```

```
            System.out.println ("Post-new CashAccount");
        }

    public static void main (String[] args)
    {
        TestHarness th = new TestHarness ();
    }
}
```

CashAccount.java

```
/*
** Name: CashAccount
** This class has been written to provide support for the bank
** of the company simulated in SimCo.
*/
import java.lang.*;
import java.text.*;
import java.util.*;


/*
** Name: CashAccount
** This method is the constructor for the class
** It assigns zeros to the balance array of the company
**
** Input: none
** Output: none
*/
public class CashAccount
{
    public CashAccount ()
    {
        System.out.println ("New CashAccount instance created");
    }
}
```

Expected Output

```
Pre-new CashAccount
New CashAccount instance created
Post-new CashAccount
```

Method Testing

This level of testing is by far the most thorough and to some the most tedious. However, there are situations where this level of testing is a basic requirement, so it would be prudent to learn how to do it.

Each method within a class is tested in isolation, and the idea of the test is to exercise the method in every conceivable fashion. The result of doing this testing is that every line of code in the method has been run during at least one of the tests. Not only that, but every combination of routes through the code has been run. This form of testing is called logic testing, as it tests the logical flow through the code.

In the output, it is important to rephrase the point in the method at which this print statement is being executed. Here are a few examples of where to use print statements, with a description of how each construct works:

- ► if–then–else
- ► for loop
- ► while loop
- ► switch statement
- ► try–catch
- ► function calls

if–then–else

This construct provides a choice between two options based on whether the test condition evaluates to either a TRUE or a FALSE.

```
if (test condition)
{
    print ("rephrase the test condition - TRUE")
    code to be executed
}
else
{
    print ("rephrase the test condition - FALSE")
    code to be executed
}
```

This construct can also be nested; for example:

```
if (<today is a workday>)
{
    print ("<today is a workday> - TRUE")
    code to be executed
}
else
{
    print ("<today is a workday> - FALSE")
    if (<today is a Saturday>)
    {
        print ("<today is a Saturday> - TRUE")
        code to be executed
    }
    else
    {
        print ("<today is a Saturday> - FALSE")
        code to be executed
    }
}
```

for Loop

This construct provides the ability to perform an action a pre-determined number of times. Although each loop normally runs to completion, it is possible to alter the way a loop runs, by using additional constructs. For example, you can use Continue to force an early finish to the current loop, and Break to force an early exit from the loop construct.

```
print ("rephrase for loop criteria - BEFORE")
for (for loop criteria 'initialization;condition;increment')
{
    print ("current value of loop variable")
    code to be executed

    <test condition>
    {
        print ("break out of the loop -\
                current value of loop variable")
        break
    }
```

```
    <test condition>
    {
        print ("continue with next loop -\
                current value of loop variable")
        continue
    }

    print ("end of loop")
}
// Because the loop could have been exited other than
// the loop condition having been met
// restate the current value of the loop count
print ("rephrase for loop criteria - AFTER")
```

while Loop

This construct provides the ability to perform an action for an undetermined number of times. The loop continues while the test condition evaluates to TRUE. Each loop normally runs to completion, although as with the *for loop* construct, it is possible to alter the way a loop runs by using additional constructs. For example, use Continue to force an early finish to the current loop, and Break to force an early exit from the loop construct.

```
print ("rephrase while loop criteria - BEFORE")
while (test condition)
{
    print ("rephrase the loop condition")
    code to be executed

    <test condition>
    {
        print ("break out of the loop")
        break
    }

    <test condition>
    {
        print ("continue with next loop")
        continue
    }

    print ("end of loop - rephrase the loop condition")
```

```
}
// Because the loop could have been exited other than
// a change in test condition result, restate the current
// value of the test condition
print ("rephrase while loop criteria - AFTER")
```

switch Statement

This construct provides a choice between multiple options. There is a test condition, which renders a value and not a TRUE or FALSE. Each value rendered has a corresponding catch point in a 'case (value)' statement. The 'default' statement catches any value not caught with a specific 'case' statement.

```
print ("switch condition - BEFORE")
switch (switch condition)
    case (value):
        print ("rephrase switch condition - switch value")
        code to be executed
    default:
        print ("rephrase switch condition - DEFAULT")
        code (if any) to be executed
print ("switch condition - AFTER")
```

try—catch

The nice thing about a try-catch construct is that it allows sections of code to have local exception handling. If an exception is generated, it unwinds the program (all of the way back to the main program, if necessary) looking for a catch designed to handle it. However, what typically happens is that a catch is set up to pick up an exception (a throw) from somewhere completely unrelated to the local code. For instance, the main program may be set up with a catch that handles generic exceptions just before the program exits. From a testing point of view, this is not very useful, as the origin of the exception is unknown, especially if there are several places that could generate this exception. So, it is very important to place print statements just before an exception is thrown.

```
try
{
    print ("Inside 'try' #n")
    code to be executed
        // whenever an exception is about to be generated
        // it is important to document it.
        print ("Just before a throw of exception 'x'")
        throw new exception_type (argument)
}
catch (exception_type and argument)
{
    print ("Inside 'catch' #n - exception 'x'")
    code to be executed
}
```

Java Addition

```
finally
{
    // This code can be reached because:
    // 1: Normal by reaching the end of the try-block
    // 2: After an exception that has been caught
    // 3: After an exception that has not been caught
    // 4: Any other reason leaving the try-block
    //    break, continue or return statement
    print ("Inside 'Finally' #n")
}
```

Around a Function Call

Just as important as tracing progress of the program through loops or if-then-else structures is the tracing of how the methods themselves are called and from where. This is important if a method can be called from different locations, as it can be used to monitor the flow of the application. If a method is called repeatedly, it could become the focus of a performance bottleneck, so monitoring the flow of the system is very important.

```
print ("'current method' - 'next method' - BEFORE")
next_method (...)
print ("'current method' - 'next method' - AFTER")
```

Example of a Single Method Test

The method tested is setBalance () from CashAccount.java.

Code Added to TestHarness.java

```
/* previous code that constructed the 'cash' object */

System.out.println ("Pre-CashAccount:setBalance-2000.0");
cash.setBalance (2000.00);
System.out.println ("Post-CashAccount:setBalance-2000.0");

/* end of TestHarness constructor */
```

Code Added to CashAccount.java

```
/*
** Name: setBalance
** This method sets the balance of the current month
**
** Input: amount to be set
** Output: none
*/
public void setBalance (double money)
{
    System.out.println ("CashAccount:setBalance-" + money);
    balance = money;
    System.out.println
        ("CashAccount:setBalance-balance=" + balance);
}
```

Expected Output

```
Pre-new CashAccount
New CashAccount instance created
New CashAccount-balance=0.0
Post-new CashAccount
Pre-CashAccount:setBalance-2000.0
CashAccount:setBalance-2000.0
CashAccount:setBalance-balance=2000.0
Post-CashAccount:setBalance-2000.0
```

Class Testing

Having successfully completed all of the method tests, the user is now in a position where s/he can guarantee the implementation of each method. The next set of tests are concerned with how a class reacts to life-cycle tests. These tests are integration tests for a class; they determine how a class reacts to being created and each of its methods being called in a typical system scenario. The test should determine if the calling of any methods has undesirable side effects or consequences for other methods. For instance, is it important that certain methods be called in a particular order, for example, first initialize environment, and only then do something. If this situation exists, it may not have been apparent when individually calling the methods using a test harness, but is now something that would cause a problem. Therefore, the designer/programmer needs to ensure that either the problematic combination of method calls is prevented, or they are handled with appropriate messaging.

The test harness now needs to be modified to run from a prepared script. Each script runs the class through a series of scenarios, in an attempt to exercise every possible combination of methods calls.

Example of a Test Using a Script

The script is designed to test one of the many combinations of method calls that could be made to the **CashAccount** class.

Rewrite of TestHarness.java

There are two additions to TestHarness.java. The first addition allows it to switch on and off the output statements, and the second addition allows the test harness to handle a script file. The output statements can be assigned a number so that different sections of the code can have their output statements enabled at different times. In addition, a file name can be specified to receive the messages that were previously displayed directly to the user. System environment variables can also be used in C++, with getenv command used to access them.

Start with the addition of global variables used throughout SimCo. The first sets the size of the arrays, while the second is used to reference the last month.

```
public final int nummonths = 6;
public final int lastmonth = 5;
```

Rather than making the *traceOut* method static in the **TestHarness** class, create the ability to reference it as an instance method. It makes the code easier to handle.

```
private static TestHarness        testH;
private static int                traceN;
private static String             traceF;
private static PrintStream        log;

private void traceOut (int number, String mesg)
{
    /*
    ** If the system environment trace level matches that of the
    ** output statement, output the message
    */
    if (number == traceN)
    {
        log.println (mesg);
    }
}

public TestHarness ()
{
    ...
    /* needs to be placed inside the constructor for TestHarness */
    testH = this;
    ...
}

public static void main (String[] args)
{
    /*
    ** Read the trace level system environment variable,
    ** if the value is not set, return "0"
    */
    String traceNstr = System.getProperty ("TRACEN", "0");
    /* Parse the returned value to return the integer value */
    traceN = Integer.parseInt (traceNstr);
    /*
    ** Read the file system environment variable,
```

```
    ** if the value is not set,
    ** use "test.out" to create a file in the current directory
    */
    traceF = System.getProperty ("TRACEF", "test.out");

    /* if the trace level is not the default open the file */
    if (traceN != 0)
    {
        try
        {
            log = new PrintStream
                (new FileOutputStream (traceF), true);
        }
        catch (FileNotFoundException e) { System.err.println (e); }
    }
    TestHarness th = new TestHarness ();
}

public static TestHarness GetThis ()
{
    return testH;
}
```

To set the environment variables for the application, use:

```
java -DTRACEN=1 -DTRACEF=Test1.dat TestHarness
```

Next are the variables used to read the script file and parse it ready to use:

String	line	The line is read from the script file into this variable.
StringTokenizer	t	This variable parses the line into separate tokens.
int	classNum	The class number allows switch statements to be used.
String	className	This is the name of the class being tested.
int	methodNum	The method number allows switch statements to be used.
String	method	This is the name of the method being tested.
String	args	This is the string of arguments specified in the script file.
int	intVal	This is an 'int' used when required.
Double	Dval	In order to extract a double from a string it must first become a Double.
double	dVal	This is a 'double' used when required.

The opening of a file must be surrounded by a try and catch for an IOException:

```
try
{
    /* open the script file */
    BufferedReader script =
    new BufferedReader (new FileReader ("script.dat"));

    /* close the script file */
    script.close ();
}
catch (IOException e)
{ System.err.println (e); }
```

The reading of the script file is inside a never-ending for-loop. This loop will only exit if there is an error reading the file, the end of the file is reached, or a pre-defined marker is encountered. The pre-defined marker is a single ':' by itself at the beginning of a line.

```
for (;;)
{
    /* read a line and break if it is empty */
    line = script.readLine();
    if (line == null) break;

    /*
    ** count the number of tokens there are on the line
    ** if the line consists of a solitary ':', break
    */
    t = new StringTokenizer (line, ":");
    if (t.countTokens () == 0) break;

    /* parse each line */
}
```

The class number is the first token to be extracted from the line. It is extracted as a number so that it can be used in a switch statement. If the class number equals zero, then this line is a comment.

```
/* if the classNum == 0, it is a comment, ignore it */
classNum = Integer.parseInt (t.nextToken ());
if (classNum == 0)
    continue;
```

Subsequent pieces of information can now be extracted from the line. First of these is the name of the class which is a string. The second piece of information is the number of the method to be tested; this is extracted as a number as it can be used in a switch statement. Next comes the name of the method to be tested; this is a string. Finally, there is a string that contains a comma-separated list of arguments.

```
/* process the remainder of the line */
className = t.nextToken ();
methodNum = Integer.parseInt (t.nextToken ());
routine = t.nextToken ();
args = t.nextToken ();
```

In this example script the class being tested is the **CashAccount** class; there are six methods that could possibly be tested.

```
case 1: cash = new CashAccount (); break;
case 2:
{
    /* balanceByIndex takes an int argument */
    intVal = Integer.parseInt(args);
    cash.balanceByIndex (intVal);
    break;
}
case 3:
{
    /* credit takes a double argument */
    DVal = Double.valueOf (args);
    dVal = DVal.doubleValue ();
    cash.credit (dval);
    break;
}
case 4:
{
    /* debit takes a double argument */
    DVal = Double.valueOf (args);
    dVal = DVal.doubleValue ();
    cash.debit (dVal);
    break;
}
```

```
case 5:
{
    /* setBalance takes a double argument */
    DVal = Double.valueOf (args);
    dVal = DVal.doubleValue ();
    cash.setBalance (dVal);
    break;
}
case 6: cash.adjustMonth(); break;
```

Between each section of output generated, insert a blank line, just to make the output a little easier to read:

```
/* print a separator between line of output */
traceOut (1, " ");
```

CashAccount.java

To be able to reference the global variables declared as part of the **TestHarness** class, you need to create an object of the **TestHarness** class.

```
TestHarness    parent;
```

The information about the balances of the current month and previous months is kept in an array of doubles:

```
double    balance [];
```

The constructor for the **CashAccount** class obtains the reference to the **TestHarness** to create the array of doubles and then assigns zero to each location:

```
public CashAccount ()
{
    int    i;

    /*
    ** Get the reference of the test harness
    */
```

```
    parent = (TestHarness)TestHarness.GetThis();

    parent.traceOut (1, "New CashAccount instance created");

    balance = new double [parent.nummonths];
    parent.traceOut (1, "Pre-for loop:i < parent.nummonths=" +
        parent.nummonths);
    for (i = 0; i < parent.nummonths; i++)
    {
        parent.traceOut (1, "start:i < parent.nummonths:i=" + i);
        balance [i] = 0;
        parent.traceOut (1, "balance [" + i + "]=" + balance [i]);
        parent.traceOut (1, "end:i < parent.nummonths");
    }
    parent.traceOut
        (1, "Post-for loop:i=" + i + " < parent.nummonths");
}
```

The *balanceByIndex* method returns the balance at a particular index in the array:

```
public double balanceByIndex (int index)
{
    parent.traceOut (1, "CashAccount:balanceByIndex-balance [" +
        index + "]=" + balance [index]);
    return balance [index];
}
```

The *credit* method adds to the balance of the current month the amount specified:

```
public void credit (double money)
{
    parent.traceOut (1, "CashAccount:crebit-balance=" +
        balance [parent.lastmonth] + " money " + money);
    balance [parent.lastmonth] = balance [parent.lastmonth] + money;
    parent.traceOut (1, "CashAccount:crebit-balance=" +
        balance [parent.lastmonth]);
}
```

The *debit* method subtracts an amount specified from the balance of the current month, as shown next.

```
public void debit (double money)
{
    parent.traceOut (1, "CashAccount:debit-balance=" +
        balance [parent.lastmonth] + " money " + money);
    balance [parent.lastmonth] = balance [parent.lastmonth] - money;
    parent.traceOut (1, "CashAccount:debit-balance=" +
        balance [parent.lastmonth]);
}
```

The *setBalance* method sets the balance of the current month to the amount specified:

```
public void setBalance (double money)
{
    parent.traceOut (1, "CashAccount:setBalance-" + money);
    balance [parent.lastmonth] = money;
    parent.traceOut (1, "CashAccount:setBalance-balance=" +
        balance [parent.lastmonth]);
}
```

The *adjustMonth* method rotates the balances held in the array by one month. The oldest month is removed from the array, while the balance for the current month becomes the balance for last month:

```
public void adjustMonth ()
{
    int    i;

    parent.traceOut (1, "Pre-for loop:i < parent.lastmonth=" +
        parent.lastmonth);
    for (i = 0; i < parent.lastmonth; i++)
    {
        parent.traceOut (1, "start:i < parent.lastmonth:i=" + i);
        balance [i] = balance [i + 1];
        parent.traceOut (1, "balance [" + i + "]=" + balance [i]);
        parent.traceOut (1, "end:i < parent.lastmonth");
    }
    parent.traceOut
        (1, "Post-for loop:i=" + i + " < parent.lastmonth");
}
```

Script File—Expected Output

This table shows the script passed to the test harness on the left and the expected output on the right:

0: This script is designed to test the 0: creation of a CashAccount object 1:CashAccount:1:new:-:	New CashAccount instance created Pre-for loop:i < parent.nummonths=6 start:i < parent.nummonths:i=0 balance [0]=0.0 end:i < parent.nummonths start:i < parent.nummonths:i=1 balance [1]=0.0 end:i < parent.nummonths start:i < parent.nummonths:i=2 balance [2]=0.0 end:i < parent.nummonths start:i < parent.nummonths:i=3 balance [3]=0.0 end:i < parent.nummonths start:i < parent.nummonths:i=4 balance [4]=0.0 end:i < parent.nummonths start:i < parent.nummonths:i=5 balance [5]=0.0 end:i < parent.nummonths Post-for loop:i=6 < parent.nummonths
0: Then to check that it is full of zeros 1:CashAccount:2:balanceByIndex:0: 1:CashAccount:2:balanceByIndex:1: 1:CashAccount:2:balanceByIndex:2: 1:CashAccount:2:balanceByIndex:3: 1:CashAccount:2:balanceByIndex:4: 1:CashAccount:2:balanceByIndex:5:	CashAccount:balanceByIndex-balance [0]=0.0 CashAccount:balanceByIndex-balance [1]=0.0 CashAccount:balanceByIndex-balance [2]=0.0 CashAccount:balanceByIndex-balance [3]=0.0 CashAccount:balanceByIndex-balance [4]=0.0 CashAccount:balanceByIndex-balance [5]=0.0
0: To set the balance of the current month 1:CashAccount:5:setBalance:2000.0:	CashAccount:setBalance-2000.0 CashAccount:setBalance-balance=2000.0

0: Rotate the months 1:CashAccount:6:adjustMonth:-:	Pre-for loop:i < parent.lastmonth=5 start:i < parent.lastmonth:i=0 balance [0]=0.0 end:i < parent.lastmonth start:i < parent.lastmonth:i=1 balance [1]=0.0 end:i < parent.lastmonth start:i < parent.lastmonth:i=2 balance [2]=0.0 end:i < parent.lastmonth start:i < parent.lastmonth:i=3 balance [3]=0.0 end:i < parent.lastmonth start:i < parent.lastmonth:i=4 balance [4]=2000.0 end:i < parent.lastmonth Post-for loop:i=5 < parent.lastmonth
0: Credit the balance of the current month 0: with 360.0 1:CashAccount:3:credit:360.0:	CashAccount:crebit-balance=2000.0 money 360.0 CashAccount:crebit-balance=2360.0
0: Rotate the months 1:CashAccount:6:adjustMonth:-:	Pre-for loop:i < parent.lastmonth=5 start:i < parent.lastmonth:i=0 balance [0]=0.0 end:i < parent.lastmonth start:i < parent.lastmonth:i=1 balance [1]=0.0 end:i < parent.lastmonth start:i < parent.lastmonth:i=2 balance [2]=0.0 end:i < parent.lastmonth start:i < parent.lastmonth:i=3 balance [3]=2000.0 end:i < parent.lastmonth start:i < parent.lastmonth:i=4 balance [4]=2360.0 end:i < parent.lastmonth Post-for loop:i=5 < parent.lastmonth
0: Debit the balance of the current month 0: with 340.0 1:CashAccount:4:dedit:340.0:	CashAccount:debit-balance=2360.0 money 340.0 CashAccount:debit-balance=2020.0

0: Rotate the months 1:CashAccount:6:adjustMonth:-:	Pre-for loop:i < parent.lastmonth=5 start:i < parent.lastmonth:i=0 balance [0]=0.0 end:i < parent.lastmonth start:i < parent.lastmonth:i=1 balance [1]=0.0 end:i < parent.lastmonth start:i < parent.lastmonth:i=2 balance [2]=2000.0 end:i < parent.lastmonth start:i < parent.lastmonth:i=3 balance [3]=2360.0 end:i < parent.lastmonth start:i < parent.lastmonth:i=4 balance [4]=2020.0 end:i < parent.lastmonth Post-for loop:i=5 < parent.lastmonth
0: Re-display the array of monthly balances 1:CashAccount:2:balanceByIndex:0: 1:CashAccount:2:balanceByIndex:1: 1:CashAccount:2:balanceByIndex:2:	CashAccount:balanceByIndex-balance [0]=0.0 CashAccount:balanceByIndex-balance [1]=0.0 CashAccount:balanceByIndex-balance [2]=2000.0
1:CashAccount:2:balanceByIndex:3:	CashAccount:balanceByIndex-balance [3]=2360.0
1:CashAccount:2:balanceByIndex:4:	CashAccount:balanceByIndex-balance [4]=2020.0
1:CashAccount:2:balanceByIndex:5:	CashAccount:balanceByIndex-balance [5]=2020.0
.	<end of script>

Integration Testing

In the same way that problems could arise when the methods of a class are tested in combination, this set of testing is designed to ensure that when classes are used in combination, everything works as expected. It is during this phase that the stubs used in the test harness can be replaced by previously successfully tested classes. The tests using real classes should render the same set of results as those tests run against stubs. Obviously if the test differs, there is a problem.

It could be possible that the stubs themselves do not correctly mimic the real classes. If this is the case, then the stubs need to be rewritten and all tests that use them have to be re-run as they have become invalid.

Example of Integration Testing

To make integration testing possible, the test harness source code needs to be modified so that more than one class is supported. This support is made possible by changing the manner in which the script file is processed. Each class is processed with its own method.

In the example below, two new classes have been added. The script being run, will create a **:CashAccount** object, create a **:Factory** object and then a new **:Machine** object, which is added to the **:Factory**.

Modified TestHarness.java

```
public          Factory          factory;

public TestHarness ()
{
...
    /* Process each class in its own method */
    switch (classNum)
    {
        case 1: processCashAccount (methodNum, args); break;
        case 2: processFactory (methodNum, args); break;
        case 3: processMachine (methodNum, args); break;
    }
...
}
```

This is an example of the new class based method:

```
private void processFactory (int methodNum, String args)
{
    int          intVal;
    Double       DVal;
    double       dVal;
    int          retI;
    switch (methodNum)
```

```
    {
        case 1: factory = new Factory (); break;
        /*
        ** factory methods 2,3 and 4 are not tested by this script
        */
        case 5:
        {
            /*
            ** howManyMachines returns the number of
            ** machines already owned
            */
            retI = factory.howManyMachines ();
            parent.traceOut
                (1, "processFactory:howManyMachines=" + retI);
            break;
        }
    }
}
```

Factory.java

```
import java.lang.*;
import java.text.*;
import java.util.*;

public class Factory
{
    TestHarness     parent;

    /*
    ** A Factory keeps a record of how many machines it currently
    ** contains it also keeps a record of how much stock it had at
    ** the start of a manufacturing cycle 'instock' and at the end
    ** of the run 'endstock'
    */
    Vector          machines;
    public int      instock [];
    public int      endstock [];

    public Factory ()
    {
        int     i;
```

```
parent.traceOut (1, "New Factory");
parent = (TestHarness)TestHarness.GetThis();
```

Create the objects:

```
machines = new Vector();
instock = new int [parent.nummonths];
endstock = new int [parent.nummonths];
```

Initialize the 'instock' and 'endstock' arrays:

```
parent.traceOut
    (1, "Factory:Pre-for loop:i < parent.lastmonth=" +
    parent.lastmonth);
for (i = 0; i < parent.nummonths; i++)
{
    parent.traceOut (1, "start:i < parent.nummonths:i=" + i);
        instock [i] = 0;
    parent.traceOut (1, "instock [" + i + "]=0");
        endstock [i] = 0;
    parent.traceOut (1, "endstock [" + i + "]=0");
    parent.traceOut (1, "end:i < parent.nummonths");
}
parent.traceOut (1, "Factory:Post-for loop:i=" + i + " <
    parent.nummonths");
}
```

Add the incoming **:Machine** object to the vector of machines:

```
public void addMachine (Machine newMC)
{
    parent.traceOut (1, "Factory:addMachine");
    machines.add (newMC);
}
```

Return the number of machines in the vector of machine objects:

```
public int howManyMachines ()
{
    int result = machines.size ();
    parent.traceOut
    (1, "Factory:howManyMachines:result=" + result);
    return result;
}
}
```

Machine.java

```
import java.lang.*;
import java.text.*;
import java.util.*;


public class Machine
{
```

Default information that applies to every **:Machine** object:

```
private static final double cost = 2000;
private static final int output = 10;
private static final double overhead = 400;
private static final double rawcost = 220;
```

Whenever a new **:Machine** object is created, debit the **:CashAccount** object the cost of the new **:Machine** object. Then add this new **:Machine** object to the **:Factory** object inventory:

```
public Machine ()
{
    parent.traceOut (1, "New Machine");
    TestHarness parent = TestHarness.GetThis();
    parent.traceOut (1, "Machine:Pre-cash.debit (" + cost + ")");
    parent.cash.debit (cost);
    parent.traceOut (1, "Machine:Pre-addMachine");
    parent.factory.addMachine (this);
}
```

Return the static cost of a machine:

```
static public double mccost ()
{
    parent.traceOut (1, "Machine:mccost:return cost");
    return cost;
}
```

Return the static output of a machine. This is the maximum number of units a machine can manufacture every manufacturing cycle:

```
static public int mcoutput ()
{
    parent.traceOut (1, "Machine:mcoutput:return output");
    return output;
}
```

Return the static overhead of a machine. This is the overhead cost of every machine used to calculate the expenses of manufacturing cycle:

```
static public double mcoverhead ()
{
    parent.traceOut (1, "Machine:mcoverhead:return overhead");
    return overhead;
}
```

Return the static cost of the raw materials used to calculate the expenses of a manufacturing cycle:

```
static public double mcrawcost ()
{
    parent.traceOut (1, "Machine:mcrawcost:return rawcost");
    return rawcost;
}
}
```

Script File—Expected Output

This table shows the script passed to the test harness on the left and the expected output on the right:

0: Create a CashAccount object 1:CashAccount:1:new:-:	New CashAccount instance created Pre-for loop:i < parent.nummonths=6 start:i < parent.nummonths:i=0 balance [0]=0.0 end:i < parent.nummonths start:i < parent.nummonths:i=1 balance [1]=0.0 end:i < parent.nummonths start:i < parent.nummonths:i=2 balance [2]=0.0 end:i < parent.nummonths start:i < parent.nummonths:i=3 balance [3]=0.0 end:i < parent.nummonths start:i < parent.nummonths:i=4 balance [4]=0.0 end:i < parent.nummonths start:i < parent.nummonths:i=5 balance [5]=0.0 end:i < parent.nummonths Post-for loop:i=6 < parent.nummonths
0: To set the balance of the current month 1:CashAccount:5:setBalance:2000.0:	CashAccount:setBalance-2000.0 CashAccount:setBalance-balance=2000.0

0: Create a Factory object 2:Factory:1:new:-:	New Factory Factory:Pre-for loop:i < parent.lastmonth=5 start:i < parent.nummonths:i=0 instock [0]=0 endstock [0]=0 end:i < parent.nummonths start:i < parent.nummonths:i=1 instock [1]=0 endstock [1]=0 end:i < parent.nummonths start:i < parent.nummonths:i=2 instock [2]=0 endstock [2]=0 end:i < parent.nummonths start:i < parent.nummonths:i=3 instock [3]=0 endstock [3]=0 end:i < parent.nummonths start:i < parent.nummonths:i=4 instock [4]=0 endstock [4]=0 end:i < parent.nummonths start:i < parent.nummonths:i=5 instock [5]=0 endstock [5]=0 end:i < parent.nummonths Factory:Post-for loop:i=6 < parent.nummonths
0: Display the last monthly balance 1:CashAccount:2:balanceByIndex:5:	CashAccount:balanceByIndex-balance [5]=2000.0
0: Obtain the static information 3:Machine:2:mccost:-: 3:Machine:3:mcoutput:-: 3:Machine:4:mcoverhead:-: 3:Machine:5:mcrawcost:-:	 Machine:mccost:return cost processMachine:mccost=2000.0 Machine:mcoutput:return output processMachine:mcoutput=10 Machine:mcoverhead:return overhead processMachine:mcoverhead=400.0 Machine:mcrawcost:return rawcost processMachine:mcrawcost=220.0
0: Return the number of machines already purchased 2:Factory:5:howManyMachines:-:	Factory:howManyMachines:result=0 processFactory:howManyMachines=0

0: Purchase a machine 3:Machine:1:new:-:	New Machine Machine:Pre-cash.debit (2000.0) CashAccount:debit-balance=2000.0 money 2000.0 CashAccount:debit-balance=0.0 Machine:Pre-addMachine Factory:addMachine
0: Re-display the last monthly balance 1:CashAccount:2:balanceByIndex:5:	CashAccount:balanceByIndex-balance [5]=0.0
0: Return the number of machines now purchased 2:Factory:5:howManyMachines:-:	Factory:howManyMachines:result=1 processFactory:howManyMachines=1
:	< end of script>

Graphical User Interface Testing

The previous tests have focused on testing the functionality of the application. These next tests are focused on testing the look and feel of the graphical user interface (GUI). Having established that the look and feel is correct, the next phase of testing replaces the previous test harness with this new GUI.

The following two examples cover the basic window, which has minimal interaction with the application via a menu item. Full interaction testing is described in "System Testing," later in this chapter.

Basic Windows

This test is designed to confirm that the GUI looks the way that it should and that the window can be closed. The full window is shown in Figure 6-1.

SimCo.java

```
public class SimCo
{
public static SimCo        simco;
public         Display     disp;
```

There are six months of records kept:

```
public final int nummonths = 6;
```

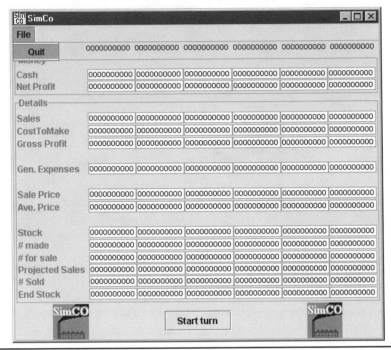

Figure 6-1   *Full SimCo window*

The main class method that creates the **:Display** object is as follows:

```
public SimCo ()
{
    simco = this;
    disp = new Display("SimCo");
}
```

This is the starting method for the application:

```
public static void main (String[] args)
{
    SimCo co = new SimCo ();
}
```

The Global Object method as described in Chapter 5, that allows this **:SimCo** object to be referenced from anywhere, is as follows:

```
public static SimCo GetThis ()
    {
        return simco;
    }
}
```

Display.java

```
public class Display      extends Jframe
                          implements ActionListener
{
    SimCo          parent;
```

Declare the menu items:

```
JMenuBar       menuBar;
JMenu          file;
JMenuItem      miQuit;
```

Declarations for the remaining class variables occur here:

- ▶ Declare the data panels.
- ▶ Declare the text field arrays; each array has six elements.
- ▶ Declare the ImageIcons.

This is main method of the Display class:

```
public Display(String title)
{
    super (title);
```

This window listener will be invoked by the Quit button:

```
addWindowListener(new WindowAdapter ()
{
    public void windowClosing(WindowEvent we) { System.exit (0); }
});
```

Obtain the number of months from the main **:SimCo** object:

```
count = SimCo.GetThis().nummonths;
```

Create the menuBar and attach it to the frame:

```
menuBar = new JMenuBar ();
setJMenuBar (menuBar);
```

Create the menu button and add it to the menu bar:

```
file = new JMenu ("File");
menuBar.add (file);
```

Create a menu drop-down item, add an action listener, add an action keyword, and then add the action keyword to the menu button:

```
miQuit = new JMenuItem ("Quit");
miQuit.addActionListener (this);
miQuit.setActionCommand ("QUIT");
file.add (miQuit);
```

The main display starts with the creation of the JPanel, which will contain the other visual elements:

```
months = new JPanel ();
months.setLayout(new GridBagLayout());
months.setBorder(empty);
```

Create the following items:

- ▶ Label, and position it.
- ▶ Text fields associated with the months.
- ▶ A money panel to hold the cash and net profit data.
- ▶ Details panel to hold the rest of the data.
- ▶ Icon buttons and position the icon buttons around the Start turn button.

Put everything together; using the content pane's BorderLayout set the windows icon.

This is the action method implementation for the Quit menu button:

```
public void actionPerformed (ActionEvent e)
{
    String str = e.getActionCommand ();

    if (str.compareTo (new String ("QUIT")) == 0)
    {
        System.exit (0);
    }
}
}
```

Using Menus

This next section shows the code required to implement the purchasing of a machine.
The functionality is exactly the same as that tested in the integration example, as will
be shown with a comparison of the test output.

The new user window is shown here:

Modified SimCo.java

As part of the class declaration add support for the two new objects,

```
public          CashAccount     cash;
public          Factory         factory;
```

The array is 6 long (nummonths), but the last element is #5:

```
public final int lastmonth = 5;
```

In the main class method, create the **cash:CashAccount** and **factory:Factory**
objects. Initialize the cash:CashAccount to 2000.00:

```
cash = new CashAccount();
cash.setBalance (2000.00);
factory = new Factory ();
```

Modified Display.java

To the class declaration, add two new menu items: admin and miMachine, so that is looks as follows:

```
Jmenu        file, admin;
JMenuItem    miQuit, miMachine;
```

Add two methods that format text strings to fit a text field ten characters wide:

```
DecimalFormat ten_two_f = new DecimalFormat ("###,##0.00");
DecimalFormat ten_d = new DecimalFormat ("##,###,###");
```

Modify the main class string to support the new menu option:

```
public Display(String title)
{
    ...
    parent = SimCo.GetThis();
    count = parent.nummonths;
    ...
    admin = new JMenu ("Admin");
    menuBar.add (admin);
    ...
    miMachine = new JMenuItem ("Machine");
    miMachine.addActionListener (this);
    miMachine.setActionCommand ("MACHINE");
    admin.add (miMachine);
    ...
}
```

Implementation of the method to update the cash text field:

```
public void updateCash ()
{
    cashV [parent.lastmonth].setText
        (ten_two_f.format
            (parent.cash.balanceByIndex (parent.lastmonth)));
}
```

Modify this method to support the machine menu item:

```
public void actionPerformed (ActionEvent e)
{
    String str = e.getActionCommand ();

    if (str.compareTo (new String ("QUIT")) == 0)
    {
        System.exit (0);
    }
    else if (str.compareTo (new String ("MACHINE")) == 0)
    {
        purchaseMachine ();
    }
}
```

Add a new method to respond to the machine menu button being pressed:

```
public void purchaseMachine ()
{
    final JDialog machine = new JDialog (this, "Buy a machine",
        true);
```

Create the contents of the window and the action buttons:

```
JButton buyB = new JButton ("Buy");
buyB.addActionListener (new ActionListener()
{
    public void actionPerformed(ActionEvent e)
    {
        Machine newMC = new Machine ();
        machine.hide ();
        updateCash ();
    }
});
```

Define a Cancel button to close the window without purchasing a new machine:

```
JButton cancelB = new JButton ("Cancel");
cancelB.addActionListener (new ActionListener()
{
    public void actionPerformed(ActionEvent e)
    {
        parent.traceOut (1, "purchaseMachine:cancelled");
        machine.hide ();
    }
});
```

Load the window with available information:

```
cashV.setText (ten_two_f.format
    (parent.cash.balanceByIndex (parent.lastmonth)));
mccostV.setText (ten_two_f.format (Machine.mccost ()));
mcoutV.setText (ten_two_f.format (Machine.mcoutput ()));
mcohV.setText (ten_two_f.format (Machine.mcoverhead ()));
mcrawV.setText (ten_two_f.format (Machine.mcrawcost ()));
ownedV.setText (ten_d.format (parent.factory.howManyMachines ()));
```

Comparison of Test Output

This table shows the responses to similar tests. The left side shows the textual output for a script that simulates user interaction, while the right side shows the response to the user interaction.

Integration Output	GUI Menu Test Output
…	…
Machine:mccost:return cost	Machine:mccost:return cost
ProcessMachine:mccost=2000.0 (TestHarness output)	
Machine:mcoutput:return output	Machine:mcoutput:return output
ProcessMachine:mcoutput=10 (TestHarness output)	

Integration Output	GUI Menu Test Output
Machine:mcoverhead:return overhead	Machine:mcoverhead:return overhead
ProcessMachine:mcoverhead=400.0 (TestHarness output)	
Machine:mcrawcost:return rawcost	Machine:mcrawcost:return rawcost
ProcessMachine:mcrawcost=220.0 (TestHarness output)	
Factory:howManyMachines:result=0	Factory:howManyMachines:result=0
processFactory:howManyMachines=0 (TestHarness output)	
	CashAccount:balanceByIndex-balance [5]−2000.0 (action method checking the cash balance)
	Machine:mccost:return cost (action method checking machine cost)
New Machine	New Machine
Machine:Pre-cash.debit (2000.0)	Machine:Pre-cash.debit (2000.0)
CashAccount:debit-balance=2000.0 money 2000.0	CashAccount:debit-balance=2000.0 money 2000.0
CashAccount:debit-balance=0.0	CashAccount:debit-balance=0.0
Machine:Pre-addMachine	Machine:Pre-addMachine
Factory:addMachine	Factory:addMachine
CashAccount:balanceByIndex-balance [5]=0.0	CashAccount:balanceByIndex-balance [5]=0.0
Factory:howManyMachines:result=1 (Script output)	
ProcessFactory:howManyMachines=1 (TestHarness output)	

Error Handling in the GUI

You can add error handling to the machine window by checking the amount of money available to spend on new machines.

```
buyB.addActionListener (new ActionListener ()
{
    public void actionPerformed(ActionEvent e)
    {
        /*
        ** check the amount of money available against the cost
        ** of a new machine
        */
        if (parent.cash.balanceByIndex (parent.lastmonth) <
            Machine.mccost ())
        {
            parent.traceOut (1, "purchaseMachine:not enough money");
            JOptionPane.showMessageDialog
                (Display.this, "Not enough money");
        }
        else
        {
            /*
            ** create a new machine, hide this window and
            ** update the cash text field to reflect the new balance
            */
            Machine newMC = new Machine ();
            machine.hide ();
            updateCash ();
        }
    }
}
```

Stress Testing

Stress testing can and should be done at all stages of testing. The basic premise is to test every component to the extreme.

An example of a stress test could be the repetitive creation and deletion of a complex object. If a single creation and deletion cycle results in a 1-byte memory leak, this memory leak is almost undetectable by itself. However, if the creation and deletion cycle is repeated several thousand times in a single test, the leak becomes a discernible amount.

Stress testing should focus on areas of the application where resources are created and deleted, with each test focusing on a specific feature. For instance, if an application manages its own resources, whether it is memory, network connections, or some other resource; stress testing uncovers situations when the system does not make best use of those resources, sometimes with dramatic results. Problems such as these could show that the resource management algorithm is flawed.

System Testing

The next step in testing is to remove the test harness and test the system as a whole. The results of the final integration are immediately visible in the applications main window shown next. The information is shown with the most current month shown in the right-hand column of elements. The row containing the month information has five elements that contain '...' with the sixth containing a zero; this indicates that the application is starting at month zero. The cash element is initialized to 2000.00. The only other element that has a value is the average sales price of a manufactured unit.

	SimCo					_ □ ×
File Admin						
Months >>	...	...	...	...	...	0
Money						
Cash	0.00	0.00	0.00	0.00	0.00	2,000.00
Net Profit	0.00	0.00	0.00	0.00	0.00	0.00
Details						
Sales	0.00	0.00	0.00	0.00	0.00	0.00
CostToMake	0.00	0.00	0.00	0.00	0.00	0.00
Gross Profit	0.00	0.00	0.00	0.00	0.00	0.00
Gen. Expenses	0.00	0.00	0.00	0.00	0.00	0.00
Sale Price	0.00	0.00	0.00	0.00	0.00	0.00
Ave. Price	0.00	0.00	0.00	0.00	0.00	450.00
Stock	0	0	0	0	0	0
# made	0	0	0	0	0	0
# for sale	0	0	0	0	0	0
Projected Sales	0	0	0	0	0	6
# Sold	0	0	0	0	0	0
End Stock	0	0	0	0	0	0

Start turn

To start the manufacturing cycle, the user needs to have more money. To get more money, the user utilizes the Loan menu button to ask for a loan. The window shown next appears.

1. The user enters the amount of the loan and the number of years over which they wish to repay the loan. The example shows an amount of 3000 and a duration of 3 years.

2. The user can confirm the loan by pressing OK, or can cancel the request by pressing Cancel.

3. If the OK button is pressed, the cash element for the current month is incremented to 5000, to reflect the addition of the loan.

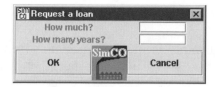

Now that the user has enough money, they now need to purchase a machine with which to manufacture units to sell. To do this the user utilizes the Machine menu button, and the window shown next appears. The user has two choices, Buy a machine or Cancel the window. If a machine is purchased, the cash element for the current month is decremented to 3000.

With enough capital and a machine on which to manufacture units, the user can now start a manufacturing cycle. The user does this by pressing the Start turn button. When this button is pressed, the Next turn window shown next appears.

The window shows the maximum number of units that can be made (this figure is based on the number of machines owned and the output potential of each machine) and the average price each manufactured unit will sell for. This window also contains two text entry fields. The first allows the user to enter the number of units they wish to have their machines manufacture. The second is the selling price of each manufactured unit. The selling price is used to adjust the average price, and the average price is used to determine the amount sold, so the user should try to stay close to the average price if possible.

This list follows the monthly accounting calculation from the number of units that can be sold to adjusting the cash balance with that month's net profit or loss.

- ▶ Number of units unsold from the previous manufacturing cycle Stock added to the number of units manufactured in this cycle (# made) equals the number available for sale in this cycle (# for sale)

- ▶ Projected sales based on selling price and average price, shown as a guide to sales trends

- ▶ Number of units actually sold (# sold) is subtracted from the number of units available (# for sale) to give the number of unsold units (End Stock) which is used in the next sales cycle

- ▶ Number of units sold (# sold) multiplied by the selling price (Sale Price) gives the gross sales for the month (Sales)

- ▶ Cost of manufacturing the units is shown in "CostToMake" which when subtracted from the gross sales (Sales) gives the gross profit for the month (Gross Profit)

- ▶ "Gen.Expenses" (the cost of the loan and general administration costs) when subtracted from the gross profit figure (Gross Profit) gives the net profit for the month

- ▶ Adding the "Net Profit" to the previous months cash amount (Cash - month 0) gives this month's cash amount (Cash - month 1)

The applications main window after one manufacturing run is shown next.

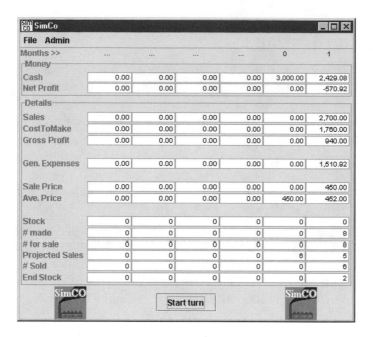

Scalability Testing

Similar to stress testing, scalability tests take everything to the extreme. This time the tests are run on the final version of the system. These tests include connecting as many users as possible to the system (concurrent users to a web site or database). These tests also test the performance of the system, by loading it with as many transactions as possible. An example would be a stock market trading application. A test could determine how many online stock market trades the system can handle before degrading performance or locking out users.

Regression Testing

The premise behind regression testing is to continually rerun the same set of tests against new versions of the product while expecting the same results. Any difference in the test results will highlight either the introduction of an error in a previously working application or the regression of the code so that an error is reintroduced.

Regression testing is very important in trying to improve the quality of the product. Also, the developers of the application should undertake the regression testing. The developers need to ensure that any work they have carried out on the application, whether it is to fix detected problems or to add new features, does not have a detrimental effect of the application.

It is vitally important that any new features added to a product provide tests that can be added to the regression test suite. The regression test suite is almost useless if it is testing only version 1 features on a version 6 product. The reason is that there are 5 versions of features that are not being tested, any one of which could fail and not be detected until the product is handed over to quality assurance.

Summary

This chapter has covered the many different levels involved in testing an application, but is by no means definitive. The chapter starts with the introduction of a test harness as a means of testing the application. The test harness is used to exercise the methods of each object of an application. Having tested each method individually, the test harness can be used to test the class as a complete entity. The final use for the test harness is to perform integration testing where classes are used in combination. The next phase in testing is to test the user interface and then to test how the user interface interacts with the application. The chapter closes with discussions on stress testing, system testing, scalability testing, and finally regression testing.

IN THIS CHAPTER:

Explain What Debugging Tools Are Used For

Show the Basic Commands of Three Widely Available Tools (DBK, GDB, and JDB)

Show an Example of Two of the Tools in Use

Debugging tools were created to help a programmer understand how an application is working and how to best fix any runtime bugs. A debugging tool provides a test environment in which to run an application under the user's control. It also allows the user to examine the changing values of variables while the application is running.

Under normal circumstances, adding output statements to the source code similar to those used during testing is enough to determine how the application is working. Output statements can determine if a section of code is ever reached, or if that code is executed, the results that are generated.

However, if the application is very complex or executes for some time, the potential size of the output is enormous, and as a consequence, this approach is not recommended, unless there is a very good reason for it. One possible reason might be to check if the application executes the same way, either on different platforms or after major re-coding. The output could then be archived and used at a later date as a regression test.

Other reasons for not using output statements are as follows:

▶   Adding a new output statement may require that the application be rebuilt, which could be time consuming.

▶   Output statements only tell the user what code has been executed without saying why it was executed. Sometimes it is more important to figure out why code was not executed, instead of what has been executed.

This chapter focuses on the commonly used commands, referencing three of the most common debugging tools. The debugging tools are usually packaged together with a compiler. For example, the Java compiler javac has the corresponding debugging tool jdb. The debugging tools used as reference are dbx, the typical UNIX debugging tool; gdb, the debugging tool provided with the GNU toolset and available on Linux releases; and jdb, the Java debugging tool. This chapter concludes with an example written in C++ that uses the two debugging tools: dbx and gdb.

The essential features of any debugging tool are as follows:

▶   To provide access to the inner workings of a running application.

▶ To allow the programmer to step through an application to determine the flow of the application.

▶ To allow the examination of the method call-stack of an application. The method call stack shows the hierarchy of methods leading from the main program to the current method. This is discussed in "Examining the Application," later in this chapter.

▶ To allow the examination of the crash (or core) file of an application. In the UNIX environment, a core file is a result of application termination caused by a server error. It contains information showing the state of the application when it crashed, including the call-stack.

▶ To allow the programmer to examine the values of variables within the application.

▶ To allow the programmer to examine the contents of memory associated with the application.

Preparing to Use the Debugging Tool

The application file passed to the debugging tool is an object (executable) file compiled with debugging instrumentation. Use the '-g' (generate symbol table) flag when compiling your application to tell the compiler to instrument debugging information into the application.

Starting the Debugging Tool

An application can be debugged in three ways, as follows:

▶ Start the debugging tool, and then start the application from within the tool. This method is used when trying to determine the cause of a problem before it happens.

▶ Attaching the debugging tool to a running (or seemingly dead) application. As an example, this method is used to determine the current state of an application that could have been running for several hours, but appears to have stopped executing.

▶ If the application has crashed and produced a core file, then the debugging tool can be used to investigate the cause of the crash.

Starting the Debugging Tool First

Starting the debugging tool with the application is a method that is used when trying to determine the cause of a problem, or to trace the flow of the logic in an application.

dbx	dbx <application name>
gdb	gdb <application name>
jdb	jdb <application name>

Attaching to a Running Application

Sometimes an application shows its problem only when running outside the debugger. The rationale is that when the application is running inside a debugger, the debugger slows down the execution of the application because it needs to trace the runtime execution, and this may hide some timing-sensitive problem. Under such a situation, someone may debug the problem by attaching the application to the debugger when the problem is about to happen or after the problem has happened. Even though this may not allow you to fully trace the cause of the problem, it still gives you enough information such as variable values and call stacks when the problem occurs. Before you attach the debugging tool to the application, you need the authority to issue a **kill** command on the application. The **kill** command is used to send a signal to the application and interrupt it.

Here are the steps that outline how to attach the debugging tool to a running application:

1. Use the **ps** command to determine the process ID.

2. If you have permission to "kill" the application, then you may use the above processed as an argument to launch the debugging tool. See the following table on what needs to be done when using different debuggers.

3. The debugging tool then interrupts the process, determines the full name of the object file, reads in the symbolic information, and prompts for commands:

AIX – dbx	dbx -a <process id>
Solaris – dbx	dbx - <process id>
gdb	gdb <application name> (gdb)attach <process id>

This can be done in Java, but is a little more complicated and will not be discussed here.

Deliberately Pausing an Application

Sometimes an application is started by another application, for example, an application started by an Internet browser. This application will start and run without any user intervention, so it is very difficult to attach a debugging tool. The technique described here deliberately pauses the application, so that it can be located using the **ps** command and the debugging tool attached. To pause the application, a piece of code is inserted into the application that causes it to loop. When the debugging tool is attached, this piece of code can be found and the value of the loop variable, 'xxx' in the example below, can have its value changed to anything that will break the loop. In the following example, the code is looping because the value of the variable 'xxx' is equal to one; changing the value to zero will break the loop.

```
// the following lines are added to pause the application
int xxx=1;
while (xxx == 1)
{
    sleep(5);
}
// pause code ends here
```

Using the Debugging Tool with a Core File

If an application crashes, it will typically create a core file. This file is very useful, because it contains information about what the application was doing when it crashed. It does this by showing you the call-stack of the application and the values of variables at different levels of the stack.

dbx	dbx <application name> core
gdb	gdb <application name> core

NOTE

The Java debugging tool does not support the use of core files.

Debugger Subcommands

The commands below have been chosen from all available commands as the most widely used. For additional help and information, either look in the system help files, or having started the debugging tool, type 'help'. The Help command is available in all three of the debugging tools discussed here. The Help command displays the list of recognized commands with a brief description.

Every debugging tool has commands that fall into five main categories:

- ▶ Making the application stop
- ▶ Running the application
- ▶ Examining the application
- ▶ Examining the data
- ▶ Line-by-line control

Making the Application Stop

Breakpoints are used to control the execution of the application. They are used to stop the application at certain points of its execution so that the values associated with variables and the contents of memory can be examined.

Setting Breakpoints

Breakpoints can be set in a debugger at line numbers or at the first instruction of a method, for example:

gdb	Set breakpoint at specified line or method.
	break <filename>:54
	This sets a breakpoint at line 54 of the specified file. The default filename is the current file.
	break <className>.<methodName>
	This sets a breakpoint at the first line of the specified method in the class specified.
dbx, jdb	**stop at <className>:22**
	This sets a breakpoint at the first instruction for line 22 of the source file (containing the class specified).
	(dbx) **stop in <className>::<methodName>**
	(jdb) **stop in <className>.<methodName>**
	This sets a breakpoint at the first line of the specified method in the class specified.

Clearing Breakpoints

dbx	**status**	Lists all breakpoints.
	clear	Removes breakpoints at a given source line.
	delete <argument>	Deletes the numbered breakpoint as shown by status.
gdb	**clear**	Clears breakpoint at specified line or function.
	delete	Deletes some breakpoints or auto-display expressions.
jdb	**clear <classname>.<method>**	
	clear <classname>:<line #>	
	clear	Lists all current breakpoints.

Additional Breakpoint Commands

| gdb | **disable** | Disable some breakpoints. |
| gdb | **enable** | Enable some breakpoints. |

Running the Application

The commands that follow are used to execute the application within the debugging tool or to terminate it.

Exit the Debugging Tool

| dbx, gdb, jdb | **quit** | Terminates the debugging tool. |
| gdb | **kill** | Kills execution of application being debugged. |

Run the Application

| dbx, gdb, jdb | **run** | After starting the debugger and setting any necessary breakpoints, you can use this command to start the execution of the debugged application. This command can be accompanied with arguments to pass to the application. |
| | **run numPhils=10** | This will pass the argument 'numPhils=10' to the application. The application then parses the argument to decide what to do. |

Rerunning the Application

dbx	**rerun** Begins execution of an application with the previous arguments.
gdb	**run** Begins execution of an application with the previous arguments.

Examining the Application

These commands are used to examine the flow of the application.

Print the Stack

gdb	**backtrace / bt** Prints backtrace of all stack frames.
dbx	**where** Displays a list of active procedures and functions.
jdb	**where** With no arguments, dumps the stack of the current thread. **where all** Dumps the stack of all threads in the current thread group. **where <threadindex>** Dumps the stack of the specified thread. If the current thread is suspended (either through an event, such as during a breakpoint or through the suspend command), local variables and fields can be displayed with the **print** and **dump** commands. The **up** and **down** commands select which stack frame is current.

Move Down the Stack

dbx, gdb, jdb	**down** Select and print stack frame called by this one. Moves the user down the application stack to the method that was called by the current method.

Move Up the Stack

dbx, gdb, jdb	**up** Select and print stack frame that called this one. Moves the user up the application stack, to the method that called the current method.

Displaying Source Code

(dbx)	**list** Displays 10 lines, beginning with the requested line. If the current line is 36, list displays lines 36–45. Typing list again displays lines 46–54. **list 36,50** Lists the lines between 36 and 50.

(gdb)	**list** Displays 10 lines, with the current line being in the middle. If the cuurent line is 36, list displays lines 31–40. Typing list again displays lines 37–46. **list 36,50** Lists the lines between 36 and 50.
(jdb)	**list** Displays 10 lines, with the current line being in the middle. So if the current line is 19, typing **list** will display lines 15–24. Typing **list** again will re-display lines 15-24. **list 30** Shows lines 26–35. List will always return to show the current line. So if the current line is 19, retyping **list** will display lines 15–24.

Examining the Data

These commands are used to examine the data in a running application.

Dump the Contents of a Variable

dbx	**dump** Displays the names and values of variables in the specified procedure.
jdb	**dump** For primitive values, this command is identical to **print**. For objects, it prints the current value of each field defined in the object. Static and instance fields are included.

Print the Contents of a Variable

NOTE

To display local variables, the containing class must have been compiled with the '-g' option.

gdb	**print**	Print value of expression EXP.
	inspect	Same as **print** command.
	output	Like **print,** but don't put in value history and don't print newline.
dbx, jdb	**print**	Displays objects and primitive values. For variables or fields of primitive types, the actual value is printed. For objects, a short description is printed.
	(dbx, jdb)	Print can also be used to run a procedure and print the return code.
	(jdb)	See the dump command below for getting more information about an object.
jdb	**printf**	C style printf format string.

Change the Value of a Variable

These commands can be used to modify the current value of a variable, while the application is running. This is useful for two reasons:

▶   To see what would happen if the value of the variable was different.

▶   To change a condition on a loop, so that the application can continue. This technique is used to start the application and then allow the debugging tool to be attached to it.

dbx	**assign <var> = <expr>**	Evaluate expression 'expr' and assign result to the variable 'var'.
gdb	**set <var> = <expr>**	Evaluate expression 'expr' and assign result to the variable 'var'.
jdb	**set <var> = <expr>**	Evaluate expression 'expr' and assign result to the variable 'var'.

Display the Data Type

dbx, gdb	**whatis var**	Print data type of expression 'var'.

Examining Memory

The formats used are

▶   **10c**   Means display 10 bytes of memory. Using 'c' also displays the content in character format.

▶ **10x (dbx)**   Means display 10 (2 byte) words of memory—see the example below. Using 'x' displays the content in hexadecimal format.

▶ **10x (gdb)**   Means display 10 (4 byte) words of memory—see the following example.

AIX - dbx	0x2ff21ed8 /10c
Solaris - dbx	examine 0x2ff21ed8 /10c
gdb	x/10c 0x2ff21ed8

Determining Line-by-Line Control

Breakpoints are used to control the large-scale flow of the application. The commands that follow are used to determine the flow on a line-by-line basis.

Continuing from a Breakpoint

dbx, gdb, jdb   **continue**   Continues execution of the debugged application after a breakpoint, exception, or step until the application finishes or another breakpoint is encountered.

Moving to the Next Statement

dbx, gdb, jdb   **next**   Command advances execution to the next line in the current stack frame (steps over).

Stepping Through the Application

dbx, gdb, jdb   **step**   Command advances execution to the next line whether it is in the current stack frame or a called method (steps into).

Completing the Method

These commands continue executing the application until the current method returns to the calling method:

AIX - (dbx)	**Return**
Solaris - (dbx)	**Step up**
(jdb)	**Step up**
(gdb)	**Finish**

This command forces an immediate exit of the *gbd* method:

gdb   **Return**   Make selected stack frame return to its caller

Examining a Multithreaded Application

In some operating systems, a single program may have more than one *thread* of execution. The precise semantics of threads differ from one operating system to another. Each thread is executing its own copy of a part of the application. Threads can share resources, but have their own execution stack and perhaps private memory, so that they can run independently of each other. Some threads may acquire the needed resources as they need them and so finish more quickly than those threads that have to wait.

Each debugging tool provides facilities for debugging a multithreaded application. When debugging, the debugging tool is only active on one thread at a time. The other threads are not halted; the debugging tool is only capable of focusing on one thread at a time. This in focus thread is called the current thread, so that the debugging commands show information in relation to the current thread. If a breakpoint is reached in another thread, the debugging tool automatically changes focus to that thread.

dbx Thread Support

```
(dbx) thread
current thread ($thread) is t@1
(dbx) help thread
thread (command)
thread                        # Display current thread
thread <tid>                  # Switch to thread <tid>.
```

In the following variations, a missing <tid> implies the current thread.

```
thread -info [ <tid> ]        # Print everything known about the given
                                  thread.
thread -hide [ <tid> ]        # Hide the given (or current) thread.
                                  It will not show up in the generic
                                  'threads' listing.
thread -unhide [ <tid> ]      # Unhide the given (or current). thread.
thread -unhide all            # Unhide all threads.
thread -suspend <tid>         # Keep the given thread from ever
```

```
                                    running. A suspended thread shows up
                                    with an 'S' in the threads list.
    thread -resume <tid>            # Undo the effect of '-suspend'.
    thread -blocks [ <tid> ]        # List all locks held by the given thread
                                    which are blocking other threads.
    thread -blockedby [ <tid> ]     # Show which synchronization object the
                                    given thread is blocked by, if any.
    (dbx) threads
    *>    t@1   a l@1   ?()    breakpoint             in main()
          t@2   b l@2   ?()    running               in _signotifywait()
          t@3   b l@3   ?()    running               in _lwp_sema_wait()
          t@4           ?()    sleep on (unknown)    in _swtch()
    (dbx) help threads
    threads (command)
    threads                         # Print the list of all known threads.
    threads -all                    # Print threads normally not printed
                                    (zombies).
    threads -mode all|filter        # Controls whether 'threads' prints all
                                    threads or filters them by default.
    threads -mode auto|manual       # Under the GUI, enables automatic
                                    updating of the thread listing.
    threads -mode                   # Echo the current modes.
```

jdb Thread Support

Select a thread to be the current thread. Many jdb commands are based on the setting of the current thread. The thread is specified with the thread index described in the **threads** command above.

```
    threads [threadgroup]       -- list threads
    thread <thread id>          -- set default thread
    suspend [thread id(s)]      -- suspend threads (default: all)
    resume [thread id(s)]       -- resume threads (default: all)
    where [thread id] | all     -- dump a thread's stack
    wherei [thread id] | all    -- dump a thread's stack, with pc info
    kill <thread> <expr>        -- kill a thread with the given exception
                                   object
    interrupt <thread>          -- interrupt a thread
    threadgroups                -- list threadgroups
    threadgroup <name>          -- set current threadgroup
```

gdb Thread Support

Set breakpoints on all threads, or on a particular thread:

break \<line-spec>   - break \<file>:54 or break \<file>.\<method>

break \<line-spec> thread \<thread #>

Example

1. Add the looping code to the application.

2. In one window, run the application.

3. In another window, type **ps –efw** to display the active processes.

4. In the same window, start the debugging tool using the following commands:

```
$> gdb 'which <application>'
GNU gdb 4.18
Copyright 1998 Free Software Foundation, Inc.
GDB is free software, covered by the GNU General Public
License, and you are welcome to change it and/or distribute
copies of it under certain conditions.
Type 'show copying' to see the conditions.
There is absolutely no warranty for GDB.  Type 'show warranty'
for details.
This GDB was configured as "i386-redhat-linux"...
(gdb)
```

5. Attach the debugging tool to the process number of the application, which uses the top thread for the \<application>, for example, 29397:

```
(gdb) attach 29397
Attaching to program: <application> 29397
Reading symbols from
<library>...done.
0x40aeb54e in __select () from /lib/libc.so.6
(gdb)
```

6. Determine which thread to use by typing **info threads**.

7. Set the breakpoint:

```
(gdb) break <file>:<line #> thread <thread #>
Breakpoint 1 at 0x405ad791: file <file>, line <line #>.
```

NOTE

The line specified is the first statement in the looping code added to the application: while (xxx == 1).

8. Type **continue**:

```
(gdb) c
Continuing.
[Switching to Thread <internal thread #>]

Breakpoint 1, <method name> (<arguments>)
 at <file>:<line #>
<line #>      while (xxx == 1)
```

9. You could now jump the loop and continue to run the application, step by step:

```
(gdb) set xxx-0
(gdb) n
<the next line in the code after the looping code>
```

Alias (dbx)

An alias is a shortcut to a command. This command is only available for dbx.

AIX - dbx	**alias l list**	Shortcut the character 'l' for the command list
Solaris - dbx	**alias p=print**	Shortcut the character 'p' for the command print

These commands can also be put into a .dbxinit (AIX) or .dbxrc (Solaris) file to be loaded every time dbx is run.

Debugging Example

This example takes the user through many of the commands supported by the debugging tools dbx and gdb. Where differences in the implementation of dbx occur, both the AIX and Solaris forms will be shown.

The example is taken from the Chapter 8 on porting, where it is used to illustrate the problems associated with different hardware architectures.

Example Code

Following is the code used in this example:

```
/*
** endian.cpp
** This application is used to test endism.
**
```

```
** Expected results:
**      Big Endian        Little Endian
**      12 34 56 78       78 56 34 12
**      12 34 56 78       34 12 78 56
**      41 42 43 00       41 42 43 00
*/
#include <stdio.h>
#include <string.h>

/*
** This structure allocates 3 variables each of 4 bytes
** Each variable is a different type, this allows the example
** to show how data is stored in memory
*/
struct endian {
    long l;
    short s[2];
    char c[4];
};

endian  temp;

/*
** This method is used to print the four bytes of each variable
** passed to it
*/
void printValue (char* ptr)
{
    int    i;

    for (i = 0; i < 4; i++)
    {
        printf ("%x ", *ptr++);
    }
    printf ("\n");
}

int main(int argc, char* argv[])
{
    char   *ptr;

    /*
```

```
** These are the values that will be stored in memory
*/
    temp.l = 305419896;                    /* 0x12345678 */
    temp.s [0] = 4660;                     /* 0x1234 */
    temp.s [1] = 22136;                    /* 0x5678 */
    strcpy (temp.c, "ABC");

/*
** Set the pointer to the long variable
** and then print the 4 bytes of memory
*/
    ptr = (char *)&temp.l;
    printValue (ptr);

/*
** Set the pointer to the short array variable
** and then print the 4 bytes of memory
*/
    ptr = (char *)&temp.s;
    printValue (ptr);

/*
** Set the pointer to the char array variable
** and then print the 4 bytes of memory
*/
    ptr = (char *)&temp.c;
    printValue (ptr);

    return 0;
}
```

Using the Debugging Tools

This section shows the endian code example that will be discussed in Chapter 8, "Porting," as it manipulated by two of the debugging tools. The tools used are dbx and gdb. Each step is documented with the output as it appears to the user.

Step 1: starting the debugging tool:

$> dbx endian

$> gdb endian

Set the breakpoint so that the application will stop at the first statement in 'main':

```
(dbx) stop in main
(2) stop in main
```

```
(gdb) break main
Breakpoint 1 at 0x80487ce: file endian.cpp, line 48.
```

Run the application:

```
(dbx) run
Running: endian
(process id 21096)
stopped in main at line 48 in file "endian.cpp"
  48      temp.l = 305419896;              /* 0x12345678 */
```

```
(gdb) run
Starting program: /home/jasmine/endian/endian
Breakpoint 1, main (argc=1, argv=0xbffffaa4) at endian.cpp:48
  48      temp.l = 305419896;              /* 0x12345678 */
```

When the application has stopped in 'main', list the code around the breakpoint:

```
(dbx) list
  48      temp.l = 305419896;              /* 0x12345678 */
  49      temp.s [0] = 4660;               /* 0x1234 */
  50      temp.s [1] = 22136;              /* 0x5678 */
  51      strcpy (temp.c, "ABC");
  52
  53   /*
  54   ** Set the pointer to the long variable
  55   ** and then print the 4 bytes of memory
  56   */
  57      ptr = (char *)&temp.l;
```

```
(gdb) list
  43      char    *ptr;
  44
  45   /*
  46   ** These are the values that will be stored in memory
  47   */
  48      temp.l = 305419896;              /* 0x12345678 */
  49      temp.s [0] = 4660;               /* 0x1234 */
  50      temp.s [1] = 22136;              /* 0x5678 */
  51      strcpy (temp.c, "ABC");
  52
```

List more of the application code:

```
(dbx) l
   58      printValue (ptr);
   59
   60   /*
   61   ** Set the pointer to the short array variable
   62   ** and then print the 4 bytes of memory
   63   */
   64      ptr = (char *)&temp.s;
   65      printValue (ptr);
   66
```

```
(gdb) l
   53   /*
   54   ** Set the pointer to the long variable
   55   ** and then print the 4 bytes of memory
   56   */
   57      ptr = (char *)&temp.l;
   58      printValue (ptr);
   59
   60   /*
   61   ** Set the pointer to the short array variable
   62   ** and then print the 4 bytes of memory
```

Step to the next statement. This will execute the code at line 48 and show the code at line 49:

```
(dbx) next
stopped in main at line 49 in file endian.cpp
   49      temp.s [0] = 4660;            /* 0x1234 */
```

```
(gdb) next
49      temp.s [0] = 4660;            /* 0x1234 */
```

Line 48 assigned a value to the long variable temp.1; print the value assigned:

```
(dbx) print temp.l
temp.l = 305419896
```

```
(gdb) print temp.l
$1 = 305419896
```

Confirm that the long variable is being processed correctly by asking the debugging tool to determine the type of 'temp.l':

```
(dbx) whatis temp.l
long l;
```

```
(gdb) whatis temp.l
type = long int
```

Step to the next statement to execute the code at line 49 and show the code at line 50:

```
(dbx) n
stopped in main at line 50 in file "endian.cpp"
   50    temp.s [1] = 22136;              /* 0x5678 */
```

```
(gdb) n
50         temp.s [1] = 22136;            /* 0x5678 */
```

Print the value assigned to the full variable. Line 49 assigned a value to the first element of the short array variable temp.s; the second element is shown as a zero:

```
(dbx) print temp.s
temp.s = (4660, 0)
```

```
(gdb) print temp.s
$2 = {4660, 0}
```

Step to the next statement, which will execute the code at line 50 and show the code at line 51:

```
(dbx) n
stopped in main at line 51 in file "endian.cpp"
   51    strcpy (temp.c, "ABC");
```

```
(gdb) n
51         strcpy (temp.c, "ABC");
```

Print the values assigned to the full variable. Line 50 assigned a value to the second element of the short array variable 'temp.s':

```
(dbx) print temp.s
temp.s = (4660, 22136)
```

```
(gdb) print temp.s
$3 = {4660, 22136}
```

Confirm that the short array variable is being processed correctly, and ask the debugging tool to determine the type of 'temp.s':

```
(dbx) whatis temp.s
short s[2];
```

```
(gdb) whatis temp.s
type = short int [2]
```

Step to the next statement; this will execute the code at line 51 and show the code at linc 57:

```
(dbx) n
stopped in main at line 57 in file "endian.cpp"
  57      ptr = (char *)&temp.l;
```

```
(gdb) n
57        ptr = (char *)&temp.l;
```

Line 51 assigned a value to the char array variable 'temp.c'; print the value assigned:

```
(dbx) print temp.c
temp.c = "ABC"
```

```
(gdb) print temp.c
$4 = "ABC"
```

To confirm that the char array variable is being processed correctly, ask the debugging tool to determine the type of 'temp.c':

```
(dbx) whatis temp.c
char c[4];
```

```
(gdb) whatis temp.c
type = char [4]
```

Print the values assigned to the structure 'temp':

```
(dbx) print temp
temp = {
    l = 305419896
    s = (4660, 22136)
    c = "ABC"
}
```

```
(gdb) print temp
$5 = {l = 305419896, s = {4660, 22136}, c = "ABC"}
```

Print the address in memory of the structure 'temp':

```
(dbx) print &temp
&temp = 0x20fe8
```

```
(gdb) print &temp
$6 = (endian *) 0x8049a10
```

Examine the memory at this address:

```
AIX - (dbx) 0x20000910/
0x20000910:  1234
```

```
Solaris - (dbx) examine 0x20fe8
0x00020fe8: temp      :      0x1234
```

```
(gdb) x 0x8049a10
0x8049a10 <temp>:      0x12345678
```

Re-examine this address using a format; dbx uses 2 bytes to display a hexadecimal number and so needs to display 6 of them for the three 4-byte variables in the structure, whereas gdb uses 4 bytes and therefore needs to display only three words:

```
AIX - (dbx) 0x20000910/6x
0x20000910:  1234 5678 1234 5678 4142 4300
```

```
Solaris - (dbx) examine 0x20fe8/6x
0x00020fe8: temp      :        0x1234 0x5678 0x1234 0x5678 0x4142 0x4300
```

```
(gdb) x/3x 0x8049a10
0x8049a10 <temp>:    0x12345678    0x56781234    0x00434241
```

Step to next statement; this will execute the code at line 57 and show the code at line 58:

```
(dbx) n
stopped in main at line 58 in file "endian.cpp"
   58      printValue (ptr);
```

```
(gdb) n
58        printValue (ptr);
```

Step into the 'printValue' method; notice that gdb shows the arguments passed to the method:

```
(dbx) s
stopped in printValue at line 34 in file "endian.cpp"
   34      for (i = 0; i < 4; i++)
```

```
(gdb) s
printValue (ptr=0x8049a10 "xV4\0224\022xVABC") at endian.cpp:34
34        for (i = 0; i < 4; i++)
```

Display the stack for the application:

```
(dbx) where
—>[1] printValue(ptr = 0x20fe8 "R4Vx"R4VxABC"), line 34 in "endian.cpp"
  [2] main(argc = 1, argv = 0xeffffb44), line 58 in "endian.cpp"
```

```
(gdb) where
#0  printValue (ptr=0x8049a10 "xV4\0224\022xVABC") at endian.cpp:34
#1  0x804880c in main (argc=1, argv=0xbffffaa4) at endian.cpp:58
```

Moving up the stack of the application will display the method from which the current method was invoked:

```
(dbx) up
Current function is main
   58      printValue (ptr);
```

```
(gdb) up
#1  0x804880c in main (argc=1, argv=0xbffffaa4) at endian.cpp:58
58          printValue (ptr);
```

Re-display the stack for the application; notice that dbx shows the stack being displayed:

```
(dbx) where
  [1] printValue(ptr = 0x20fe8 "^R4Vx^R4VxABC"), line 34 in "endian.cpp"
=>[2] main(argc = 1, argv = 0xeffffb44), line 58 in "endian.cpp"
```

```
(gdb) where
#0  printValue (ptr=0x8049a10 "xV4\0224\022xVABC") at endian.cpp:34
#1  0x804880c in main (argc=1, argv=0xbffff9d4) at endian.cpp:58
```

Go back down the stack to the current method:

```
(dbx) down
Current function is printValue
   34       for (i = 0; i < 4; i++)
```

```
(gdb) down
#0  printValue (ptr=0x8049a10 "xV4\0224\022xVABC") at endian.cpp:34
34          for (i = 0; i < 4; i++)
```

Re-display the stack for the application:

```
(dbx) where
=>[1] printValue(ptr = 0x20fe8 "^R4Vx^R4VxABC"), line 34 in "endian.cpp"
  [2] main(argc = 1, argv = 0xeffffb44), line 58 in "endian.cpp"
```

```
(gdb) where
#0  printValue (ptr=0x8049a10 "xV4\0224\022xVABC") at endian.cpp:34
#1  0x804880c in main (argc=1, argv=0xbffff9d4) at endian.cpp:58
```

Step to the next statement; this will execute the code at line 34 and will show the code at line 36:

```
(dbx) n
stopped in printValue at line 36 in file "endian.cpp"
   36        printf ("%x ", *ptr++);
```

```
(gdb) n
36          printf ("%x ", *ptr++);
```

Execute the loop two more times; notice that dbx does not stop on the closing bracket of the condition statement, whereas gdb does:

```
(dbx) n
stopped in printValue at line 36 in file "endian.cpp"
  36        printf ("%x ", *ptr++);
(dbx) n
stopped in printValue at line 36 in file "endian.cpp"
  36        printf ("%x ", *ptr++);
```

```
(gdb) n
37      }
(gdb) n
36        printf ("%x ", *ptr++);
(gdb) n
37      }
(gdb) n
36        printf ("%x ", *ptr++);
(gdb) n
37      }
```

Print the value currently in the loop condition variable 'i':

```
(dbx) p i
i = 2
```

```
(gdb) p I
$7 = 2
```

Keep stepping through the application until line #38:

```
(dbx) n
stopped in printValue at line 36 in file "endian.cpp"
  36        printf ("%x ", *ptr++);
(dbx) n
stopped in printValue at line 38 in file "endian.cpp"
  38      printf ("\n");
```

```
(gdb) n
36        printf ("%x ", *ptr++);
(gdb) n
37      }
(gdb) n
38      printf ("\n");
```

Step to the end of the 'printValue' method:

```
(dbx) n
12 34 56 78
stopped in printValue at line 39 in file "endian.cpp"
   39   }
```

```
(gdb) n
39      }
```

Step out of the method and back to the previous method:

```
(dbx) n
stopped in main at line 64 in file "endian.cpp"
   64      ptr = (char *)&temp.s;
```

```
(gdb) n
main (argc=1, argv=0xbffffaa4) at endian.cpp:64
64      ptr = (char *)&temp.s;
```

Re-display the stack of the application:

```
(dbx) where
=>[1] main(argc = 1, argv = 0xeffffb44), line 64 in "endian.cpp"
```

```
(gdb) where
#0  main (argc=1, argv=0xbffffaa4) at endian.cpp:64
```

Step to the next statement; this will execute the code at line 64 and show the code at line 65:

```
(dbx) n
stopped in main at line 65 in file "endian.cpp"
   65      printValue (ptr);
```

```
(gdb) n
65      printValue (ptr);
```

Step into the 'printValue' method; notice that gdb shows the arguments passed to the method:

```
(dbx) s
stopped in printValue at line 34 in file "endian.cpp"
   34      for (i = 0; i < 4; i++)
```

```
(gdb) s
printValue (ptr=0x8049a14 "4\022xVABC") at endian.cpp:34
34       for (i = 0; i < 4; i++)
```

Return from the method (dbx finishes the execution of the method, gdb does an immediate return); notice that dbx returns from the method and moves to the next line in the code, whereas gdb returns to the line where the method was invoked:

```
AIX - (dbx) return
12 34 56 78
stopped in main at line 71 in file "endian.cpp" ($t1)
   71    ptr = (char *)&temp.c;
```

```
Solaris - (dbx) step up
12 34 56 78
printValue returns
stopped in main at line 71 in file "endian.cpp"
   71    ptr = (char *)&temp.c;
```

```
(gdb) return
Make printValue(char *) return now? (y or n) #0  0x804881f in main (argc=1,
argv=0xbffffaa4) at endian.cpp:65
65       printValue (ptr);
(gdb) n
71       ptr = (char *)&temp.c;
```

Step to next statement; this will execute the code at line 71 and will show the code at line 72:

```
(dbx) n
stopped in main at line 72 in file "endian.cpp"
   72    printValue (ptr);
```

```
(gdb) n
72       printValue (ptr);
```

Step into the 'printValue' method:

```
(dbx) s
stopped in printValue at line 34 in file "endian.cpp"
   34    for (i = 0; i < 4; i++)
```

```
(gdb) s
printValue (ptr=0x8049a18 "ABC") at endian.cpp:34
34       for (i = 0; i < 4; i++)
```

Return and finish the method (gdb also finishes the execution of the method):

```
(dbx) step up
41 42 43 0
printValue returns
stopped in main at line 74 in file "endian.cpp"
   74      return 0;
```

```
(gdb) finish
Run till exit from #0  printValue (ptr=0x8049a18 "ABC") at endian.cpp:34
41 42 43 0
0x8048832 in main (argc=1, argv=0xbffff9d4) at endian.cpp:72
72         printValue (ptr);
(gdb) n
74         return 0;
```

Finish the application:

```
(dbx) c
execution completed, exit code is 0
```

```
(gdb) c
Continuing.
78 56 34 12
Program exited normally.
```

Exit debugging tool:

```
(dbx) quit
```

```
(gdb) quit
```

Summary

This chapter described the most common commands used by three different debugging tools. The commands examined fell into five main categories: making the application stop, running the application, examining the application, examining the data, and providing the user with line-by-line control of the debugging process. In addition, debugging a multithreaded application was covered. The chapter concludes with an example of an application being debugged with the dbx and gdb debugging tools.

IN THIS CHAPTER:

Understand that All Operating System Are Not the Same

Learn About Endianism

Learn How to Create Applications for an International Market

pplications are typically written for one hardware platform and one operating system. They are designed with a single programming language and support a single spoken language. Yet, by porting your application, you can enable it to work in a different hardware and/or software environment. While this subject is not specifically associated with object-oriented analysis and design, it is a subject that needs to be considered should you start to write applications for other people.

Of course, some platforms are easier to port to than others. Porting is not an easy part of software production and is usually passed to dedicated teams of people who specialize in porting.

The topics of interest here are porting to a new hardware platform, porting to a new operating system, and porting to a new spoken language (internationalization and localization). Some people would argue that internationalization and localization are not porting at all, but I would counter any argument by saying that as with porting to support new hardware, porting to support a new spoken or written language requires minimal changes to the original source code and user interface.

It should be noted that each of the topics above, hardware, operating system, and spoken language, affects different parts of the application. Each topic has special needs when solving its unique problems, and each is discussed in this chapter.

Porting to a New Operating System

If you are porting your application to another operating system, please read the manuals that come with that software. If the programming construct you want to use happens to mention that it is specific to only this platform, here is a tip: don't use it; use a programming construct that is portable and will work across many operating systems.

When writing a C++ application, a porting engineer can use the conditional compiler directives to help write code that work across different operating systems. These directives can be found in any C or C++ programming book and in the following list:

- ▶ #define and #undef
- ▶ #if, #elif, #else and #endif
- ▶ #ifdef, #ifndef, #else and #endif
- ▶ #if defined, #if !defined, #else and #endif

Examples of operating system differences are the basic data types. Microsoft Visual C++® defines many specific data types. These include DWORD, LPCSTR, and TCHAR. The code may be readily understandable by fellow Microsoft Visual C++ users, but these data types do not exist on any other operating system.

Fortunately most of the data types do have real C++ equivalents, but this is not always the case:

▶ DWORD = 32-bit unsigned integer

▶ LPSTR = 32-bit pointer to a character string

▶ TCHAR = The _TCHAR data type is defined conditionally in TCHAR.H. If the symbol _UNICODE is defined for your build, _TCHAR is defined as wchar_t; otherwise, for single-byte and MBCS builds, it is defined as char. (wchar_t, the basic Unicode wide character data type, is the 16-bit counterpart to an 8-bit signed char.)

Another area where problems can occur is the usage of system methods. The following example shows different versions of the same system method for accessing the time. The use of compilation directives shows how to implement a function that can be used on many operating systems.

```
/*
** The 'time.h' header file can be found in one of two places
** either '.../include/time.h'
** or '.../include/sys/time.h'
*/
#if defined(INCLUDE_SYS_TIME)
#include <sys/time.h>
#else
#include <time.h>
#endif

void getTimeOfDay (int time_secs, int time_msecs)
{
    struct timeval  t;
    struct timezone tz;

#if defined(TIMEONLY_GETTIMEOFDAY)
    gettimeofday(&t);
#elif defined(TIME_AND_TZ_GETTIMEOFDAY)
    gettimeofday(&t, &tz);
```

```
#endif

    time_secs = t.tv_sec;
    time_msecs = t.tv_usec;
}
```

The following examples show several implementations of two of the thread support methods, Psem and Vsem, in Microsoft Visual C++, UNIX C++, and Java. The UNIX version includes 'PM.h', which uses a header file that shows how different threading models can be implemented using macros to support System V threads and POSIX threads.

Microsoft Visual C++ Thread Support

```
// Psem - block while trying to obtain a specific mutex
//     mutex - the ID of the mutex being requested
//     seq - used to identify where in the program this routine
//            was called from
void Psem (HANDLE mutex, int seq)
{
    DWORD stat;
    stat = WaitForSingleObject( mutex, INFINITE );
    if(stat == WAIT_FAILED)
    {
      printf ("Error lock - %d = %d\n", seq, stat);
      exit(1);
    }
}


// Vsem - release a specific mutex
//     mutex - the ID of the mutex being released
//     seq - used to identify where in the program this routine
//            was called from
void Vsem (HANDLE mutex, int seq)
{
    DWORD stat;
    stat = ReleaseMutex ( mutex );
    if(stat == 0)
    {
      printf ("Error unlock - %d = %d\n", seq, stat);
      exit(1);
    }
}
```

UNIX Thread Support

The extract below comes from the header file 'PM.h'. This header file contains platform independent macros for common threading datatypes and system routines:

```
/*
** Porting Threads
** Macros that distinguish between the two most popular threading
** models on UNIX, System V threads and POSIX threads
**
** PM_ - PortableMutex
**
** Name: PT_MUTEX - Simplest synchronization object
**
** Description:
**     When operating system semaphores are used,
**     this is the simplest form of synchronization object.
*/
# ifdef SYS_V_THREADS
# define  PM_t                   mutex_t
# define  PM_init (mutexptr)     mutex_init(mutexptr,NULL,NULL)
# define  PM_destroy (sptr)      mutex_destroy(sptr)
# define  PM_lock (sptr)         mutex_lock(sptr)
# define  PM_trylock (sptr)      mutex_trylock(sptr)
# define  PM_unlock (sptr)       mutex_unlock(sptr)
# endif /* SYS_V_THREADS /
# ifdef POSIX_THREADS
# define  PM_t                   pthread_mutex_t
# define  PM_init (mutexptr)     pthread_mutex_init(mutexptr,NULL)
# define  PM_destroy (sptr)      pthread_mutex_destroy(sptr)
# define  PM_lock (sptr)         pthread_mutex_lock(sptr)
# define  PM_trylock (sptr)      pthread_mutex_trylock(sptr)
# define  PM_unlock (sptr)       pthread_mutex_unlock(sptr)
# endif /* POSIX_THREADS */
```

Here's how the code for the two threading methods would look:

```
// Psem - block while trying to obtain a specific mutex
//     mutex - the ID of the mutex being requested
//     seq - used to identify where in the program this routine
//           was called from
void Psem (PM_t *mutex, int seq)
{
```

```
    int stat;
    // request a lock on a specific mutex
    stat = PM_lock (mutex);
    if (stat != 0)
    {
        // if the request fails, report error to the user
        // do not try and recover
        cout << "Error PM_lock - " << seq << " = " << stat << endl;
        exit(1);
    }
}


// Vsem - release a specific mutex
//      mutex - the ID of the mutex being released
//      seq - used to identify where in the program this routine
//            was called from
void Vsem (PM_t *mutex, int seq)
{
    int stat;
    // release the lock on a specific mutex
    stat = PM_unlock (mutex);
    if (stat != 0)
    {
    // if the release fails, report error to the user
    // do not try and recover
    cout << "Error PM_unlock - " << seq << " = " << stat << endl;
        exit(1);
    }
}
```

Java Thread Support

```
// Psem - block while trying to obtain a specific mutex
//      pos - the number of the mutex being requested
public void Psem (int pos)
{
    boolean    flag;

System.out.println (threadName + " RequestLock");
synchronized (Dinner.chopstickLock [pos])
{
flag = Dinner.chopstickLock [pos].booleanValue ();
if (flag == false)
```

```
            {
                Dinner.chopstickLock [pos] = new Boolean (true);
                System.out.println (threadName + " AcquiredLock ");
                return;
            }
        }

    while (flag == true)
    {
        synchronized (Dinner.chopstickLock [pos])
        {
            flag = Dinner.chopstickLock [pos].booleanValue ();
            if (flag == false)
            {
                Dinner.chopstickLock [pos] = new Boolean (true);
                System.out.println (threadName + " AcquiredLock");
                return;
            }
        }
        try {sleep (20);}
        catch (InterruptedException e) {}
    }
}

// Vsem - release a specific mutex
//       mutex - the number of the mutex being released
public void Vsem (int pos)
{
    System.out.println (threadName + " Vsem " + pos);
    synchronized (Dinner.chopstickLock [pos])
    {
        Dinner.chopstickLock [pos] = new Boolean (false);
    }
}
```

Porting to New Hardware

Until the last few years, there were really only two hardware configurations, machines that used the Intel x86 processors and those that didn't. So for a long time, the only concern to a programmer was moving between these two different configurations.

This concern is called *endianism* and relates to the way in which data is stored in memory.

However, in the last few years, both sides have come out with new 64-bit configurations. Previously everything was 32-bit, that is to say that integers and longs both occupied 32 bits of memory, which, unfortunately, meant that programmers often used them interchangeably.

Supportting Endianism

The following section provides some history about the origins of endianism.

The names Big Endian and Little Endian are used because of the apt analogy to the bloody feud in the classic children's book *Gulliver's Travels* (*quod vide*). The feud was between the two mythical islands, Lilliput and Blefescu, over the correct end (big or little) at which to crack an egg. In Gulliver's travels, the Lilliputians liked to break their eggs on the small end and the Blefescudians on the big end. They fought wars over this. In our case, the issue has to do with the end (most significant or least significant) of a multiple-byte data type.

Those in the Big-Endian camp (most significant byte stored first) include the Java VM virtual computer, the Java binary file format, the IBM 360, and subsequent mainframes, and the Motorola 68K and most mainframes.

Blefescudians (Big-Endians) assert that this is the way integers were intended to be stored, the most important part first. When using a debugger to examine the contents of memory, Big-Endian is a lot easier to comprehend.

In the Little-Endian camp (least significant byte first) are the Intel 8080, 8086, 80286, Pentium, and the AMD 6502 popularized by the Apple II.

Lilliputians (Little-Endians) assert that putting the low order part first is more natural because when you do arithmetic manually you start at the least significant part and work toward the most significant part. When using a debugger to examine the contents of memory, Little-Endian provides a challenge.

With Big Endian ordering, the address of a multiple-byte data type is of its most significant byte (its "big end"), whereas with Little Endian ordering, the address is of its least significant byte (its "little end"). For structures declared in a high-level language, the order of bytes in memory differs depending on the byte ordering and the particular data type, in the C structure that follows.

To write code that can be compiled/assembled to execute correctly in either a Big or a Little Endian target environment, the user must follow one basic rule: either eliminate Endian-specific code or enclose it with #ifdef/else statements. Endian-specific code is whenever the data type used to store the data differs from the data type used to retrieve it. The following is somewhat confusing but shows how data can be stored using specific data types, but then accessing it using the character type. This program shows how the memory is stored as full words; with the four bytes reversed, the two half words reversed, and the full word complete on a Little Endian machine.

```
/*
** endian.cpp
** This application is used to test endism.
**
** Expected results:
**      Big Endian          Little Endian
**      12 34 56 78         78 56 34 12
**      12 34 56 78         34 12 78 56
**      41 42 43 00         41 42 43 00
*/
#include <stdio.h>
#include <string.h>


/*
** This structure allocates 3 variables each of 4 bytes
** Each variable is a different type, this allows the example
** to show how data is stored in memory
*/
struct endian {
    long l;                     /* 1 * 4-byte variable */
    short s[2];                 /* 2 * 2-byte variables */
    char c[4];                  /* 4 * 1-byte variables */
};

endian temp;

/*
** This method is used to print the four bytes of each variable
** passed to it
*/
void printValue (char* ptr)
{
    int     i;

    for (i = 0; i < 4; i++)
    {
        printf ("%x ", *ptr++);
    }
    printf ("\n");
}
```

```c
int main(int argc, char* argv[])
{
    char    *ptr;

/*
** These are the values that will be stored in memory
*/
    temp.l = 305419896;            /* 0x12345678 -> 12-34-56-78 */
    temp.s [0] = 4660;             /* 0x1234 -> 12-34 */
    temp.s [1] = 22136;            /* 0x5678 -> 56-78 */
    strcpy (temp.c, "ABC");        /* 'A'-'B'-'C'-<end of string> */

/*
** Set the pointer to the long variable
** and then print the 4 bytes of memory
*/
    ptr = (char *)&temp.l;
    printValue (ptr);

/*
** Set the pointer to the short array variable
** and then print the 4 bytes of memory
*/
    ptr = (char *)&temp.s;
    printValue (ptr);

/*
** Set the pointer to the char array variable
** and then print the 4 bytes of memory
*/
    ptr = (char *)&temp.c;
    printValue (ptr);

    return 0;
}
```

When the memory is checked using the Microsoft Visual C++ debugger, it all appears to be OK:

```
[-]temp
 |-- a              0x12345678
 |-- [-]b
 |    |-- [0x0]     0x1234
 |    |-- [0x1]     0x5678
 |-- [-]c
      |-- [0x0]     0x41         'A'
      |-- [0x1]     0x42         'B'
      |-- [0x2]     0x43         'C'
      |-- [0x3]     0x00         ' '
```

However, when the application runs the results are

```
78 56 34 12
34 12 78 56
41 42 43 00
```

When the application is built using UNIX C++ and the memory is checked using dbx on a UNIX system:

```
$ dbx endian
dbx > stop at 30
dbx > print &temp
0xeffffad8
dbx > examine 0xeffffad8 /6x
0xeffffad8: 0x1234 0x5678 0x1234 0x5678 0x4142 0x4300
```

When the application is run:

```
12 34 56 78
12 34 56 78
41 42 43 00
```

When the application is built using 'g++' on a Linux system and the memory is checked using gdb on a Linux system:

```
$ gdb endian
gdb > break 30
gdb > print &temp
$1=(endian*)0xbffffb8c
gdb > x/3x 0xbffffb8c
0xbffffb8c: 0x12345678 0x56781234 0x00434241
```

When the application is run on a Linux system:

```
78 56 34 12
34 12 78 56
41 42 43 00
```

Comparing 32-bit with 64-bit Machines

The majority of machines that people use today are known as 32-bit machines. This is because they use 32 bits to address memory. The 32 bits allow the program to address 4G. The size of both an integer and a long data type is set to 32 bits. The size of the register is different so that the movement of data is 32 or 64 bits and affects the alignment of data structures from one machine to another. Also, the address pointer is a different size than an integer on a 64-bit machine and cannot be used interchangeably with the integer to save it in memory. Having machines that now have the long data type assigned to 64-bit while leaving integers at 32-bit now means that the programmer has to be especially vigilant so as not confuse data types.

The new 64 bit machines have set the long data type to 64 bits, while the integer data type remains at 32 bits. A 64-bit machine allows the programmer to access 1.8×10^{19}.

Porting to a New Language

This section covers the importance of specifying the environment in which the application is to be executed. Topics covered range from specifying the locale, distinguishing between single-byte, multibyte, and Unicode storage systems, and concluding with message catalogues.

Internationalization can be referred to as 'i18n', which represents 'i', skip the next 18 characters, and end with 'n'. Similarly, localization can be referred to as 'l10n', which represents 'l'; skip the next 10 characters and end with 'n'.

Internationalization and Localization

Software internationalization is the process of developing software that can be specialized for a particular user community without having to deal with the program's executable code.

Localization is the process of adapting a product for use in a particular region, or by users of a specific written language. It involves translation of messages, icons/images, and so on. A good i18n design can simplify the localization process dramatically.

Software should be designed for global deployment while it is completely localizable. A good i18n project keeps the localizable material in a format other than code. Internationalizing your application should include the following:

► Implementing it so that it can be made to work in many locales.

► Making it configurable, that is, localization could be simply implemented by replacing message/resource files.

► Supporting different locales at the same time.

► Allowing nontechnical people (such as translation teams) access to information without having to open the source code to them.

► Supporting generic features so that it is possible to develop the application so that it can be ported to various platforms.

Although i18n does not require the support of Unicode, it does greatly simplify the development and maintenance of an i18n project. Some of the tasks that were prohibitively difficult before are now made much easier because of it.

Issues to Consider to Internationalize a Program

These are the basic issues you need to review to internationalize your application. They help in developing software that is independent of the language, country, and culture of the intended end-users. This results in an application that can be readily translated for multiple countries or regions. The three key steps for internationalizing programs are to:

1. Separate form from function, which means to separate how the application works from how it appears to the user.

2. Avoid making cultural assumptions.

3. Provide support for different locales.

NOTE

Although this sounds simple, the first part focuses on keeping static information (such as pictures and window layouts) separate from the program code. The second part focuses on making certain that the text that the program generates while running, such as error messages, comes out in the right language and formatted correctly for the targeted user community.

Additionally, there is the problem of processing input and output, how to handle input from different sources from keyboard to voice, and then knowing how to display them correctly back to the user. These tasks are relatively easy for English, but quite challenging for some other languages.

Separating Form from Function

To design good software applications, it is required that the programming code that implements the user interface is kept separate from the programming code that implements the underlying functionality. One advantage of this is that the application can be moved to another platform that supports a different user-interface style, with only the code for the user interface needing to be modified.

The user interface can be thought of as containing items that the user sees. These items include, but are not limited to, the following:

▶ Messages displayed to the user

▶ Buttons that contain either text or icons

▶ Menu commands that the user can use to navigate through the application

▶ Dialog box layout, icons, and colors

The programming code used to describe the user interface should be kept together, but remain separated from the body of the programming code that describes the functionality of the application.

Avoiding Cultural Assumptions

Whenever a programmer writes any piece of code, they usually make a series of basic assumptions. One could be that the audience for the product will always understand English, while another is that the input device (the keyboard) will be the same used by the user. These two assumptions alone automatically invalidate the product outside of the programmer's current environment. Although English is widely understood in many countries, it is normally a second language and not fully understood, especially if the programmer uses local phrases.

For example, when driving in both the U.S. and England, 'STOP' means stop; however, to give preference to a major road at a road junction in the U.S. and in England, one uses 'YIELD,' while the other uses 'GIVE WAY.' Any cultural assumptions made by the programmer always make it harder to port any code that interfaces with the user, without rewriting the underlying program.

Providing Support for a Different Locale

The locale is used by an application to determine how certain characteristics of the application will perform. A call to setlocale() sets or interrogates the settings for the process. The characteristics that can be controlled by environment variables are listed next.

LANG   This variable determines the locale category for native language, local customs, and coded character set in the absence of the LC_ALL and other LC_(LC_COLLATE, LC_CTYPE, LC_MESSAGES, LC_MONETARY, LC_NUMERIC, LC_TIME) environment variables. This can be used by applications to determine the programming language for error messages and instructions, collating sequences, date formats, and so forth.

LC_ALL   This variable determines the values for all locale categories. The value of the LC_ALL environment variable has precedence over any of the other environment variables starting with LC_(LC_COLLATE, LC_CTYPE, LC_MESSAGES, LC_MONETARY, LC_NUMERIC, LC_TIME) and the LANG environment variable.

LC_COLLATE – Collation   This variable determines the locale category for character collation. It determines collation information for regular expressions and sorting, including equivalence classes and multi-character collating elements in various utilities and the strcoll() and strxfrm() functions. All languages (even those using the same alphabet) do not necessarily have the same concept of alphabetical order. Even more importantly, be careful in assuming that alphabetical order is the same as the numerical order of the character's character-set values. In practice, 'a' is distinct from 'A' and 'b' is distinct from 'B'. Each has a different character-set value. This means that you cannot use a bit-wise lexical comparison, such as what strcmp() provides to sort user-visible lists. The strcmp() variable cannot be used to do bit-wise comparison. This is because the result of that is "A < B < a < b".

Not all languages consider that the same characters are equivalent, or that changing a character's case will always be a one-to-one mapping. Accent differences, the presence or absence of certain characters, and even spelling differences may be insignificant in determining whether two strings are equal.

When checking characters for membership in a particular class, do not specifically list the characters you are interested in, and do not assume they come in any particular order in the encoding scheme. For example, /A-Za-z/ does not mean all letters in most European languages. And /0-9/ does not mean all digits in many writing systems. This includes using the C interfaces such as isupper() and islower().

LC_CTYPE – Character Handling   This variable determines the locale category for character handling functions, such as, *tolower()*, *toupper()*, *isdigit()*, *isalpha()*, *mbtowc()*, *wctomb()*. This environment variable determines the interpretation of sequences of bytes of text data as characters (for example, single- as opposed to multi-byte characters), the classification of characters (for example, alpha, digit, and graph) and the behavior of character classes. Additional semantics of this variable, if any, are implementation-dependent.

LC_MESSAGE   This determines the location of the message catalog, used by gencat, catopen, catgets, and catclose. Be careful in formulating assumptions as to how individual pieces of text are glued together to create a complete sentence, such as in cases that generate error messages. The elements may go together in a different order if the message is translated into a new language. Additional semantics of this variable, if any, are implementation-dependent. The language and cultural conventions of diagnostic and informative messages whose format is unspecified by this specification set should be affected by the setting of LC_MESSAGES.

> **NOTE**
>
> *There may also be situations in which parts of the sentence change depending on other parts of the sentence (selecting between singular and plural nouns that go after a number is the most common example).*

LC_MONETARY   This determines how monetary units are displayed. Numerical representations can change with regard to measurement units and currency values. Currency values can vary by country. A good example of this is the representation of $1,000 dollars. This could be either U.S. or Canadian. U.S. dollars can be displayed as USD while Canadian dollars can be displayed as CAD, depending on the locale. This is a situation where the displayed numerical quantity may change, and where the number might also change.

```
%%%%%%%%%%
LC_MONETARY
%%%%%%%%%%
int_curr_symbol      ""
currency_symbol      ""
mon_decimal_point    ""
mon_thousands_sep    ""
mon_grouping         ""
positive_sign        ""
negative_sign        ""
```

Additional semantics of this variable, if any, are implementation-dependent.

LC_NUMERIC   This variable determines the locale category for numeric formatting (for example, thousands separator and radix character) information in various utilities, as well as the formatted I/O operations in printf() and scanf(), and the string conversion functions in strtod(). Numbers and dates are represented in different languages. In particular, do not implement routines for converting numbers into strings, and do not call low-level system interfaces like sprintf() that do not produce language-sensitive results.

```
%%%%%%%%%%
    LC_NUMERIC
%%%%%%%%%%
    decimal_point       "<period>"
    thousands_sep       " "
    grouping            " "
```

Additional semantics of this variable, if any, are implementation-dependent.

LC_TIME – Date and Time   This variable determines the locale category for date and time formatting information. It affects the behavior of the time functions in strftime(). Additional semantics of this variable, if any, are implementation-dependent. Time can be reckoned in many units, such as the lengths of months or years, which day is the first day of the week, the allowable range of values for things like month and year (with DateFormat), the time zone you are in (with TimeZone), or when daylight-savings time starts.

Here is an example of how different locale variables can be used. Ask the system to print the current settings for the various locales. Everything is set to the default for the operating system:

```
$ locale
LANG=en_US
LC_CTYPE="C"
LC_NUMERIC="C"
LC_TIME="C"
LC_COLLATE="C"
LC_MONETARY="C"
LC_MESSAGES="C"
LC_ALL=
```

Set the language locale to British English and redisplay the various locales:

```
$ setenv LANG en_UK
$ locale
LANG=en_UK
LC_CTYPE="en_UK"
LC_NUMERIC="en_UK"
LC_TIME="en_UK"
LC_COLLATE="en_UK"
LC_MONETARY="en_UK"
LC_MESSAGES="en_UK"
LC_ALL=
```

Change the setting of the collation locale:

```
$ setenv LC_CTYPE "en_US"
$ locale
LANG=en_UK
LC_CTYPE="en_US"
LC_NUMERIC="en_UK"
LC_TIME="en_UK"
LC_COLLATE="en_UK"
LC_MONETARY="en_UK"
LC_MESSAGES="en_UK"
LC_ALL=
```

Reset everything to the system default:

```
$ setenv LANG en_US
LANG=en_US
LC_CTYPE="C"
LC_NUMERIC="C"
LC_TIME="C"
LC_COLLATE="C"
LC_MONETARY="C"
LC_MESSAGES="C"
LC_ALL=
```

Single- and Double-Byte Character Sets

A single-byte character set allocates one byte or 8 bits to the storage of characters. This character set can store a maximum of 256 characters. The ASCII character set is a single-byte character set. A double-byte character set allocates two bytes or 16 bits to the storage of characters. This character set can therefore store up to 2^{16} characters.

Issues Specific to the Double-Byte Character Set

The *double-byte character set* (DBCS) was created to handle East Asian languages that use ideographic characters, which require more than the 256 characters supported by ANSI. Characters in DBCS are addressed using a 16-bit notation, using 2 bytes. With 16-bit notation you can represent 65,536 characters, although far fewer characters are defined for the East Asian languages. For instance, Japanese character sets today define over 10,000 characters.

In locales where DBCS is used—including China, Japan, and Korea—both single-byte and double-byte characters are included in the character set. The single-byte characters used in these locales conform to the 8-bit national standards for each country and correspond closely to the ASCII character set. Certain ranges of codes in these single-byte character sets (SBCS) are designated as *lead bytes* for DBCS characters. A consecutive pair made of a lead byte and a trail byte represents one double-byte character. The code range used for the lead byte depends on the locale.

NOTE

DBCS is a different character set from Unicode.

When developing a DBCS-enabled application, you should consider the following:

► Differences between Unicode, ANSI, and DBCS

► DBCS sort orders and string comparison

► DBCS string manipulation functions

► DBCS string conversion

► How to display and print fonts correctly in a DBCS environment

► How to process files that include double-byte characters

► DBCS identifiers

► DBCS-enabled events

► How to call Windows APIs

TIP

Developing a DBCS-enabled application is good practice, whether or not the application is run in a locale where DBCS is used. This approach helps you develop a flexible, portable, and truly international application.

Wide Character String

A wide character (wchar_t) is typically a two-byte multilingual character code. However, some operating systems, example being Solaris, have defined the wchar_t to be four bytes in length. Any character used in modern computing worldwide, including technical symbols and special publishing characters, can be represented according to the Unicode specification as a wide character. Because each wide character is always represented in a fixed size of 16 bits, using wide characters simplifies programming with international character sets.

A wide character string is represented as a wchar_t[] array and is pointed to by a wchar_t* pointer. Any ASCII character can be represented as a wide character by prefixing the letter L to the character. For example, L'\0' is the terminating wide (16-bit) NULL character. Similarly, any ASCII string literal can be represented as a wide character string literal by prefixing the letter L to the ASCII literal (L"Hello").

Generally, wide characters take more space in memory than multibyte characters, but are faster to process. In addition, only one locale can be represented at a time in multibyte encoding, whereas all character sets in the world are represented simultaneously by the Unicode representation.

Unicode

A 16-bit character encoding that includes all of the world's commonly used alphabets and ideographic character sets in a "unified" form (that is, a form from which duplications among national standards have been removed). Unicode characters are manipulated in an application by using the 'wchar_t' data type. Here are some points to consider about Unicode:

▶   In its current version, the Unicode standard contains over 30,000 distinct coded characters derived from 24 supported scripts. These characters cover the principal written languages of the Americas, Europe, the Middle East, Africa, India, Asia, and the Pacific.

▶   Unicode is the trademark of the Unicode Consortium and further information can be found at http://unicode.org/. Several programming languages use Unicode internally; two of these languages are Visual Basic and Java.

▶ Unicode allows a program to standardize on a single encoding scheme for all textual data within the program's environment. Conversion only has to be done with incoming and outgoing data. Operations on the text, while it is in the environment, are simplified because you do not have to take into account (or keep track of) the encoding of a particular text.

▶ Unicode supports multilingual data because it encodes characters for all the languages of the world. You do not have to tag pieces of data with their encoding to enable the right characters, and you can mix languages within a single piece of text. ASCII and Latin-1 characters may be mapped to Unicode characters.

Localizing Strings in Messages

The localization of strings using message catalogs is discussed below, followed by resource files for Microsoft™ programming languages. The Java localization and internationalization kit are not discussed; however, I believe that the documentation that comes with the kit is self-explanatory.

Creating a Message Catalogue—UNIX

A message catalog is a method of providing the same messages in different languages. These messages can then be made available to any program. The program makes the determination of which message catalog to use based on the user's locale settings.

The message catalog files start with source files that are created by the programmer and contain the messages required by the application. The messages can be used by the user interface or to provide information.

After the message source files have been created, they are converted into message catalogs. These catalogs are then used by the applications to retrieve and display the messages. The translation of the text in the message source files does not require the application to be changed or recompiled.

The following are the steps involved in creating, converting, and using the message file:

▶ Creating a Message Source File

▶ Creating a Message Catalog—UNIX utility using gencat

▶ Displaying Messages with an Application—C language methods using catopen, catgets, and catclose

Creating a Message Source File

To create a message-text source file, open a file using any text editor. Enter a message identification number. It is possible with some message catalog utilities to create message source files that have symbolic identifiers instead of numbers, although these utilities are beyond the scope of this basic introduction and are not discussed here. Finally, enter the message text. An example is shown here:

```
1 message-text          $ (This message is numbered)
2 message-text          $ (This message is numbered)
OUTMSG message-text     $ (This message has a symbolic identifier \
                            called OUTMSG)
4 message-text          $ (This message is numbered)
```

There are some basic rules that you need to follow when creating a message source file.

▶ One blank character must exist between the message I.D. number or identifier and the message text.

▶ Message I.D. numbers must be assigned in ascending order within a single message set, but need not be contiguous. The number 0 (zero) is not a valid message I.D. number.

Adding Comments to the Message Source File   You can include a comment anywhere in a message source file except within message text. Leave at least one space or tab (blank) after the $ (dollar sign). The following is an example of a comment:

```
$ This is a comment.
```

Comments do not appear in the message catalog generated from the message source file. Comments should be used whenever sensible to do so; there can never be too many comments. A comment should be added so that the programmer knows where in the application this message can be appropriately used. An additional comment should be added so that the translator knows the context in which a message would be used. A simple phrase when used in two different contexts may result in two different translations. This last point is very important. Do not overload messages. If there is the remotest possibility of a message being translated into different messages, then the original message should appear multiple times. Comments should be used to identify what variables, such as %s, %c, and %d, represent. For clarity, comments should be placed adjacent to the message to which it refers.

Continuing Messages on the Next Line   All text following the blank character after the message I.D. number is included as message text, up to the end of the line. The escape character \ (backslash) is used to continue message text on the following line. The \ (backslash) must be the last character on the line as shown in the example below:

```
5 This is the text associated with \
message number 5.
```

The example above results in the following single-line message:

```
This is the text associated with message number 5.
```

Including Special Characters in the Message Text   Other special characters can be inserted into the message text by using the escape character \ (backslash). These special characters are listed here:

\n	Code for a new-line character.
\t	Code for a horizontal tab character.
\v	Code for a vertical tab character.
\b	Code for a backspace character.
\r	Code for a carriage-return character.
\f	Code for a form-feed character.
\\	Code for a \ (backslash) character.
\ddd	Code for a single-byte character associated with the octal value represented by the valid octal digits ddd. Up to three octal digits can be specified.

If octal byte character is used as part of a string, then it must be fully padded to avoid confusing it with the following characters. For example, the octal value for $ (dollar sign) is 44. To display $2.00, use \0442.00, not \442.00, or the 2 will be parsed as part of the octal value. |
| \xdd | Code for a single-byte character associated with the hexadecimal value represented by the two valid hexadecimal digits dd. You must include a leading zero to avoid parsing errors (see the note about \ddd). |
| \xdddd | Code for a double-byte character associated with the hexadecimal value represented by the four valid hexadecimal digits dddd. You must include a leading zero to avoid parsing errors (see the note about \ddd). |

Reviewing Informative Message Text   It is important that the message text provide useful information to the user. It is not sufficient to tell the user that an error occurred. Users should be told exactly how the error occurred and how they can possibly fix it. An example of two different messages is shown here:

```
Unhelpful Message:      Value out of range
Informative Message:    The range for the value is between 1 and 99.
```

The message "Value out of range" does not help users much; whereas the message "The range for the value is between 1 and 99" informs the users exactly the range of values involved.

Examples of message source file code is as follows:

```
$ This is a message source file sample.
$ This is a set of messages.
1 The specified file does not have read permission on\n
2 The %1$s file and the %2$s file are same\n
3 Hello world!\n
$ This is another set of messages
11 fieldef: Cannot open %1$s \n
12 Hello world\n
```

Creating a Message Catalog

A programmer creates a message source file containing application messages and converts it to a message catalog. Translating message source files into other languages and then converting the files to message catalogs does not require changing or recompiling a program. To create a message catalog, process your completed message source file with the system command **gencat**. The **gencat** command is used to process a message source file containing message I.D. numbers and associated text. The following example uses the information in the message source file 'messages.msg' to generate the catalog file 'messages.cat':

```
gencat messages.cat messages.msg
```

If the catalog file 'messages.cat' already exists, the **gencat** command modifies the catalog with the statements in the message source file. If the catalog file does not exist, the **gencat** command creates it.

You can specify any number of message text source files. Multiple files are processed in the sequence you specify. Each successive source file modifies the catalog. If you do not specify a source file, the **gencat** command accepts message source data from standard input.

Displaying Messages with an Application Program

To access the message catalog from an application, the following items must be included:

- ▶ The limits.h and nl_types.h files
- ▶ A call to initialize the locale environment
- ▶ A call to open a catalog
- ▶ A call to read a message
- ▶ A call to display a message
- ▶ A call to close the catalog

The following methods provide the facilities necessary for an application to display the messages in a message catalog:

setlocale	Sets the locale. Specify the **LC_ALL** or **LC_MESSAGES** environment variable in the call to the **setlocale** subroutine for the preferred message catalog language.
catopen	Opens a specified messages catalog and returns a catalog descriptor, which is used to retrieve messages from the catalog.
catgets	Retrieves a message from a catalog after a successful call to the **catopen** subroutine.
catclose	Closes a specified message catalog.

The following C program, 'hello', shows how to open the 'hello.cat' message catalog with the **catopen** method, retrieving messages from the catalog with the **catgets** method, displaying the messages with the **printf** method, and closing the catalog with the **catclose** method.

```
/* program: hello */
#include <nl_types.h>
#include <locale.h>
nl_catd catd;
main()
{
    /*  initialize the locale  */
    setlocale (LC_ALL, "");
    /* open the catalog */
    catd=catopen("hello.cat",NL_CAT_LOCALE);
```

```
    printf(catgets(catd,1,1,"Hello World!"));
    catclose(catd);                           /* close the catalog */
    exit(0);
}
```

In the example above, the **catopen** method refers to the 'hello.cat' message catalog by name. The **NLSPATH** environment variable defines the location of the message catalog. If the message catalog is successfully opened by the **catopen** method, the **catgets** method returns a pointer to the specified message in the 'hello.cat' catalog. If the message catalog is not found or the message does not exist in the catalog, the **catgets** method returns the Hello World! default string.

Understanding the NLSPATH Environment Variable   The **NLSPATH** environment variable specifies the directories to search for message catalogs. The **catopen** method searches these directories in the order specified when called to locate and open a message catalog. If the message catalog is not found, the message-retrieving routine returns the program-supplied default message. See the **/etc/environment** file for the **NLSPATH** default path.

Retrieving Program-Supplied Default Messages   All message-retrieving routines return the program-supplied default message text if the desired message could not be retrieved for any reason. Program-supplied default messages are generally brief one-line messages that contain no message numbers in the text. Users who prefer these default messages can set the **LC_MESSAGES** category to the C locale or unset the **NLSPATH** environment variable. When none of the **LC_ALL** , **LC_MESSAGES**, or **LANG** environment variables are set, the **LC_MESSAGES** category defaults to the C locale.

Resource Files—Microsoft

Microsoft provides resource files that can be compiled into a dynamic library that is used by the application at execution time. There are two approaches to including localized strings into an application. The first involves including all strings in one resource file, the second requires multiple resource files, and both are shown below.

A Single Resource File

Within the development environment, open a resource file and insert a 'String Table'. By default this string table will be used to hold the native message strings. This string table can then be copied and the associated language changed. Changing the language allows the messages to be translated in the new string table. These new messages are referenced in the application by using the same I.D.s as the original string table; the application merely has to change the language it is using.

A possible string table is shown, as follows:

```
String Table
   |
   +---[abc]  String Table
   +---[abc]  String Table [English (U.K.)]
   +---[abc]  String Table [French (France)]
```

Multiple Resource Files

The difference with the above example is that each of the three string tables would be built into three separate resource files. The decision of which to use is made at compile time and not at execution time. The decision could look like this:

```
#ifdef _FRENCH
#include "resourceFile_f.rc
#elif _ENGLISH_UK
#include "resourceFile_uk.rc
#else // default USA
#include "resourceFile_us.rc
#endif
```

Developing International Applications

To support the world market, applications must be designed so that it is equally effective internationally and domestically. This section describes how to use international features to produce applications for selected locales, including both planning a international application and designing its interface. It also discusses related topics of entering international data, sorting data in international applications, working with double-byte characters sets, and so on.

Planning an International Application

Preparing an international application usually involves three steps: creating data, writing code, and designing a user interface. Before you take these steps, however, you need to consider the following questions:

- ▶ What data is acceptable?
- ▶ How do you write code for an international application?
- ▶ What should you consider when designing a user interface?

The following sections address these questions and pose others that you need to consider before you prepare your application.

TIP

You can reduce the cost of developing an international application and bring it to market more quickly by designing it as an international application initially rather than modifying it for international use later on.

Determining Which Data to Accept

To decide which data is acceptable, first consider the locales in which the application will be used. The locales determine the cultural content of the data, as well as the languages in which the data is prepared.

In addition, the languages affect the code page with which the data is prepared. A code page is a character set that a computer uses to display data properly, often to handle *international characters*. International characters include characters that have diacritical marks. Diacritical marks are placed over, under, or through letters to indicate sound changes from the unmarked form. The most common diacritical marks are the grave accent (` as in à), acute accent (´ as in á), circumflex (^ as in â), tilde (~ as in ã), umlaut (¨ as in ä), ring (° as in å), and slash (/ as in ø), all used in conjunction with vowels.

Some languages, such as Chinese, Korean, and Japanese, use DBCS to represent their data. If your application might run in these environments, you might need to use special string-handling functions and collation sequences for the application to work properly.

Writing the Code

An application consists of a user interface component and an application component. The user interface component contains graphics, text strings, and settings related to various locales, such as dates, currencies, numeric values, and separators. The application component contains the code that is run for all locales, including code that processes the strings and graphics used in the user interface. When designing your application, keep the application and user interface components separate, because independent components make the application easier to localize and maintain. For example, with separate components you don't have to browse the source code to localize interface elements.

Designing the User Interface

The menus, forms, controls, toolbars, and bitmaps used in the user interface must serve the locales for which you are designing the application. For example, if you design the application for users in Germany and France, dialog boxes must be large enough to display instructions properly when the instructions are localized in German and French. In addition, the images used in icons and bitmaps must be culturally correct so that they are understood in the target locales.

Testing the Application

To test an international application, you need to check the country or region and language dependencies of the locale for which the application is designed. Testing involves checking the application's data and user interface to ensure that they conform to the locale's standards for date and time, numeric values, currency, list separators, and measurements.

Designing the Interface

Because text tends to increase when you localize an application, be careful when designing the following user interface components:

- ▶ Application messages
- ▶ Menus and forms
- ▶ Icons and bitmaps

Creating Application Messages

When messages are created for the application, the English text strings are usually shorter than their equivalent text strings in other languages. The table that follows shows the average growth of translated strings, compared against their initial English string length.

English length (in characters)	Growth for localized strings
1 to 4	200 percent
5 to 10	180 percent
11 to 20	160 percent
21 to 30	140 percent
31 to 50	120 percent
over 50	110 percent

Designing Menus and Forms

As previously mentioned with messages, the localized text displayed within menus and forms may not fit unless the size difference is taken into account during design. By allowing extra room for localized text, localizers do not have to waste time adjusting the size of controls nor redesigning the interface.

Using Icons and Bitmaps

When used properly, images in the form of icons and bitmaps can be an important part of the user interface of an application. Unfortunately, the meaning that is conveyed by using icons and bitmaps can be more ambiguous than if words were used. The saying 'A picture paints a thousand words' is true, unless the picture also needs to be translated. You should follow these guidelines when using icons and bitmaps:

▶ Use images that are universally recognized. For example, use an envelope to represent mail, but don't use a mailbox, because it's not a universal symbol.

▶ Use color and patterns appropriately. For example, certain color combinations could have regional significance. Also, understand the needs of the color-blind. Traffic lights at road junctions sometimes flash to indicate priority: red indicates stop and check for a clear road, while orange means caution. Color-blind people always stop at these lights, as they cannot tell red from orange.

▶ Try not to use bitmaps that contain text, because when translated the new size of the text could be a problem, as it can elsewhere in the interface.

▶ Do not use anything that does not translate across cultures. Typically this includes jargon, slang, and humor.

▶ Use ToolTips to help explain icons, which have the added advantage of expanding automatically to the size of the text they display.

▶ If men and women are to be shown, ensure that the roles in which you portray them are appropriate for the culture in which the application is to be used.

If you're not sure whether an icon or bitmap is appropriate, consult someone in the locale for which you're designing the application.

Establishing a Directory Structure for a Ported Application

This directory structure allows the programmer to separate the portable components of an application from the remainder of the application. Chapter 9 discusses how this directory structure is integrated into an overall project directory structure. The directory structure is divided into the necessary portable components of an application. The 'i18n' components have their own directory away from the components that vary between operating systems.

```
porting
    |-- exposed porting header files
    |-- package
        |-- private header files specific to package
        |-- component
            |-- source files directories
        |-- object files directory
        |-- library directory
```

Example

```
porting
    |-- exposed porting header files
    |-- messages
        |-- private header files specific to package
        |-- Unix message source files
            |-- source files directories
        |-- Microsoft resource files
        |-- object files directory
        |-- library directory
```

Summary

This chapter has covered the fundamental aspects of porting. The topics covered have included the following:

- ► Porting to new operating systems
- ► Porting to new hardware platforms
- ► Porting to new spoken languages 'i18n' and 'l10n'
- ► Localizing strings in messages
- ► Designing international applications
- ► Designing the interface

Finally, a directory structure is introduced for supporting the portable components of an application.

Application Lifecycle

IN THIS CHAPTER:

Learn About a Standard for Documenting Code

Understand the Need for a Structured Directory Layout

Learn About the Make Utility

Learn About Source Code Control

Learn How to Document Aspects of an Application Other than the Source Code

T he three stages of an application lifecycle are analysis, design, and implementation. This chapter focuses on the final stage of this process, the implementation stage. Although we do not discuss which languages to use, we do describe some techniques to improve maintainability, including two widely used utilities for maintaining the application source code: make and source code control.

In this chapter we also discuss four techniques to help keep track of error reports and enhancement requests, and to record both fixes and regression tests. These techniques help you when managing larger projects.

Documenting Your Source Code

In previous chapters, the topic of documentation has been discussed on a project-wide scale, documenting the analysis and design. This section discusses the documenting of the implementation of the source code, and techniques to make the source code more readable.

Good documentation is essential for two reasons:

▶ If people understand what tasks a class has been designed to perform, they are better able to make decisions about when to reuse the class in their own projects. Imprecise or vague documentation impedes class reuse, as people do not reuse classes they are not able to understand.

▶ Class modifications and support are made easier if the documentation clearly indicates a class function, which methods carry out specific functions and how they are implemented. Trying to extend the functionality of a method is almost impossible if there is no documentation describing how the task is currently implemented.

General Comments

Comments should be used to explain important steps in a method, for example, a comment explaining why the source code implemented in a particular way. A comment telling the reader that a variable is about to be incremented is a waste of everyone's time, unless the reason for the increment is given. (In the following example, C-style comments are used for no particular reason.)

```
/* comment */
```

or

```
/*
** comment
** another comment
*/
```

Examples of comments around code are shown here:

```
/* comment */
code
```

or

```
code                                    /* comment */
```

or

```
if (test == 0)
{
    code                                /* comment */
}
else
{
    code                                /* comment */
}
```

C++ File Documentation

This section shows how a C++ source file should be documented. The documentation includes the following:

► An introductory header explaining why this file exists, including a history of changes

► Which external header files are used

► Which internal header files are used

Each method then has its own explanatory documentation.

```
/*
** Name of file
** What classes does this file provide implementations for
** What are the responsibilities of these classes
** Who created the file
** Change History
**      dd-mmm-yyyy (who made the change)
**          what is this change
*/


/*
** System include files
** include files from outside of the project environment
*/


/*
** Local include files
** Done in this order so that local include files do not try to
** define something that could be declared by the system include
** files include files from the project environment
*/


/*
** Method Header
** Method Name
** Purpose of method
**      Describe any algorithms used in this method
** Input
**      method takes no arguments
**      Arg1 - purpose and range of variable value
** Output/Return
**      method is void
**      return value 1 - when it succeeds
**      return value 2 - when it fails
** Change History
**      dd-mmm-yyyy (who made the change)
**          what is this change
*/
<return type>
method name (data_type argument_name, ...)
{
    /*
    ** local variables
    */
}
```

C++ Header File Syntax

All header files should begin with a conditional compilation flag, as shown next. The first time the compiler includes this header file, the flag __HEADER_FILE_NAME_H is checked. If the flag has not been defined, the compiler proceeds with including the file. The next line in the header file defines the flag, so that should the compiler try to include this header file again, it will fail. This prevents the same file from being included multiple times when compiling one source file. For each new source file that is compiled, the flag is assumed to be undefined until a header file defines it. It is important that each header file uses a different name for its flag. By using the name of the file, this issue is addressed. If different names are not used, one header file could stop the processing of other files as they will fail when the flag is checked:

```
#ifndef __HEADER_FILE_NAME_H
#define __HEADER_FILE_NAME_H


/*
**   Who created the file
**   Change History
**       dd-mmm-yyyy (who made the change)
**            what is this change
*/
/*
**   forward declaration of classes
*/
class <class name>;


/*
**   What is the super class of this class (if any)
*/
public class <classname>
{
    public:
        /*
        **   document the methods of this class that are for public
        **   consumption
        */
    protected:
        /*
        **   document the methods of this class that are for use
        **   by this and derived classes
        */
```

```
    private:
        /*
        **   document the methods of this class that are for use
        **   by this class only
        */
        /*
        **   For each variable (the scope if hopefully private)
        **       what is the variable used for
        **       what is it data type
        **       is the variable a class or instance variable
        */
};


#endif /* __HEADER_FILE_NAME_H
```

Java File Documentation

The documentation for a Java source file follows along similar lines to that used to document a C++ source file.

```
/*
**   Name of file
**   What are the responsibilities of this class
**   Who created the file
**   Change History
**       dd-mmm-yyyy (who made the change)
**           what is this change
*/


/*
**   import files
*/


/*
**   The class definition statement.
**   Does this class extend another class?
**   Does this class implement any interfaces?
*/
public class <classname>

/*
**   For each variable:
**       what is the variable used for
**       what is its scope: public, private or protected
```

```
**      what is it data type
**      is the variable a class or instance variable
*/


/*
**   Method Name
**   Purpose of method
**       Describe any algorithms used in this method
**   Input
**       method takes no arguments
**       Arg1 - purpose and range of variable value
**   Output/Return
**       method is void
**       return value 1 - when it succeeds
**       return value 2 - when it fails
**   Change History
**       dd-mmm-yyyy (who made the change)
**           what is this change
*/
<scope><return type>
method name (data_type argument_name, ...)
{
    /*
    ** local variables
    */
}
```

Statement Layout

The following are examples of how to write source code that is easily readable.

Conditions

Whether the condition is listed in an if-then-else statement, a while loop, or a for loop, always test the result against a known value. This statement:

```
if (method_call () == some_value)
```

is better than a test that relies on the result of the method being positive:

```
if (method_call ())
```

as the preceding statement relies on a result that may change should the method_call be modified.

if-then-else

This statement:

```
if (condition)
{
    <code statements>
}
else
{
    <code statements>
}
```

is a lot easier on the eye when checking matching brackets than the following:

```
if (condition) {
    <code statements>
}
else {
    <code statements>
}
```

for Loops and while Loops

As with if-then-else, keep the brackets out front:

```
for (<initialization>; <condition_is_false>; <increment>)
{
    <code statements>
}
```

and

```
while (<condition_is_true>)
{
    <code statements>
}
```

If a for loop or a while loop is being run just for its side-effect, label it as having no body:

```
for (;*dst++ != *src++; )
    ;     /* void body */
```

and

```
while (*dest++ != *src++)
    ;     /* void body */
```

Organizing Your Project Directories

The following is an example of how to organize a project into directories for ease of administration and management. Essentially, a project has a number of distinct components that are better served if they have their own directories.

Each project has the following components:

► Tools and control files to build the application.

► Facilities that can be ported.

► Facilities that are common to other components.

► The back-end, or engine, of the application.

► The front-end, or external interface, of the application.

► A build directory structure in which to put the built components of the application.

► A dummy installation directory that mimics an installation of the application. This will be similar to the build directory, but could contain configuration information.

► Finally, a directory that contains all of the test programs.

```
project
    |-- tools
        |-- makefiles
        |-- build scripts
    |-- porting
        |-- exposed porting header files
        |-- package
            |-- private header files specific to package
            |-- source files directories
                |-- component_1
                |-- component_2
            |-- object files directory
            |-- library directory
    |-- common
        |-- exposed common header files
        |-- package
            |-- private header files specific to package
            |-- source files directories
                |-- component_1
                |-- component_2
```

```
            |-- object files directory
            |-- library directory
    |-- back-end
        |-- exposed back-end header files
        |-- package
            |-- private header files specific to package
            |-- source files directories
                |-- component_1
                |-- component_2
            |-- object files directory
            |-- library directory
    |-- front-end
        |-- exposed porting header files
        |-- package
            |-- private header files specific to package
            |-- source files directories
                |-- component_1
                |-- component_2
            |-- object files directory
            |-- executables directory
    |-- buildArea
        |-- executabls
        |-- libraries
        |-- message_catalogs / resource files
    |-- dummy_installation_area
        |-- executabls
        |-- libraries
        |-- message_catalogs / resource files
        |-- other_files (configuration_files, header_files
                        - if needed)
    |-- test_suite
        |-- test1
            |-- project
                |-- test1 source files
                |-- test1 object files
                |-- test1 library - if needed
                |-- test1 executable - if needed
```

Using the make Utility

The make utility is used to keep a series of files (the targets) up-to-date. The utility uses a file called a makefile to contain the instructions. The instructions describe how to create a target from its source and the commands used. The source of each target may itself be a target and may have instructions for its own creation.

The make utility recursively checks each target against its sources. If, after processing all of the source files, a target file is found to be either missing or older than any of its source files, the make utility rebuilds it.

To build a given target, the make utility executes the list of commands, called a *rule*. This rule may be listed explicitly in the target's makefile entry, or it may be supplied implicitly by make.

If no *target* is specified on the command line, make uses the first target defined in the makefile. This is usually defined as 'all'.

Options

The following options are supported:

-f *makefile*	The usual name for the file used by the make utility is makefile. However, '-f' allows the file to be otherwise named, as shown here:
	make –f <name>
	Use the description file *makefile*. A '-' as the *makefile* argument denotes the standard input. The contents of *makefile*, when present, override the standard set of implicit rules and predefined macros. When more than one '-f *makefile*' argument pair appears, make uses the concatenation of those files, in order of appearance.
-n	No execution mode. Print commands, but do not execute them. Even lines beginning with an @ are printed. However, if a command line contains a reference to the $(MAKE) macro, that line is always executed. When in POSIX mode, lines beginning with a "+" are executed.
-s	Silent mode. Do not print command lines before executing them. Equivalent to the special-function target .SILENT:.

NOTE

If there is a file named makefile in the working directory, make uses that file. If, however, there is an SCCS history file (SCCS/s.makefile) which is newer, make attempts to retrieve and use the most recent version.

In the absence of the above file(s), if a file named Makefile is present in the working directory, make attempts to use it. If there is a newer SCCS history file (SCCS/s.Makefile), make attempts to retrieve and use the most recent version. When no makefile is specified, /usr/ccs/bin/make in POSIX mode and /usr/xpg4/bin/make try the following files in sequence:

./makefile, ./Makefile
s.makefile, SCCS/s.makefile
s.Makefile, SCCS/s.Makefile

Other options exist but are beyond the scope of this book.

Operands

The make utility can be passed specific targets, as follows:

```
make target
```

An example of this is 'make clean' to remove objects, libraries, and executables so that everything can be rebuilt.

TIP

Macro definition. This definition overrides any regular definition for the specified macro within the makefile itself, or in the environment. However, this definition can still be overridden by conditional macro assignments.

```
make macro=value
```

An example of this is 'make DEBUG=1'. With the appropriate instructions as shown in "OS_SPECIFIC.defs" in the "Example of Makefiles" section later in this chapter, this macro can be used to invoke compilation with the debug flag '-g', which adds information for use with the debugging tool.

Reading Makefiles and the Environment

The make utility then reads the command line for additional options, which also take effect. Next, make reads in a default makefile that typically contains predefined macro definitions, target entries for implicit rules, and additional rules, such as the rule for retrieving SCCS files.

The make utility then imports variables from the environment and treats them as defined macros. Because make uses the most recent definition it encounters, a macro definition in the makefile normally overrides an environment variable of the same name.

The make utility reads any makefiles you specify with -f, or one of files makcfile or Makefile, as previously described in "Options."

The make utility finally reads in any macro definitions supplied as command line arguments. These override macro definitions in both the makefile and the environment, but only for the make command itself.

Makefile Target Entries

The entries in the makefile have the following format:

```
## the '->' is used to indicate a tab character
target... [:|::] [dependency] ... [; command] ...
    ->    [command]
```

The first line contains the name of a target, or a space-separated list of target names, terminated with a colon. If a list of targets is given, this is equivalent to having a separate entry of the same form for each target. The colon is generally followed by a dependency, or a dependency list. The make utility checks this list before building the target. The dependency list may be terminated with a semicolon (;), which in turn can be followed by a single Bourne shell command. Subsequent lines in the target entry begin with a TAB, and contain Bourne shell commands. These commands comprise the rule for building the target.

Shell commands may be continued across input lines by escaping the newline character with a backslash (\), like this: \n . The continuing line must then start with a tab character.

To rebuild a target, the make utility expands macros, strips off initial tab characters and either executes the command directly (if it contains no shell metacharacters) or passes each command line to a Bourne shell for execution.

The first line that does not begin with a tab or '#' begins another target or macro definition.

Special Characters

What follows is a simplified list of makefile characters.

Special Characters	Description
Global	
#	Start a comment. The comment ends at the next newline character. If the '#' follows the tab character in a command line, that line is passed to the shell (which also treats '#' as the start of a comment).
include *filename*	If the word *include* appears as the first seven letters of a line and is followed by a space or tab, the string that follows is taken as a filename to interpolate at that line. You can nest include files to a depth of no more than about 16. If *filename* is a macro reference, it is expanded.
Targets and Dependencies	
:	Target list terminator. Words following the colon are added to the dependency list for the target or targets. **An example** clean : src_clean
%	Pattern matching wild card metacharacter. Like the '*' shell wild card, '%' matches any string of zero or more characters in a target name or dependency, in the target portion of a conditional macro definition, or within a pattern replacement macro reference. Note that only one '%' can appear in a target, dependency-name, or pattern-replacement macro reference. **An example** %.o:%.c
Macros	
=	Macro definition. The word to the left of this character is the macro name; words to the right comprise its value. Leading and trailing white space characters are stripped from the value. A word break following the = is implied.
$	Macro reference. The following character, or the parenthesized or bracketed string, is interpreted as a macro reference: make expands the reference (including the $) by replacing it with the macro's value.

Special Characters	Description
Macros (continued)	
( ) or { }	Macro-reference name delimiters. A parenthesized or bracketed word appended to a $ is taken as the name of the macro being referred to. Without the delimiters, make recognizes only the first character as the macro name.
$$	A reference to the dollar-sign macro, the value of which is the character $. Used to pass variable expressions beginning with $ to the shell, to refer to environment variables, which are expanded by the shell, or to delay processing of dynamic macros within the dependency list of a target, until that target is actually processed.
\$	Escaped dollar-sign character. Interpreted as a literal dollar sign within a rule.
+=	When used in place of '=', appends a string to a macro definition (must be surrounded by white space, unlike '=').
Rules	
@	If the first non-TAB character is a @, make does not print the command line before executing it. This character is not passed to the shell.
?	Escape command-dependency checking. Command lines starting with this character are not subject to command dependency checking.
!	Force command-dependency checking. Command-dependency checking is applied to command lines for which it would otherwise be suppressed. This checking is normally suppressed for lines that contain references to the '?' dynamic macro (for example, '$?').

When any combination of '@', '?', or '!' appears as the first characters after the tab character, all that are present apply. None are passed to the shell.

Special-Function Targets

When incorporated in a makefile, the following target names perform special functions:

.INIT:	If defined in the makefile, this target and its dependencies are built before any other targets are processed.
.SILENT:	Run silently. When this target appears in the makefile, make does not echo commands before executing them. When used in POSIX mode, it could be followed by target names, and only those target names will be executed silently.

Suffix Replacement Macro References

Substitutions within macros can be made, as follows:

$(name:string1=string2)

An example is shown here:

```
SRC = x.c y.c z.c
OBJ = $(SRC:.c=.o)
# which gives x.o y.o and z.o
```

where <u>string1</u> is either a suffix or a word to be replaced in the macro definition, and <u>string2</u> is the replacement suffix or word. Words in a macro value are separated by space, tab, and escaped newline characters.

Dynamic Macros

There are several dynamically maintained macros that are useful as abbreviations within rules. They are shown here as references; if you were to define them, make would simply override the definition.

$*	The base name of the current target, derived as if selected for use with an implicit rule.
$<	The name of a dependency file, derived as if selected for use with an implicit rule.
$@	The name of the current target. This is the only dynamic macro whose value is strictly determined when used in a dependency list. (In which case, it takes the form '$$@'.)

$?	The list of dependencies that are newer than the target. Command-dependency checking is automatically suppressed for lines that contain this macro, just as if the command had been prefixed with a '?'. See the previous description of '?', under "Special Characters." You can force this check with the ! command-line prefix. An example:
	`print : *.c`
	`  -> $(PRINT) $?`
	`  -> touch print`
	The variable '$?' is used to print only those files that have changed.

To refer to the $@ dynamic macro within a dependency list, precede the reference with an additional '$' character (as in, '$$@'). Because make assigns $< and $* as it would for implicit rules (according to the suffixes list and the directory contents), they may be unreliable when used within explicit target entries.

Implicit Rules

When a target has no entry in the makefile, make attempts to determine its class (if any) and apply the rule for that class. An implicit rule describes how to build any target of a given class from an associated dependency file. The class of a target can be determined either by a pattern or by a suffix, the corresponding dependency file (with the same basename) from which such a target might be built. In addition to a predefined set of implicit rules, make allows you to define your own, either by pattern or by suffix.

Command Execution

Command lines are executed one at a time, *each by its own process or shell*. Shell commands, notably *cd*, are ineffectual across an unescaped newline in the makefile. A line is printed (after macro expansion) just before being executed. This is suppressed if it starts with a '@', if there is a '.SILENT:' entry in the makefile, or if make is run with the -s option. Although the -n option specifies printing without execution, lines containing the macro $(MAKE) are executed regardless, and lines containing the @ special character are printed. The -t (touch) option updates the modification date of a file without executing any rules. This can be dangerous when sources are maintained by more than one person.

Bourne Shell Constructs

To use the Bourne shell if control structure is for branching, use a command line of the form:

```
if expression ; \
then command ; \
... ; \
else command ; \
... ; \
fi
```

Although composed of several input lines, the escaped newline characters ensure that make treats them all as one (shell) command line.

To use the Bourne shell for control structure for loops, use a command line of the form:

```
for var in list ; \
do command; \
... ; \
done
```

To refer to a shell variable, use a double dollar sign ($$). This prevents expansion of the dollar sign by make.

Diagnostics

Don't know how to make target *target*	There is no makefile entry for *target*, and none of make's implicit rules apply (there is no dependency file with a suffix in the suffixes list, or the target's suffix is not in the list).
*** *target* removed	The make was interrupted while building *target*. Rather than leaving a partially-completed version that is newer than its dependencies, make removes the file named *target*.
*** *target* not removed	The make was interrupted while building *target*, and *target* was not present in the directory.
*** *target* could not be removed, *reason*	The make was interrupted while building *target*, which was not removed for the indicated reason.
Read of include file *file* failed	The makefile indicated in the include directive was not found, or was inaccessible.
Loop detected when expanding macro value *macro*	A reference to the macro being defined was found in the definition.
*** Error code *n*	The previous shell command returned a nonzero error code.
Conditional macro conflict encountered	Displayed only when -d is in effect, this message indicates that two or more parallel targets currently being processed depend on a target, which is built differently for each by virtue of conditional macros. Since the target cannot simultaneously satisfy both dependency relationships, it is conflicted.

Example of Makefiles

This makefile says that pgm depends on two files, a.o and b.o, and that they in turn depend on their corresponding source files (a.c and b.c) along with a common file incl.h.

Simple Explicit Makefile

```
pgm: a.o b.o
$(LINK.c) -o $@ a.o b.o
a.o: incl.h a.c
cc -c a.c
b.o: incl.h b.c
cc -c b.c
```

Simple Implicit Makefile

The following makefile uses implicit rules to express the same dependencies:

```
pgm: a.o b.o
cc a.o b.o -o pgm
a.o b.o: incl.h
```

Example of Porting Makefiles

The example makefiles that follow show generic definitions, operating specific definitions, generic rules, and operating specific rules, and then makefiles for each of the levels in the application directory structure, including different makfiles for libraries and executables. ' -> ' is used to indicate the eight-character tab required lines that continue previous lines.

genericMakefile.defs

```
## Setup the macro to include to commonly used values
INCLUDE            = -I$(PROJECT_SRC)/$(part)/hdr
DEFINES           =


## Add extra header files if the package is only 'pack1' or 'pack2'
## The test below searches for the package name in the
## comma separated list, which consists of 'pack1' and 'pack2'.
## If the result is positive, the package name does not equal the
## first argument of the 'ifneq', which by default is an empty string
## and so the commands are executed
ifneq (,$(findstring $(package), pack1, pack2))
    CUSTOM_INCLUDE    = \
  ->    -I$(PROJECT_SRC)/$(part)/$(another_package)/hdr
    CUSTOM_DEFINES    = -DANSI
    CUSTOM_LIBRARIES  = -l<package1lib>
endif


## Setup aliases for libraries
## example for the shared library 'libpackage1'
## and the static library 'libpackage2'
package1name      = libpackage1.$(SH_lib_EXT)
package1lib       = $(PROJECT_BUILD_LIB)/$(package1name)

package2name      = libpackage2.$(SH_lib_EXT)
package2lib       = $(PROJECT_BUILD_LIB)/$(package2name)

include $(PROJECT_MAKE_DIR)/${OS_SPECIFIC}.dets
```

OS_SPECIFIC.defs

```
PROJECT_SOURCE      = <some directory>
PROJECT_BUILD       = $(PROJECT_SOURCE)/build
PROJECT_BUILD_BIN   = $(PROJECT_BUILD)/bin
PROJECT_BUILD_LIB   = $(PROJECT_BUILD)/lib
PROJECT_MAKE_DIR    = $(PROJECT_BUILD)/makefiles


ST_lib_EXT          = a
SH_lib_EXT          = so


OBJ_EXT             = o


#
# Platform dependant include dirs
#
INCLUDE             += -I/usr/include -I/usr/ucbinclude -I.

ifdef DEBUG
OPTFLAGS            += -g
CPP_OPTFLAGS        += -g
else
OPTFLAGS            += -xO5
CPP_OPTFLAGS        += -xO5
endif

ifneq (,$(findstring $(package), package1))
DEFINES            += -D<operating_specific_define>
endif

## library archive command
AR                  = /usr/ccs/bin/ar
## compilers
CC                  = <compiler location>/cc
CPP                 = <compiler location>/CC
## copy files
CP                  = /bin/cp
## directory manipulation
MKDIR               = /bin/mkdir -p
RMDIR               = /bin/rm -rf
## remove files
RM                  = /bin/rm -rf
```

```
## Compiler flags
cflags          += ...
CCFLAGS         += ...

## AIX specific flag to force characters to be signed
CCFLAGS         += -qchars=signed
cflags          += -qchars=signed

CC.options      = $(OPTFLAGS) $(INCLUDE) $(DEFINES) $(CFLAGS)
CPP.options     = $(CPP_OPTFLAGS) $(INCLUDE) $(DEFINES) $(CFLAGS)
## Compiler command
CC.comp         = $(CC) -c $(CC.options)
CPP.comp        = $(CPP) -c $(CPP.options)

## Library flags
LDFLAGS         = ...
## Building library command
CC.link         = $(CC) $(OPTFLAGS) $(LDFLAGS)

## Standard libraries = usulaly system libraries
STDLIBS         = ... -lpthread -lm
```

genericMakefile.rules

```
all-packages:
    ->    for package in boo $(packages); do \
    ->        if [ -d "$$package" ]; then \
    ->        ->    (cd $$package && \
    ->        ->    $(MAKE) all && exit 1);\
    ->        fi;\
    ->    done; exit 0;


all-clean:
    ->    for package in boo $(packages); do \
    ->        if [ -d "$$package" ]; then \
    ->        ->    (cd $$package;\
    ->        ->    ($(MAKE) clean || exit 1));\
    ->        fi;\
    ->    done; exit 0;


src-clean:
    ->    (cd $(PROJECT_SOURCE)/$(part)/$(package); \
    ->    for objfile in boo $(OBJ_FILES); do \
```

```
->        if [ -f "$$objfile" ]; then \
->     ->   $(RM) $$objfile; \
->        fi; \
->   done;)
```

```
include $(PROJECT_MAKE_DIR)/${OS_SPECIFIC}.rules
```

OS_SPECIFIC.rules

```
## the rules the build to a library can either be placed here if it
## has operating specific needs
```

Part Makefile

```
##
##  Makefile for top of tree part e.g. back
##
##  History:
##      <date> <author>
##          <description>
##

export part    = <part>

include $(PROJECT_MAKE_DIR)/genericMakefile.defs

packages = package_1 package_2

all:    all-components
clean:  all-clean

include $(PROJECT_MAKE_DIR)/genericMakefile.rules
```

Library Package Makefile

```
##
##  makefile for the <part>/<package> library
##
##  History:
##      <date> <author>
##          <description>
##
part              = <part>
```

```
package          = <package>

include $(PROJECT_MAKE_DIR)/genericMakefile.defs

SRC_FILES        = \
    src/<component>/<source_file_1> \
    src/<component>/<source_file_2>

OBJ_FILES        = \
    obj/<object_file_1> \
    obj/<object_file_2>

OBJDIR           = ./obj
BINDIR           = ./bin
LIBDIR           = ./lib
INCDIR           = ./hdr
SRCDIR           = ./src

INCLUDE          += $(CUSTOM_INCLUDE)

LIBS             += $(CUSTOM_LIBS) $(STDLIBS)

all : $(OBJDIR) $(package1lib)
clean: src-clean

$(package1lib): $(OBJ_FILES)
    ->   $(CPP.link) -o $(LIBDIR)/$(package1name) $(LDFLAGS) \
    ->        $(OBJ_FILES) $(LIBS)
    ->   $(CP) $(LIBDIR)/$(package1name) $(package1lib)

obj/%.o: src/<component>/%.c
    ->   $(CC.comp) $(CCFLAGS) $(DEFINE) $(INCLUDE) $< -o $@

include $(PROJECT_MAKE_DIR)/genericMakefile.rules
```

Executable Package Makefile

```
##
##  makefile for the <part>/<package> executable
##
##  History:
##      <date> <author>
##          <description>
```

```
##

part              = <part>
package           = <package>

include $(PROJECT_MAKE_DIR)/genericMakefile.def

SRC_FILES         = \
    src/<component>/<source_file_1> \
    src/<component>/<source_file_2> \
    src/<component>/<source_file_3> \
    src/<component>/<source_file_4>

OBJ_FILES         = \
    obj/<object_file_1> \
    obj/<object_file_2> \
    obj/<object_file_3> \
    obj/<object_file_4>

OBJDIR            = ./obj
BINDIR            = ./bin
LIBDIR            = ./lib
INCDIR            = ./hdr
SRCDIR            = ./src

INCLUDE           += $(CUSTOM_INCLUDE)

LIBS              += $(CUSTOM_LIBS) $(STDLIBS)

all : $(OBJDIR) <executable1>
clean:  src-clean

$(PROJECT_BUILD_BIN)/<executable1>: $(OBJ_FILES)
    ->    $(CC.comp) -o $(BINDIR)<executable1> $(OBJ_FILES) \
    ->        -L$(PROJECT_BUILD_LIB) $(LIBS)
    ->    $(CP) $(BINDIR)<executable1> $(PROJECT_BUILD_BIN)

obj/<component_name>.$(OBJ_EXT): src/<component_name>/<source_file_1>
    ->    $(CC) $(CCFLAGS) $(DEFINE) $(INCLUDE) \
    ->        src/<component_name>/<source_file_1>

include $(PROJECT_MAKE_DIR)/genericMakefile.rules
```

Making Dependencies

When dependencies for a file are created, the lines in the makefile that follow the user commands are shown here. There is a statement that declares that the dependencies are to follow. The object file is shown on the left, with the file on which it is dependent on the right. Should the file on the right be updated, it will cause the file on the left to be rebuilt.

```
# DO NOT DELETE THIS LINE — make depend depends on it.
obj/<object_file_1>: $(PROJECT_SRC)/$(<part>)/$(<package>)/hdr/<header_file>.h
```

Using the Source Code Control Utility

Source code control is a useful utility, as it allows the programmer to keep track of changes made to the source code files of an application. A source code control system is used to record the differences between different versions of a file, with associated comments that explain why a change was made.

The source code control system discussed here is the system used on UNIX, called SCCS.

Source Code Control System

This section consists of a description of the Source Code Control System (SCCS) , the various commands that can be used, and finally a simple example showing how SCCS can be used.

Description

The *sccs* command is a comprehensive, straightforward front end to the various utility programs of the SCCS. The *sccs* applies the indicated subcommand to the history file associated with each of the indicated files.

The name of an SCCS history file is derived by pre-pending the 's.' prefix to the filename of a working copy. The *sccs* command normally expects these s.files to reside in an SCCS subdirectory. Thus, when you supply sccs with a *file* argument, it normally applies the subcommand to a file named s.*file* in the SCCS subdirectory. If *file* is a path name, *sccs* looks for the history file in the SCCS subdirectory of that file's parent directory. If *file* is a directory, however, *sccs* applies the subcommand to every s.*file* file it contains. Thus, the command

```
example% sccs get program.c
```

would apply the get subcommand to a history file named

```
SCCS/s.program.c
```

while the command

```
example% sccs get SCCS
```

would apply it to every s.file in the SCCS subdirectory.

Options for the *sccs* command itself must appear before the subcommand argument. Options for a given subcommand must appear after the subcommand argument. These options are specific to each subcommand, and are described along with the subcommands themselves (see the explanation of subcommands in the next section).

Operands

The following operands are supported:

▶   **Subcommand**   An SCCS utility name or the name of one of the pseudo-utilities listed in USAGE.

▶   **Options**   An option or option-argument to be passed to subcommand.

▶   **Operands**   An operand to be passed to subcommand.

Usage

Many of the following *sccs* subcommands invoke programs that reside in /usr/ccs/bin. Many of these subcommands accept additional arguments that are documented in the reference page for the utility program that the subcommand invokes.

check [-b]	Check for files currently being edited. Like info and tell, but returns an exit code, rather than producing a listing of files. The check returns a non-zero exit status if a file is being edited. -b Ignore branches
clean [-b]	Remove everything in the current directory that can be retrieved from an SCCS history. Do not remove files that are being edited. -b Do not check branches to see if they are being edited. The clean -b subcommand is dangerous when branch versions are kept in the same directory.
create	Create (initialize) history files. The *create* subcommand performs the following steps: 1. Renames the original source file to ,program.c in the current directory. 2. Creates the history file called s.program.c in the SCCS subdirectory. 3. Performs an 'sccs get' on program.c to retrieve a read-only copy of the initial version.

deledit [-s] [-y[*comment*]]	Equivalent to an 'sccs delta' and then an 'sccs edit'. deledit checks in a delta, and checks the file back out again, but leaves the current working copy of the file intact. -s Silent. Do not report delta numbers or statistics. -y[*comment*] Supply a comment for the delta commentary. If -y is omitted, delta prompts for a comment. A null *comment* results in an empty comment field for the delta.
delget [-s] [-y[*comment*]]	Perform an 'sccs delta' and then an 'sccs get' to check in a delta and retrieve read-only copies of the resulting new version. See the *deledit* subcommand for a description of -s and -y. The *sccs* command performs a delta on all the files specified in the argument list, and then a get on all the files. If an error occurs during the delta, the get is not performed.
delta [-s] [-y[*comment*]]	Check in pending changes. Records the line-by-line changes introduced while the file was checked out. The effective user I.D. must be the same as the I.D. of the person who has the file checked out. Refer to sccs-delta(1). See the deledit subcommand for a description of -s and -y.
diffs [-c*date-time*] [-r*sid*]	Compare the working copy of a file that is checked out for editing, with a version from the SCCS history. Use the most recent checked-in version by default. -c*date-time* Use the most recent version checked in before the indicated date and time for comparison. The *date-time* subcommand takes the form: *yy*[*mm*[*dd*[*hh*[*mm*[*ss*]]]]]. Omitted units default to their maximum possible values; that is -c7502 is equivalent to -c750228235959. -r*sid* Use the version corresponding to the indicated delta for comparison.
edit	Retrieve a version of the file for editing. The *sccs* edit command extracts a version of the file that is writable by you, and creates a p.file in the SCCS subdirectory as lock on the history, so that no one else can check that version in or out. I.D. keywords are retrieved in unexpanded form. The *edit* subcommand accepts the same options as get, below.
enter	Similar to create, but omits the final sccs get. This may be used if an 'sccs edit' is to be performed immediately after the history file is initialized.
get [-ek] [-c*date-time*] [-r[*sid*]]	Retrieve a version from the SCCS history. By default, this is a read-only working copy of the most recent version; I.D. keywords are in expanded form. -e Get the file out for edit -k Suppress expansion of I.D. keywords. -k is implied by the flag –e.
help *message-code* | *sccs-command*	help stuck Supply more information about SCCS diagnostics. The *help* subcommand displays a brief explanation of the error when you supply the code displayed by an SCCS diagnostic message. If you supply the name of an SCCS command, it prints a usage line. The help command also recognizes the keyword stuck. Refer to sccs-help(1).

info [-b]	Display a list of files being edited, including the version number checked out, the version to be checked in, the name of the user who holds the lock, and the date and time the file was checked out. -b Ignore branches
print	Print the entire history of each named file.
prs [-el] [-c*date-time*] [-r*sid*]	Peruse (display) the delta table, or other portion of an s.file. -e Display information of deltas created before the delta indicated by the –r or –c. -l Display information of deltas created after the delta indicated by the –r or –c.
sact	Show editing activity status of an SCCS file. Refer to sccs-sact(1).
sccsdiff -r*old-sid* -r*new-sid*	Compare two versions corresponding to the indicated SIDs (deltas) using diff.
tell [-b]	Display the list of files that are currently checked out, one file per line. -b Ignore branches
unedit or unget	"Undo" the last edit or 'get -e', and return the working copy to its previous condition. Unedit backs out all pending changes made since the file was checked out.

Environment

See environ(5) for descriptions of the following environment variables that affect the execution of sccs: LC_CTYPE, LC_MESSAGES, and NLSPATH.

If it begins with a slash (an absolute path name), sccs searches for SCCS history files in the directory given by that variable. If PROJECTDIR does not begin with a slash, it is taken as the name of a user, and sccs searches the src or source subdirectory of that user's home directory for history files. If such a directory is found, it is used. Otherwise, the value is used as a relative path name.

SCCS—Files

The following is a list of files and directories typically associated with the SCCS utility:

► SCCS SCCS subdirectory

► SCCS/d.<u>file</u> temporary file of differences

► SCCS/p.<u>file</u> lock (permissions) file for checked-out versions

► SCCS/q.<u>file</u> temporary file

► SCCS/s.<u>file</u> SCCS history file

- ► SCCS/x.<u>file</u> temporary copy of the s.file
- ► SCCS/z.<u>file</u> temporary lock file
- ► /usr/ccs/bin/* SCCS utility programs

SCCS Keywords

In the absence of -e or -k, get expands the following I.D. keywords by replacing them with the indicated values in the text of the retrieved source.

Keyword	Value
%A%	Shorthand notation for an I.D. line with data for what(1): %Z%%Y% %M% %I%%Z%
%B%	SID branch component
%C%	Current line number. Intended for identifying messages output by the program, such as "this shouldn't have happened" type errors. It is *not* intended to be used on every line to provide sequence numbers.
%D%	Current date: *yy/mm/dd*
%E%	Date newest applied delta was created: *yy/mm/dd*
%F%	SCCS s.file name
%G%	Date newest applied delta was created: *mm/dd/yy*
%H%	Current date: mm/dd/yy
%I%	SID of the retrieved version: %R%.%L%.%B%.%S%
%L%	SID level component
%M%	Module name: the name of the s.file less the prefix
%P%	Fully qualified o.file name
%Q%	Value of the q flag in the s.file
%R%	SID Release component
%S%	SID Sequence component
%T%	Current time: *hh:mm:ss*
%U%	Time the newest applied delta was created: *hh:mm:ss*
%W%	Shorthand notation for an I.D. line with data for what: %Z%%M% %I%
%Y%	Module type: value of the t flag in the s.file
%Z%	4-character string: '@(#)', recognized by what

Examples of SCCS

Create the source safe file. The file has 79 lines and the version is 1.1:

```
>> sccs create endian.cpp
endian.cpp:
No id keywords (cm7)
1.1
79 lines
No id keywords (cm7)
```

Print the directory:

```
>> ls
,endian.cpp  SCCS          endian        endian.cpp
```

Check to see if any files are open for editing:

```
>> sccs check
```

Check for differences between the file in the directory and the file under source code control:

```
>> sccs diffs endian.cpp

------- endian.cpp -------
```

Check the file out for editing. The previous version was 1.1, the new version is 1.2:

```
>> sccs edit endian.cpp
1.1
new delta 1.2
79 lines
```

Check that the file is able to be edited:

```
>> ls -l
total 36
-rw-r--r--   1 jasmine  jasii            941 Feb  1 15:20 ,endian.cpp
drwxrwxr-x   2 jasmine  jasii            512 Feb 16 14:25 SCCS
-rwxr-xr-x   1 jasmine  jasii          11052 Feb  1 15:20 endian
-rw-r--r--   1 jasmine  jasii            941 Feb 16 14:25 endian.cpp
```

Check the SCCS directory:

```
>> ls SCCS
p.endian.cpp   s.endian.cpp
```

Unget the file, so that it is removed from the directory:

```
>> sccs unget endian.cpp
1.2
```

Recheck the directory:

```
>> ls -l
total 34
-rw-r--r--    1 jasmine   jasii         941 Feb  1 15.20 ,endian.cpp
drwxrwxr-x    2 jasmine   jasii         512 Feb 16 14:26 SCCS
-rwxr-xr-x    1 jasmine   jasii       11052 Feb  1 15:20 endian
```

Print the file with some revision history:

```
>> sccs print endian.cpp
SCCS/s.endian.cpp:


D 1.1 01/02/16 14:23:23 jasmine 1 0     00079/00000/00000
MRs:
COMMENTS:
date and time created 01/02/16 14:23:23 by jasmine


1.1     /*
1.1     ** endian.cpp
1.1     ** This application is used to test endism.
1.1     **
1.1     ** Expected results:
1.1     **      Big Endian        Little Endian
1.1     **      12 34 56 78       78 56 34 12
1.1     **      12 34 56 78       34 12 78 56
1.1     **      41 42 43 00       41 42 43 00
1.1     */
...
1.1     int main(int argc, char* argv[])
1.1     {
...
```

```
1.1      /*
1.1      ** Set the pointer to the long variable
1.1      ** and then print the 4 bytes of memory
1.1      */
1.1          ptr = (char *)&temp.l;
1.1
1.1          printValue (ptr);
1.1
1.1      /*
1.1      ** Set the pointer to the short array variable
1.1      ** and then print the 4 bytes of memory
1.1      */
1.1          ptr = (char *)&temp.s;
1.1
1.1          printValue (ptr);
1.1
1.1      /*
1.1      ** Set the pointer to the char array variable
1.1      ** and then print the 4 bytes of memory
1.1      */
1.1          ptr = (char *)&temp.c;
1.1
1.1          printValue (ptr);
1.1
1.1          return 0;
1.1      }
```

Check the file out for editing:

```
>> sccs edit endian.cpp
```

Edit the file:

```
>> vi endian.cpp
```

Show the editing activity of this file:

```
>> sccs sact endian.cpp
1.1 1.2 jasmine 01/02/16 14:28:24
```

Check for differences between the file in the directory and the file under source code control:

```
>> sccs diffs endian.cpp

------- endian.cpp -------
58d57
<
66d64
<
74d71
<
```

Show the file being edited:

```
>> sccs tell
endian.cpp
```

Show more history of the file being edited:

```
>> sccs info
   endian.cpp: being edited: 1.1 1.2 jasmine 01/02/16 14:28:24
```

Unedit the file (removes any edits made to the file):

```
>> sccs unedit endian.cpp
   endian.cpp: removed
1.1
79 lines
No id keywords (cm7)
```

Reshow the history of any files being edited:

```
>> sccs info
Nothing being edited
```

Check the file out again for editing. The previous version was 1.1, the new version is 1.2:

```
>> sccs edit endian.cpp
1.1
new delta 1.2
79 lines
```

Submit the changes (the delta) and then get the file out, read-only:

```
>> sccs delget endian.cpp
comments? this change removes the blank lines between the assignments
statements and the method invocation
No id keywords (cm7)
1.2
0 inserted
3 deleted
76 unchanged
1.2
76 lines
No id keywords (cm7)
```

Print the file with some revision history:

```
>> sccs print endian.cpp
SCCS/s.endian.cpp:


D 1.2 01/02/16 14:38:56 jasmine 2 1     00000/00003/00076
MRs:
COMMENTS:
this change removes the blank lines between the assignment statements
and the method invocation


D 1.1 01/02/16 14:23:23 jasmine 1 0     00079/00000/00000
MRs:
COMMENTS:
date and time created 01/02/16 14:23:23 by jasmine


1.1     /*
1.1     ** endian.cpp
1.1     ** This application is used to test endism.
1.1     **
...
1.1         ptr = (char *)&temp.l;
1.1         printValue (ptr);
...
1.1         ptr = (char *)&temp.s;
1.1         printValue (ptr);
...
1.1         ptr = (char *)&temp.c;
```

```
1.1            printValue (ptr);
1.1
1.1            return 0;
1.1        }
```

Check the file out again for editing:

```
>> sccs edit endian.cpp
sccs edit endian.cpp
1.2
new delta 1.3
76 lincs
```

Edit the file:

```
>> vi endian.cpp
```

Submit the changes (the delta) and then retrieve the file, read-only:

```
>> sccs delget endian.cpp
comments? put blank lines back
No id keywords (cm7)
1.3
3 inserted
0 deleted
76 unchanged
1.3
79 lines
No id keywords (cm7)
```

Print the file with some revision history:

```
>> sccs print endian.cpp
SCCS/s.endian.cpp:


D 1.3 01/02/16 14:41:38 jasmine 3 2      00003/00000/00076
MRs:
COMMENTS:
put blank lines back


D 1.2 01/02/16 14:38:56 jasmine 2 1      00000/00003/00076
MRs:
```

```
COMMENTS:
this change removes the blank lines between the assignment statements
and the method invocation

D 1.1 01/02/16 14:23:23 jasmine 1 0     00079/00000/00000
MRs:
COMMENTS:
date and time created 01/02/16 14:23:23 by jasmine

1.1     /*
1.1     ** endian.cpp
1.1     ** This application is used to test endism.
1.1     **
...
1.1          ptr = (char *)&temp.l;
1.3
1.1          printValue (ptr);
...
1.1          ptr = (char *)&temp.s;
1.3
1.1          printValue (ptr);
...
1.1          ptr = (char *)&temp.c;
1.3
1.1          printValue (ptr);
1.1
1.1          return 0;
1.1     }
```

Show differences in the file between the first and last versions:

```
>> sccs sccsdiff -r 1.1 -r 1.3 endian.cpp
SCCS/s.endian.cpp: No differences
```

Show differences in the file between the first and second versions:

```
>> sccs sccsdiff -r 1.1 -r 1.2 endian.cpp
58d57
<
66d64
<
74d71
<
```

Show differences in the file between the second and third versions:

```
>> sccs sccsdiff -r 1.2 -r 1.3 endian.cpp
57a58
>
64a66
>
71a74
>
```

Show the history of the file:

```
>> sccs prs endian.cpp
SCCS/s.endian.cpp:

D 1.3 01/02/16 14:41:38 jasmine 3 2     00003/00000/00076
MRs:
COMMENTS:
put blank lines back

D 1.2 01/02/16 14:38:56 jasmine 2 1     00000/00003/00076
MRs:
COMMENTS:
this change removes the blank lines between the assignments
statements and the method invocation

D 1.1 01/02/16 14:23:23 jasmine 1 0     00079/00000/00000
MRs:
COMMENTS:
date and time created 01/02/16 14:23:23 by jasmine
```

Reporting Errors

An error is an event that results in a failure of a facility, in that it does not work as planned. When you report an error to the development team, certain information needs to be provided. Each new error report needs to have a unique number. The information required in the error report is listed as follows:

► **Error date**   The date the error was reported.

► **Error reporter**   The name of the person reporting the error and the name of the person to be notified when it has been fixed.

▶ **Error priority**   The priority with which the error is regarded. The higher the priority the greater the importance assigned to this error by its reporter.

▶ **Error description**   A brief and full description of the error so that the readers of this report know all about the error.

▶ **Error re-creation steps**   A description of the steps taken to reproduce the error and any scripts that can be used to help reproduce the error.

Requesting an Enhancement

An enhancement is a request for either an additional feature or the extension of an existing feature. The information required is as follows:

▶ A unique number so that it can be uniquely referenced

▶ The name of the requester

▶ The description of the enhancement: what the enhancement is for and why it is needed

Recording a Fix

This technique can also be used to record requests that have been fulfilled, as well as recording fixes to existing errors. The information recorded is as follows:

▶ The unique number of the error or enhancement that is related to this fix.

▶ A description of how the fix was implemented.

▶ The date and author of this fix.

▶ A description of how this fix was tested in relation to the original error or request.

▶ A description of the impact of this fix. Does it require a local component to be rebuilt or does it require other areas of the project to be rebuilt?

▶ A list of all of the parts-packages-components affected by this fix, used to determine the impact of this fix.

▶ A specific list of files changed when implementing this fix.

▶ Finally, a list of the changes made, file-by-file, line-by-line. The list should show lines of source code added, changed, and deleted.

Testing Regression

It is important to provide a regression test whenever a change is made to the source code. Regression tests provide a mechanism for ensuring that when the source code is changed, previously working facilities continue to work. The information required is as follows:

- ▶ A unique test number
- ▶ The author of the test
- ▶ The date the test was created
- ▶ What facilities are being tested
- ▶ Which fix numbers are associated with this test
- ▶ The steps to follow to carry out this test and any scripts that accompany the test. Steps include configuring the application of the environment, as well as the application itself, including loading any data.

Summary

This chapter has introduced you to:

- ▶ A standard for documenting code
- ▶ A structured directory layout, which separates logical components of an application
- ▶ The make utility, used to build the application
- ▶ Source code control, essential for managing the source code of nontrivial applications
- ▶ Documentation for recording errors, requested enhancements, code fixes, and regression tests

Case Studies

OBJECTIVES

► See the Analysis documents used in the development of a simple application

► Understand the problems and solutions of developing a multithreaded application

Case Study 1—
Simulated Company

IN THIS CHAPTER:

Analyze the Game SimCo

Show Each of the Chapter 2 Analysis Documents in the Context of SimCo

T his is an example that shows the documents produced when undertaking the analysis and design of an application that simulates a small manufacturing company. The application is called SimCo; it stands for simulated company.

Project Requirements

This application simulates a small manufacturing company. The resulting application will enable the user to take out a loan, purchase a machine, and over a series of monthly production runs, follow the performance of their company.

As part of this case study, the following analysis diagrams will be created:

1. Produce use cases for the system.

2. Produce class diagrams for the initially identified classes.

3. Create CRC cards showing how every class fits into the system.

4. Use class relationship diagrams to show how the classes relate to each other.

5. Use activity diagrams to show flow for each use case.

6. Use scripts to document the interaction between instances, following each use case.

7. Derive sequence diagrams and collaboration diagrams from the scripts.

8. Use statechart diagrams to model long-term objects.

Use Cases

I have identified five use cases for our business application:

▶ **Filing a loan application**   The simulated company may require a loan to purchase more machines, or just to stay afloat.

▶ **Purchasing a machine**   In order to do anything the company must purchase a machine on which to manufacture goods.

▶ **Doing a production run**   During the production run is when the user decides how many goods to manufacture and at what price to sell them. The user is given an indication of projected sales and the average price that can be expected for the goods sold.

▶ **Working out the company details**   The company accounts are updated for a given month. The accounts take into account the Gross Profit from sales, general expenses such as salary and rent, to calculate the Net Profit for the company. In addition, details such as inventory and sales details are updated.

▶ **Displaying company details**   Display to the user a summary of the dealings of the company for this month and the five previous months.

Recap of the Use Case Template

This use case template was first introduced in Chapter 2. The usc case template is used to detail the high-level aspects of the application.

Use case number		<short name>
Description		Full explanation of the use case
Preconditions		For this use case to function, what condition does the system need to be in, for example, the shop needs to be open to sell goods.
Trigger		What is it that starts the use case? For example, the customer needs food and enters the shop.
Success		When the use case is finished, what condition should the system be in? For example, the customer has all of their goods and they are happy. The money is in the register, and someone is restocking the shelves for the next customer.
Abort		What happens if the use case is abandoned? For example, if the customer puts the basket down and leaves the shop without buying anything, somebody needs to see this and put the goods back on the shelf.
Actors	Primary	Who plays the lead roles, for example, customer and checkout clerk?
	Secondary	Who plays the secondary roles, for example, store clerk?

As mentioned in Chapter 2, the following sections of the template show the process to bc followed, as well as any variations in this process and any exceptions that may occur.

Process	Step #	Short Name <action>	Description
Variations	Step #	<action>	Description
Exceptions	Step #	<action> or use case	Description

Here is some additional information that provides a fuller description of each use case.

- ► What is the priority of this use case?
- ► How long is it expected to take?
- ► How often does it happen?
- ► The interface with the actors:
    - ► **Interactive**   For example, each customer has a 'conversation' with the shop.
    - ► **Static**   For example, price of scanned goods. The price for the most part is static.
    - ► **Scheduled**   For example, the restocking of shelves happens during certain shifts by specific workers.
- ► **Open issues**   Many things that could affect this use case, such as more customers, more staff, and larger shop.
- ► **Delivery date**   When does the system have to be implemented?
- ► **Related use cases**   For example, the use case that handles the restocking of the shelves or the collecting of abandoned baskets.

Use Case #1—Loan Application

The simulated company may require a loan to purchase more machines, or just to stay afloat. This illustration shows the use case for acquiring a loan, and the table that follows shows the use case as a template.

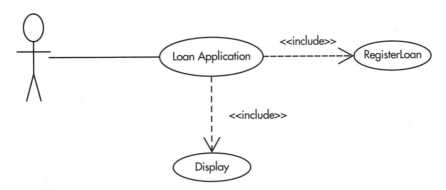

Use case #1	Loan application		
Description	Ask the system for a loan, and then enter an amount and the number of months' repayment period. Have the money entered into the company's cash account.		
Preconditions	There are no preconditions.		
Trigger	The user needs to have selected this option.		
Success	A loan is created and registered with the company's accounts. The money is credited to the company's cash account.		
Abort	No loan is created and no money is credited to the company's cash account.		
Actors	Primary	User	
	Secondary	None	
Process	Step #	Short Name <action>	Description
	1	PromptAmount	Prompt the user for the amount of the loan.
	2	CheckAmount	Check that the amount requested is greater than zero.
	3	PromptDuration	Prompt the user for the duration of the loan.
	4	CheckDuration	Check that the duration entered is greater than zero.
	5	PromptConfirm	Prompt the user to confirm the details of the loan, detailing the total amount of the loan including interest and the repayment schedule.
	6	ConfirmLoan	Tell the user the loan has been confirmed.
	7	CreditMoney	Credit the company's cash account with the money.
	8	RegisterLoan	Register with the company's accounts the duration of the loan and the repayment schedule.
Variations	Step #	<action>	Description
	1	UseGUI	Instead of a text-based interaction, use a GUI to display a dialog box.

Exceptions	Step #	<action> or use case	Description
	2a	BadAmount	If the amount is less than or equal to zero, it can be used to signal an intention not to continue with the loan application.
	2b	Exit	Leave the loan application.
	4a	BadDuration	If the duration is less than or equal to zero, it can be used to signal an intention not to continue with the loan application.
	4b	Exit	Leave the loan application.
	6a	Decline	Decline the loan application.
	6b	Exit	Leave the loan application.

Use Case #2—Purchasing a Machine

In order for the company to stay in business, it must purchase a machine to manufacture goods. This illustration shows the use case for purchasing a machine, and the table that follows shows the use case as a template.

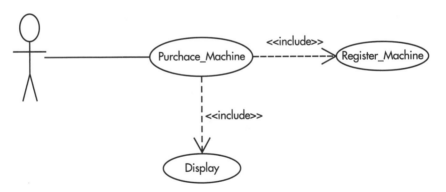

Use case #2	Purchasing a machine.
Description	Ask the system for an additional machine on which to make products.
Preconditions	Needs to be enough money in the company's cash account to spend without going into debt.
Trigger	The user needs to have selected this option.
Success	A machine is bought and registered with the factory. The money is debited from the company's cash account.

Abort	No machine is bought and no money is debited from the company's cash account.		
Actors	Primary	User	
	Secondary	None	
Process	Step #	Short Name <action>	Description
	1	DisplayDetails	Display the details of the machine.
	2	PromptPurchase	Prompt the user to buy the machine.
	3	ConfirmPurchase	Tell user the purchase has been confirmed.
	4	DebitMoney	Debit the money from the company's cash account.
	5	RegisterMachine	Register the machine with the factory.
Variations	Step #	<action>	Description
	1	UseGUI	Instead of a text-based interaction, use a GUI to display a dialog box.
Exceptions	Step #	<action> or use case	Description
	3a	Decline	Decline the purchase.
	3b	Exit	Leave the machine purchase.

Use Case #3—Production Run

During the production run the user decides how many goods to manufacture and at what price to sell them. The user is given an indication of projected sales and the average price that can be expected for the goods sold. This illustration shows the use case for the production run, and the table that follows shows the use case as a template.

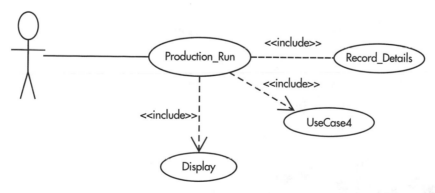

Use case #3	Production run		
Description	Produce goods, set a sale price, and sell them.		
Preconditions	A machine must exist on which to make the goods.		
Trigger	The user needs to have selected this option.		
Success	Goods are made and sold.		
Abort	Nothing has changed.		
Actors	Primary	User	
	Secondary	None	
Process	Step #	Short Name <action>	Description
	1	ShowProjectedSales	Display to the user the projected sales for the goods to be made.
	2	NumberToMake	Prompt the user for quantity to be manufactured.
	3	CheckAmount	Check that the amount is greater than or equal to zero, as zero allows the existing stock to be sold.
	4	CheckMax	Check that the number to be produced does not exceed the production capacity of the existing machines.
	5	ShowAvePrice	Display the average market price for the goods.
	6	SalePrice	Prompt the user for the sale price of the goods.
	7	CheckPrice	Check that the price entered is greater than zero.
	8	NumberForSale	Add the number of goods made to the existing stock.
	9	NumberSold	Calculate the number of goods sold.

	10	RecordSold	Record the number of goods sold.
	11	RecordUnsold	Record the number unsold, as this figure becomes next month's stock.
	12	AdjustMarket	Adjust the projected sales and average price for next month.
	13	RecordSales	Record the amount of money made from sales.
	14	CalcCostToMake	Calculate the cost of the raw materials.
	15	PayCostToMake	Debit the cash account for the cost of the raw materials used to make the goods.
	16	CalcGrossProfit	Calculate the gross profit, sales minus production expenses.
Variations	Step #	<action>	Description
	1	UseGUI	Instead of a text-based interaction, use a GUI to display a dialog box.
Exceptions	Step #	<action> or use case	Description
	3a	BadAmount	If the amount is less than zero, it can be used to signal an intention not to continue with production run.
	3b	Exit	Leave production run.
	4a	TooMany	If the amount is greater than the production capacity, then re-prompt.
	4b	Exit	Leave production run.

6a		BadPrice	If the amount is less than or equal to zero, it can be used to signal an intention not to continue with the production run.
6b		Exit	Leave production run.

This is information that can be added to the use case to aid in its description:

▶ *What is the priority of this use case?*   Second highest priority.

▶ *How often does it happen?*   Every time the user takes a turn.

▶ The interface with the actors:

   ▶ **interactive**   e.g., the user defined number of goods to be made and the selling price

   ▶ **static**   e.g., the capacity of the factory to produce goods

   ▶ **scheduled**   e.g., the running of 'Working out company details' once this use case has completed

▶ *What are the related use cases?*   Working out the company details and displaying company details.

Use Case #4—Processing the Company Accounts

The company accounts are updated for a given month. The accounts take into consideration the Gross Profit from sales, general expenses such as salary and rent to calculate the Net Profit for the company. In addition details such as inventory and sales details are updated. This illustration shows the use case for processing the company accounts, and the table that follows shows the use case as a template.

Use case #4	Working out the Company Details
Description	At the end of every production run, calculate the accounts for the company.
Preconditions	None
Trigger	End of production run

Success	The accounts have been updated.		
Abort	Nothing has been updated.		
Actors	Primary	Production run	
	Secondary	None	
Process	Step #	Short Name \<action\>	Description
	1	GetLoan	From the existing loans calculate the monthly repayments.
	2	GetOtherExpenses	Calculate the other monthly expenses.
	3	CalcExpenses	Calculate the total monthly expenses.
	4	GetGrossProfit	From sales accounting get the gross profit.
	5	CalcNetProfit	Subtract the expenses from the gross profit.
	6	GetCash	From the cash account get the balance.
	7	AddNetProfit	Add the net profit to the cash balance.
	8	RecordBalance	Record the new cash balance.
	9	AdjustLoan	Adjust the number of loan repayments.

Here is a piece of additional information:

What are the related use cases?   Production run.

Use Case #5—Display Company Details

Display to the user a summary of the dealings of the company for this month and the five previous months. This illustration shows the use case for displaying the financial details of the company, and the table that follows shows the use case as a template.

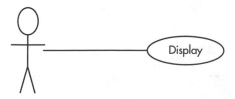

Use case #5	Display company details		
Description	Display to the user full company details. Show a table where each column represents a month.		
Preconditions	There are no preconditions.		
Trigger	The user needs to have selected this option.		
Success	All of the details of the company have been displayed.		
Abort	N/A		
Actors	Primary	User	
	Secondary	None	
Process	Step #	Short Name <action>	Description
	1	ShowMonth	
	2	ShowBalance	Display the closing cash balance for a month.
	3	ShowNetProfit	Display the net profit for a month.
	4	ShowSales	Display the sales for a month.
	5	ShowCost	Display the cost of making the goods.
	6	ShowGrossProfit	Display the profit from sales.
	7	ShowExpenses	Display the expenses.
	8	ShowAvePrice	Display the average market price for the goods.
	9	ShowSalePrice	Display the price the user set.
	10	ShowInstock	Display the number of goods in stock.
	11	ShowMade	Display the number of goods made.
	12	ShowForSale	Display the number of goods for sale.
	13	ShowProjectedSales	Display the projected sales for the goods.
	14	ShowSold	Display the number of goods sold.
	15	ShowEndStock	Display the number of goods unsold.

Analysis Documents—Static Aspects of Classes

The following are the documents that provide information about classes. They also document how these classes interact with the system. They are as follows:

▶ Class diagrams

▶ CRC cards

▶ Scripts

Class Diagrams

From the five use cases described in the preceding section, it can be determined by looking at the use case components that the application consists of nine classes, as shown in Figure 10-1.

CRC Cards

Having decided on the classes for the application, here are the CRC cards that I will use to document the proposed responsibilities and collaborations between the classes.

Class:	Loan
Responsibilities:	Manage the details of a loan.
Collaborators:	Display, CompanyDetails, CashAccount
Class:	CashAccount
Responsibilities:	Manage the cash for the company.
Collaborators:	Loan, CompanyDetails, Machine, Display
Class:	CompanyDetails
Responsibilities:	Manage the details of the company.
Collaborators:	Display, Loan, CashAccount, Sales, Factory
Class:	Machine
Responsibilities:	Manage the machine details.
Collaborators:	Display, Factory, CashAccount
Class:	Factory
Responsibilities:	Manage the factory subsystem.
Collaborators:	Display, ProductionRun, Machine, CompanyDetails
Class:	ProductionRun
Responsibilities:	Manage the production run.
Collaborators:	Display, Factory, Market, Sales
Class:	Market
Responsibilities:	Manage the external influence on sales.
Collaborators:	Display, ProductionRun
Class:	Sales

Responsibilities:	Manage the sales account.
Collaborators:	Display, ProductionRun, CompanyDetails
Class:	Display
Responsibilities:	Manage the user interface.
Collaborators:	CashAccount, CompanyDetails, Factory, Market, Sales, ProductionRun, Machine

Loan
-duration, -repayment
+Loan(void) : Loan   +showRepayment(void) : double   +adjustDuration(void) : void

Company Details
-numberOfLoans, -salary, -overhead, -month,   -generalExpenses, -netProfit
CompanyDetails (void) : CompanyDetails   +addLoan (Loan) : void   +doMonthlyAccounts (void) : void   +genExpenses (void) : double   +netProfit(void) : double   +month(void) : int

Factory
-numberOfMachines, -numberInStock,   -numberEndStock
+Factory (void) : Factory   +adMachine (void) : void   +howManyMachines (void) : int   +setEndStock (int) : void   +getInStock (void) : int   showInStock (void) : int   +showEndStock (void) : int   +showCapacity (void) : int   +machineOverhead (void) : int

Market
-projectedSales, -averagePrice
+Market (void) : Market   +getProjectedSales (void) : int   +getAveragePrice (void) : double   +adjustProjectedSales (void) : void   +adjustAveragePrice (void) : void

Display
+Display(void) : Display   +requestLoan(void) : void   +purchaseMachine(void) : void   +nextTurn(void) : void   +displayDetails(void) : void   +updateCash(void) : void

CashAccount
-balance
+CashAccount (void) : CashAccount   +credit (double) : void   +balance (void) : double   +debit (double) : void   +setBalance (double) : void   +adjustMonth (void) : void

Machine
-cost, -output, -overhead, -costOfRaw
+Machine (void) : Machine $+cost (void) : double $+output (void) : int $+overhead (void) : double $+costOfRaw (void) : double

ProductionRun
-numberMade, -numberForSale
+Production (void) : ProductionRun   +nextTurn (void) : void   +numberMade (void) : int   +numberForSale (void) : int

Sales
-numberSold, -salePrice, -sales,   -costToMake, -grossProfit
+Sales (void) : Sales   +recordNemberMade (int) : void   +recordNujmberSold (int) : void   +recordSalePrice (double) : void   +calcGrossProfit (void) : void   +grossProfit (void) : double   +sales (void) : double   +costToMake (void): double   +salePrice (void) : double   +numberSold (void) : int

Figure 10-1 *Class diagrams of the nine classes of the application*

Scripts

Each script documents how a single class interacts with other classes of the system.

User

The **User** class is the external entity that drives the application.

Caller	Method	Called	Result	Use Case #
:User	RequestLoan ()	:Display	Select loan option	1
:User	PurchaseMachine ()	:Display	Select new machine option	2
:User	NextTurn ()	:Display	Select next turn	3
:User	DisplayDetails ()	:Display	Select display details option	5

Display

This class passes the requests made by the user onto the other classes in the system.

Caller	Method	Called	Result	Use Case #
:Display	Loan ()	:Loan	Create a new loan.	1
:Display	Balance ()	:CashAccount	Display the newly updated balance.	1,2,5
:Display	Machine::mccost ()	:Machine	Display the cost of a machine.	2
:Display	Machine::mcoutput ()	:Machine	Display the output of a machine.	2
:Display	Machine::mcoverhead ()	:Machine	Display the overhead of running a machine.	2
:Display	Machine::mcrawcost ()	:Machine	Display the cost of the raw materials.	2
:Display	Machine ()	:Machine	Create a new machine.	2
:Display	HowManyMachines ()	:Factory	Display the number of machines already owned.	2
:Display	Capacity ()	:Factory	Get the capacity of the machines in the factory.	3

Caller	Method	Called	Result	Use Case #
:Display	*ShowInstock ()*	**:Factory**	Display the number of goods unsold from last month.	5
:Display	*ShowEndStock ()*	**:Factory**	Display how many goods remain unsold.	5
:Display	*NextTurn ()*	**:ProductionRun**	Start a new production run	5
:Display	*NumberMade ()*	**:ProductionRun**	Display the number of goods made this month.	5
:Display	*NumberForSale ()*	**:ProductionRun**	Display the total number of goods for sale.	5
:Display	*month ()*	**:CompanyDetails**	Display the month.	5
:Display	*NetProfit ()*	**:CompanyDetails**	Display the net profit from sales minus all expenses.	5
:Display	*GeneralExpenses ()*	**:CompanyDetails**	Display other expenses e.g., wages.	5
:Display	*sales ()*	**:Sales**	Display the amount made from sales.	5
:Display	*CostToMake ()*	**:Sales**	Display how much the raw materials cost to make the goods.	5
:Display	*GrossProfit ()*	**:Sales**	Display the gross profit from sales minus cost to make.	5
:Display	*SalePrice ()*	**:Sales**	Display the sale price of the goods for sale.	5
:Display	*numberSold ()*	**:Sales**	Display the number of goods sold this month.	5

Caller	Method	Called	Result	Use Case #
:Display	*averagePrice ()*	**:Market**	Display the average market price of the goods for sale.	5
:Display	*projectedSales ()*	**:Market**	Display the projected sales for the goods.	5

Loan

This class drives two external interactions, adding the loan to the cash balance of the company and incrementing the total number of loans owned by the company.

Caller	Method	Called	Result	Use Case #
:Loan	*credit ()*	**:CashAccount**	Add the money to the cash account of the company.	1
:Loan	*addLoan ()*	**:CompanyDetails**	Register the loan with the company details.	1

Machine

This class drives two external interactions, debiting the cost of the machine from the cash balance of the company and incrementing the total number of machines owned by the company.

Caller	Method	Called	Result	Use Case #
:Machine	*debit ()*	**:CashAccount**	Remove the money from the cash account of the company.	2
:Machine	*addMachine ()*	**:Factory**	Register the loan with the company details.	2

Production Run

This class drives several interactions, each of them concerned with calculating the information related to manufacturing goods.

Caller	Method	Called	Result	Use Case #
:ProductionRun	*recordNumberMade ()*	**:Sales**	Save the number of goods to be made.	3
:ProductionRun	*recordSalePrice ()*	**:Sales**	Save the price at which the goods are to be sold.	3
:ProductionRun	*recordNumberSold ()*	**:Sales**	Save the number of goods sold this month.	3
:ProductionRun	*calcGrossProfit ()*	**:Sales**	Calculate from the sales and the cost of manufacture the gross profit.	3
:ProductionRun	*getInstock ()*	**:Factory**	Get the number of goods unsold from last month.	3
:ProductionRun	*setEndStock ()*	**:Factory**	Set the number of goods unsold this month.	3
:ProductionRun	*projectedSales ()*	**:Market**	Get the projected sales for the goods to be made.	3
:ProductionRun	*averagePrice ()*	**:Market**	Get the average price for the goods to be made.	3
:ProductionRun	*adjustAvePrice ()*	**:Market**	Adjust the average price by a random factor.	3
:ProductionRun	*adjustProjSales ()*	**:Market**	Adjust the projected sales by a random factor.	3

Company Details

This class drives information regarding the calculating of month end accounts.

Caller	Method	Called	Result	Use Case #
:CompanyDetails	*machineOverhead ()*	**:Factory**	Retrieve the overhead of running a machines.	4

Caller	Method	Called	Result	Use Case #
:CompanyDetails	adjustDuration ()	:Loan	Reduce the duration of all loans by one month.	4
:CompanyDetails	showRepayment ()	:Loan	Get the loan repayments for the month.	4
:CompanyDetails	grossProfit ()	:Sales	Get the gross profit from sales of goods.	4
:CompanyDetails	adjustMonth ()	:CashAccount	Get the balance from the previous month.	4
:CompanyDetails	credit ()	:CashAccount	Record profit or loss in the cash balance.	4

Factory

This class responds to requests for machine overhead.

Caller	Method	Called	Result	Use Case #
:Factory	mcoverhead ()	:Machine	Return the overhead of running a machine.	4

Analysis Documents—Dynamic Aspects of Classes

The documents that are used to show the dynamic aspects of classes are statechart diagrams.

Statechart Diagrams

Each class is shown in its own diagram. Objects of this class once created exist with no change of state until the application terminates.

The **Loan** class:

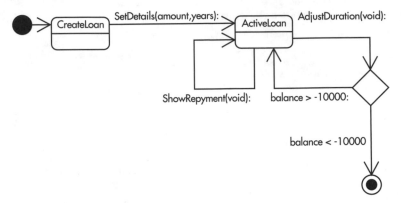

The **CashAccount** class:

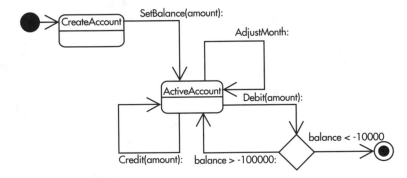

The **ProductionRun** class:

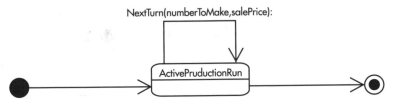

The **Market** class:

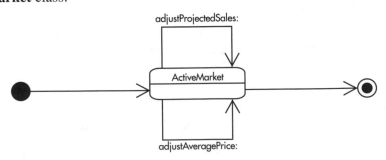

The **Sales** class:

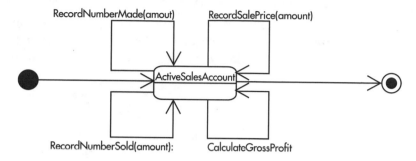

The **CompanyDetails** class:

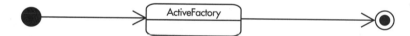

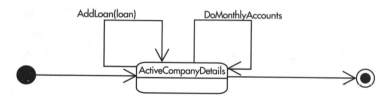

The **Machine** class:

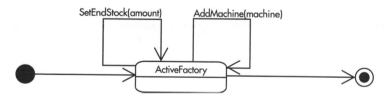

The **Factory** class:

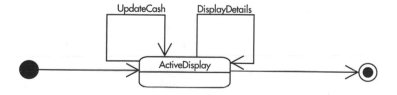

The **Display** class:

Analysis Documents—Static Aspects of the System

The documents in this section provide information about the static aspects of the system. That is to say that the following shows how the classes interact and react to specfic stimuli. These documents do not show how the system reacts over time. The documents are as follows:

▶ Class relationship diagrams
▶ Collaboration diagrams (instance and specification)

Class Relationship Diagrams

The application setup and each use case have a diagram. The application setup is shown in Figure 10-2.

The class relationship diagram for use case #1—Loan Application is shown here:

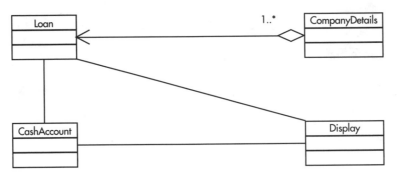

The class relationship diagram for use case #2—Purchasing a Machine is shown here:

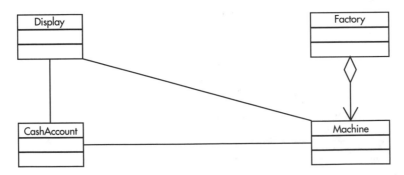

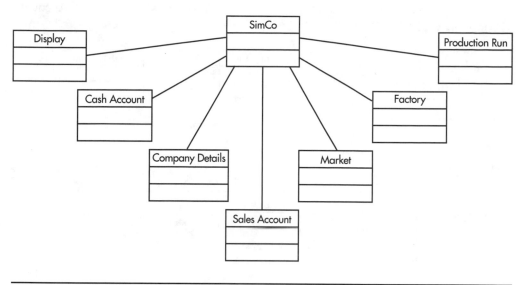

Figure 10-2   *The application setup*

The class relationship diagram for use case #3—Production Run is shown here:

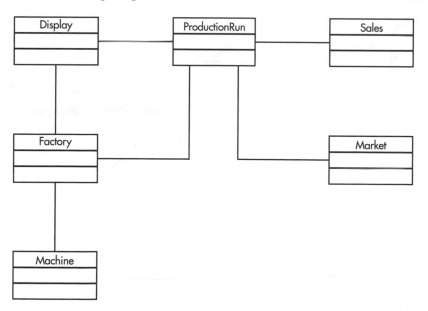

The class relationship diagram for use case #4—Processing the Company Accounts is shown here:

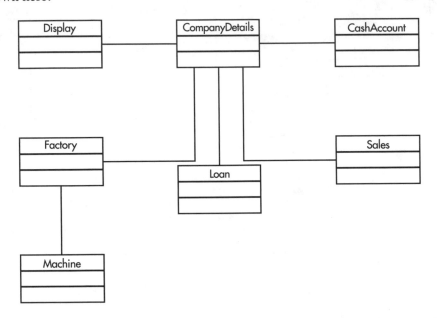

The class relationship diagram for use case #5—Display the Company Details is shown here:

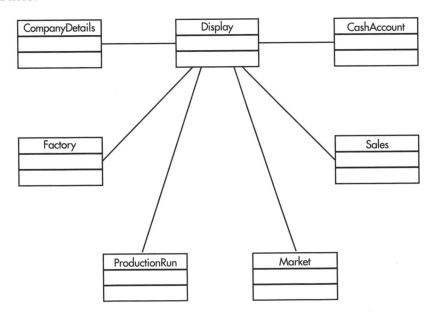

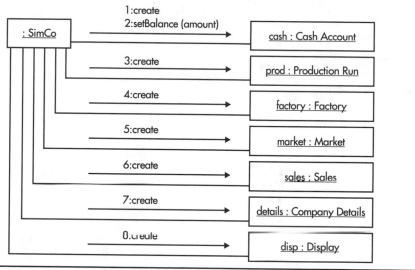

Figure 10-3   *Instance level collaboration diagram*

Collaboration Diagrams

The application setup and each use case have two diagrams. The first diagram shows the instance level collaboration and the second shows the specification level collaboration.

The instance level collaboration diagram for the application setup is shown in Figure 10-3.

The specification level collaboration diagram for the application setup is shown here:

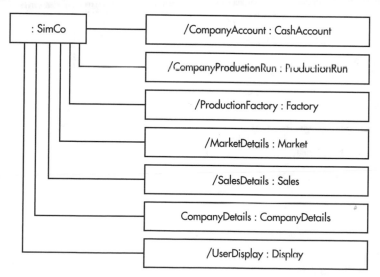

The instance level collaboration diagram for the use case #1—Loan Application is shown here:

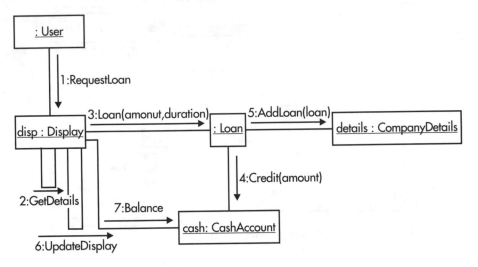

The specification level collaboration diagram for the use case #1—Loan Application is shown here:

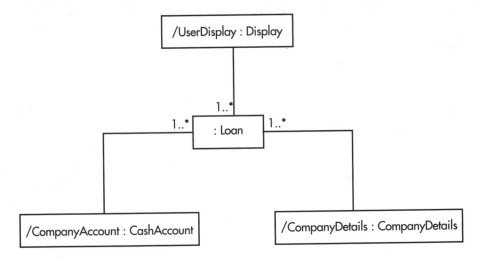

The instance level collaboration diagram for the use case #2—Purchasing a Machine is shown here:

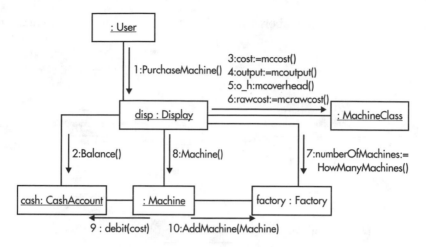

The specification level collaboration diagram for the use case #2—Purchasing a Loan is shown here:

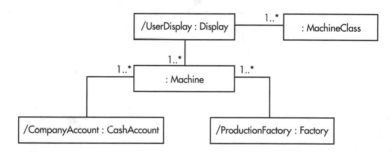

The instance level collaboration diagram for the use case #3—Production Run is shown here:

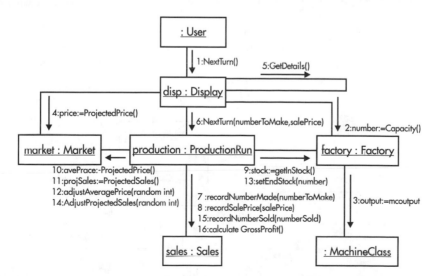

The specification level collaboration diagram for the use case #3—Production Run is shown here:

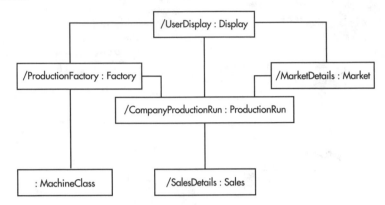

The instance level collaboration diagram for the use case #4—Processing the Company Accounts is shown here:

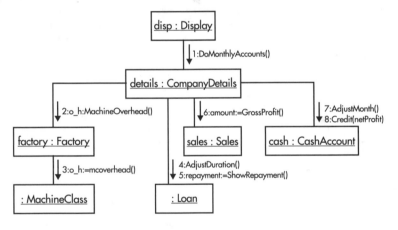

The specification level collaboration diagram for the use case #4—Processing the Company Accounts is shown here:

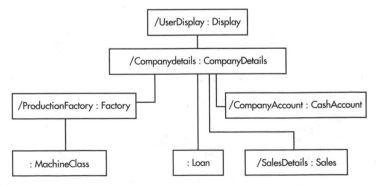

The instance level collaboration diagram for the use case #5—Displaying the Company Details is shown here:

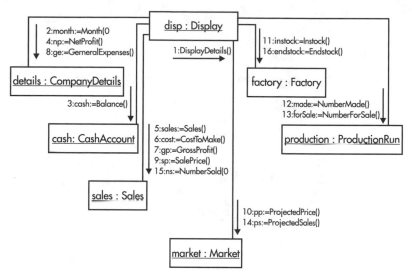

The specification level collaboration diagram for the use case #5—Displaying the Company Details is shown here:

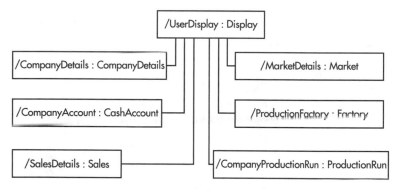

Analysis Documents—Dynamic Aspects of the System

The documents in this section provide descriptions of the system as it performs over time.

▶ **Activity diagrams** These diagrams show use case as it progress from start to finish.

▶ **Sequence scripts and diagrams**   The script and sequence diagrams show the methods that are used in the interactions between objects, and the order in which they are used.

Activity Diagrams

Each use case has an activity diagram, shown in Figures 10-4 through 10-8.

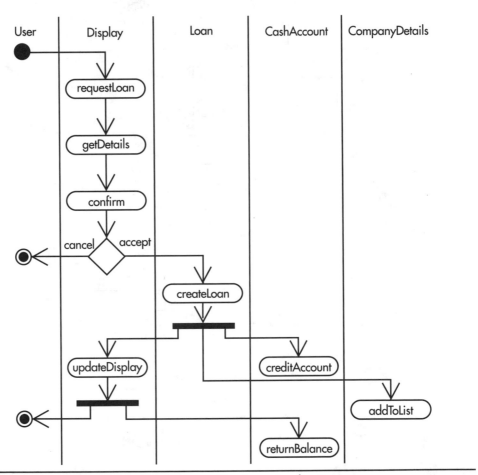

Figure 10-4   *Activity diagram for use case #1—Loan Application*

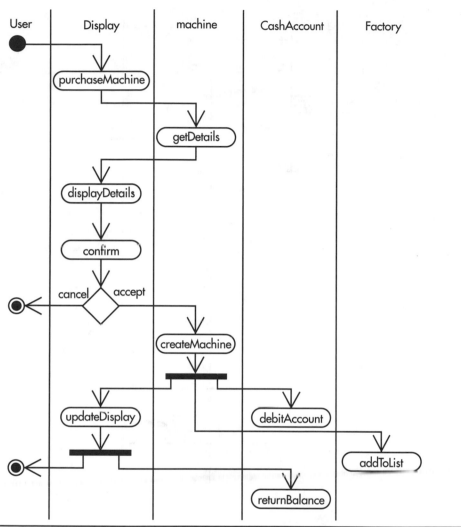

Figure 10-5   *Activity diagram for use case #2—Purchasing a Machine*

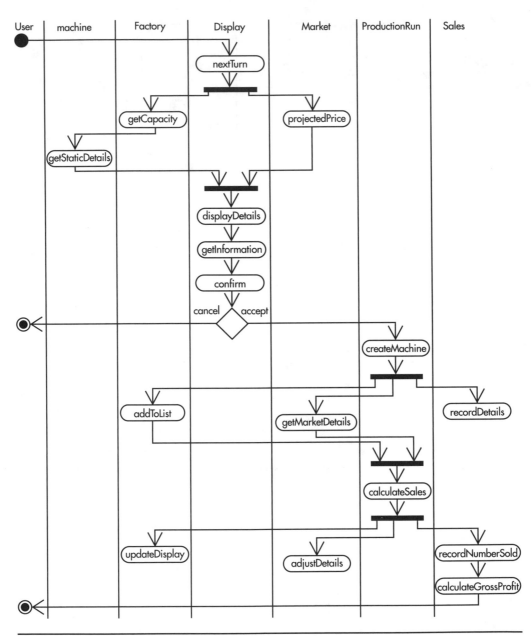

Figure 10-6   *Activity diagram for use case #3—Production Run*

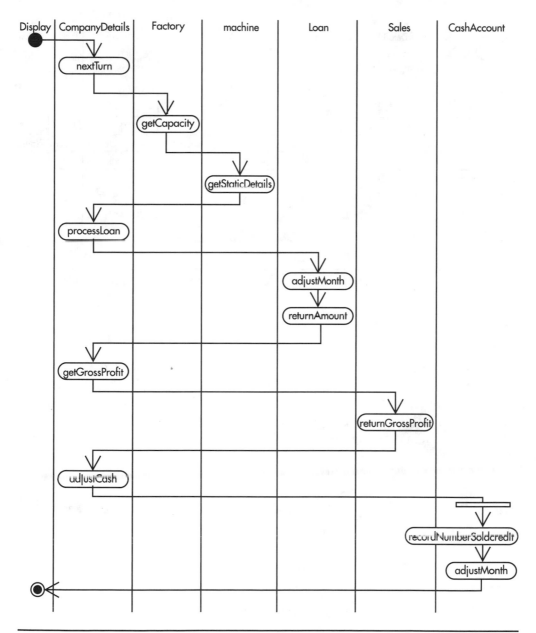

Figure 10-7 *Activity diagram for use case #4—Processing the Company, Accounts*

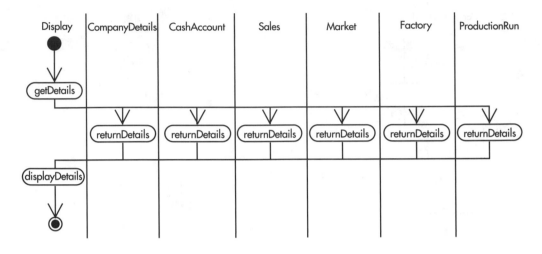

Figure 10-8 *Activity diagram for use case #5—Displaying the Company, Details*

Sequence Scripts

Tables 10-1 through 10-5 show the scripts for each of the previously described use cases. Each script takes the reader from a user interaction with the system to its conclusion. The syntax of these scripts is shown in Chapter 2. This syntax is not part of the UML v1.4 standard; however, I find it not only very descriptive but also very useful in detailing the flow of the system in terms that are understandable by everyone associated with the project.

Ref #	Source	Method	Destination	Next Ref #
1	User	requestLoan (void)	Display	1.a
1.a	Display	"Enter amount"	User	1.b
1.b	User	<amount <= 0>	Display	1.1
1.b	User	<amount > 0>	Display	1.2
1.1	Display	{end}		

Table 10-1 *UC#1—Loan Application*

Ref #	Source	Method	Destination	Next Ref #
1.2	Display	"Enter duration of loan"	User	1.2.a
1.2.a	User	<duration <= 0>	Display	1.2.1
1.2.a	User	<duration > 0>	Display	1.2.2
1.2.1	Display	{end}		
1.2.2	Display	"Confirm Loan"	User	1.2.2.a
1.2.2.a	User	<Reject>	Display	1.2.2.1
1.2.2.a	User	<Accept>	Display	1.2.2.2
1.2.2.1	Display	{end}		
1.2.2.2	Display	Loan (amount, duration)	Loan	1.2.2.2.a
1.2.2.2.a	Loan	credit (amount)	CashAccount	1.2.2.2.b
1.2.2.2.b	CashAccount	{return void}	Loan	1.2.2.2.c
1.2.2.2.c	Loan	addLoan (self)	Company Details	1.2.2.2.d
1.2.2.2.d	Company Details	{return void}	Loan	1.2.2.2.e
1.2.2.2.e	Loan	{return void}	Display	1.2.2.2.f
1.2.2.2.f	Display	updateCash (void)	Display	1.2.2.2.g
1.2.2.2.g	Display	balance (void)	CashAccount	1.2.2.2.h
1.2.2.2.h	CashAccount	{return double}	Display	1.2.2.2.i
1.2.2.2.i	Display	{end}		

Table 10-1   *UC#1—Loan Application* (continued)

Ref #	Source	Method	Destination	Next Ref #
2	User	purchaseMachine (void)	Display	2.a
2.a	Display	balance (void)	CashAccount	2.b
2.b	CashAccount	{return double}	Display	2.c
2.c	Display	Machine::mccost (void)	Machine	2.d
2.d	Machine	{return double}	Display	2.e
2.e	Display	Machine::mcoutput (void)	Machine	2.f
2.f	Machine	{return int}	Display	2.g
2.g	Display	Machine::mcoverhead (void)	Machine	2.h
2.h	Machine	{return double}	Display	2.i
2.i	Display	Machine::mcrawcost (void)	Machine	2.j
2.j	Machine	{return double}	Display	2.k
2.k	Display	howManyMachines (void)	Factory	2.l
2.l	Factory	{return int}	Display	2.m
2.m	Display	"Confirm Purchase"	User	2.n
2.n	User	<Reject>	Display	2.1
2.n	User	<Accept>	Display	2.2
2.1	Display	{end}		
2.2	Display	Machine (void)	Machine	2.2.a

Table 10-2   *UC#2—Purchasing a Machine*

Ref #	Source	Method	Destination	Next Ref #
2.2.a	Machine	debit (cost)	CashAccount	2.2.b
2.2.b	CashAccount	{return void}	Machine	2.2.c
2.2.c	Machine	addMachine (this)	Factory	2.2.d
2.2.d	Factory	{return void}	Machine	2.2.e
2.2.e	Machine	{return void}	Display	2.2.f
2.2.f	Display	updateCash(void)	Display	2.2.g
2.2.g	Display	balance (void)	CashAccount	2.2.h
2.2.h	CashAccount	{return double}	Display	2.2.i
2.2.i	Display	{end}		

Table 10-2   *UC#2—Purchasing a Machine* (continued)

Ref #	Source	Method	Destination	Next Ref #
3	User	nextTurn (void)	Display	3.a
3.a	Display	capacity (void)	Factory	3.b
3.b	Factory	{return int}	Display	3.c
3.c	Display	projectedPrice (void)	Market	3.d
3.d	Market	{return double}	Display	3.e
3.e	Display	"Enter number to make"	User	3.f
3.f	User	<amount < 0>	Display	3.1
3.f	User	<amount => 0>	Display	3.2
3.1	Display	{end}		

Table 10-3   *UC#3—Production Run*

Ref #	Source	Method	Destination	Next Ref #
3.2	Display	"Enter sale price"	User	3.2.a
3.2.a	User	<price <= 0>	Display	3.2.1
3.2.a	User	<price > 0>	Display	3.2.2
3.2.1	Display	{end}		
3.2.2	Display	"Confirm next turn"	User	3.2.2.a
3.2.2.a	User	<Reject>	Display	3.2.2.1
3.2.2.a	User	<Accept>	Display	3.2.2.2
3.2.2.1	Display	{end}		
3.2.2.2	Display	nextTurn (numberToMake, salePrice)	ProductionRun	3.2.2.2.a
3.2.2.2.a	ProductionRun	recordNumberMade (int)	Sales	3.2.2.2.b
3.2.2.2.b	Sales	{return void}	ProductionRun	3.2.2.2.c
3.2.2.2.c	ProductionRun	recordSalePrice (double)	Sales	3.2.2.2.d
3.2.2.2.d	Sales	{return void}	ProductionRun	3.2.2.2.e
3.2.2.2.e	ProductionRun	getInstock (void)	Factory	3.2.2.2.f
3.2.2.2.f	Factory	{return int}	ProductionRun	3.2.2.2.g
3.2.2.2.g	ProductionRun	projectedPrice (void)	Market	3.2.2.2.h
3.2.2.2.h	Market	{return double}	ProductionRun	3.2.2.2.i
3.2.2.2.i	ProductionRun	projectedSales (void)	Market	3.2.2.2.j
3.2.2.2.j	Market	{return int}	ProductionRun	3.2.2.2.k
3.2.2.2.k	ProductionRun	adjustAvePrice (double)	Market	3.2.2.2.l
3.2.2.2.l	Market	{return void}	ProductionRun	3.2.2.2.m

Table 10-3   *UC#3—Production Run* (continued)

Ref #	Source	Method	Destination	Next Ref #
3.2.2.2.m	ProductionRun	setEndStock (int)	Factory	3.2.2.2.n
3.2.2.2.n	Factory	{return void}	ProductionRun	3.2.2.2.o
3.2.2.2.o	ProductionRun	adjustProjSales (double)	Market	3.2.2.2.p
3.2.2.2.p	Market	{return void}	ProductionRun	3.2.2.2.q
3.2.2.2.q	ProductionRun	recordNumberSold (int)	Sales	3.2.2.2.r
3.2.2.2.r	Sales	{return void}	ProductionRun	3.2.2.2.s
3.2.2.2.s	ProductionRun	calcGrossProfit (void)	Sales	3.2.2.2.t
3.2.2.2.t	Sales	{return void}	ProductionRun	3.2.2.2.u
3.2.2.2.u	ProductionRun	{return void}	Display	3.2.2.2.v
3.2.2.2.v	Display	{end}		

Table 10-3   *UC#3—Production Run* (continued)

Ref #	Source	Method	Destination	Next Ref #
4	Display	doMonthlyAccounts (void)	CompanyDetails	4.a
4.a	CompanyDetails	machineOverhead (void)	Factory	4.b
4.b	Factory	{return double}	CompanyDetails	4.c
4.c	CompanyDetails	adjustDuration (void)	Loan	4.d
4.d	Loan	{return void}	CompanyDetails	4.e
4.e	CompanyDetails	showRepayment (void)	Loan	4.f
4.f	Loan	{return void}	CompanyDetails	4.g

Table 10-4   *UC#4—Processing the Company Accounts*

Ref #	Source	Method	Destination	Next Ref #
4.g	CompanyDetails	grossProfit (int)	Sales	4.h
4.h	Sales	{return double}	CompanyDetails	4.i
4.i	CompanyDetails	adjustMonth (void)	CashAccount	4.j
4.j	CashAccount	{return void}	CompanyDetails	4.k
4.k	CompanyDetails	credit (netProfit)	CashAccount	4.l
4.l	CashAccount	{return void}	CompanyDetails	4.m
4.m	CompanyDetails	{return void}	Display	4.n

Table 10-4   *UC#4—Processing the Company Accounts* (continued)

Ref #	Source	Method	Destination	Next Ref #
5	User	displayDetails (void)	Display	5.a
5.a	Display	month (void)	CompanyDetails	5.b
5.b	CompanyDetails	{return int}	Display	5.c
5.c	Display	balance (void)	CashAccount	5.d
5.d	CashAccount	{return double}	Display	5.e
5.e	Display	netProfit (void)	CompanyDetails	5.f
5.f	CompanyDetails	{return double}	Display	5.g
5.g	Display	sales (void)	Sales	5.h
5.h	Sales	{return double}	Display	5.i
5.i	Display	costToMake (void)	Sales	5.j

Table 10-5   *UC#5—Displaying the Company Details*

Ref #	Source	Method	Destination	Next Ref #
5.j	Sales	{return double}	Display	5.k
5.k	Display	grossProfit (void)	Sales	5.l
5.l	Sales	{return double}	Display	5.m
5.m	Display	generalExpenses (void)	CompanyDetails	5.n
5.n	CompanyDetails	{return double}	Display	5.o
5.o	Display	salePrice (void)	Sales	5.p
5.p	Market	{return double}	Display	5.q
5.q	Display	projectedPrice (void)	Market	5.r
5.r	Sales	{return double}	Display	5.s
5.s	Display	showInstock (void)	Factory	5.t
5.t	Factory	{return int}	Display	5.u
5.u	Display	numberMade (void)	ProductionRun	5.v
5.v	ProductionRun	{return int}	Display	5.w
5.w	Display	numberForSale (void)	ProductionRun	5.x
5.x	ProductionRun	{return int}	Display	5.y
5.y	Display	projectedSales (void)	Market	5.z
5.z	Market	{return int}	Display	5.aa

Table 10-5   *UC#5—Displaying the Company Details* (continued)

Ref #	Source	Method	Destination	Next Ref #
5.aa	Display	numberSold (void)	Sales	5.bb
5.bb	Sales	{return double}	Display	5.cc
5.cc	Display	showEndStock (void)	Factory	5.dd
5.dd	Factory	{return int}	Display	5.ee
5.ee	Display	{end}		

Table 10-5   *UC#5—Displaying the Company Details* (continued)

Sequence Diagrams

Each use case has a sequence diagram, shown in Figures 10-9 through 10-13.

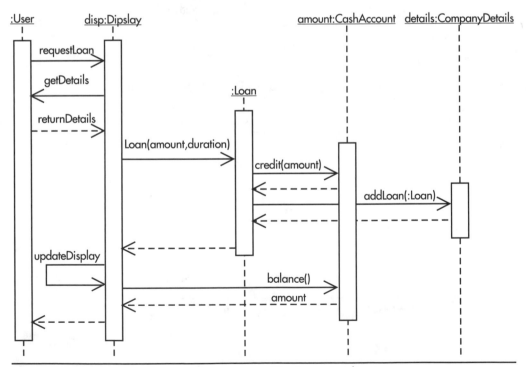

Figure 10-9   *Sequence diagram for use case #1—Loan Application*

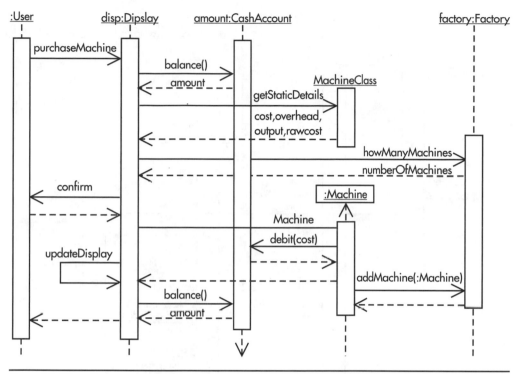

Figure 10-10   *Sequence diagram for use case #2—Purchasing a Machine*

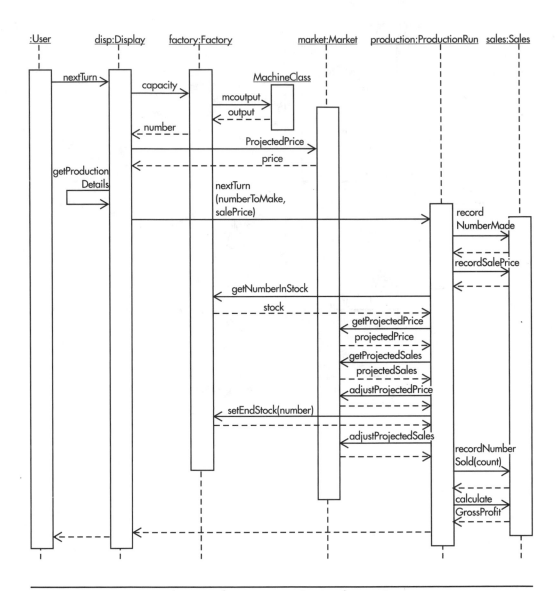

Figure 10-11   *Sequence diagram for use case #3—Production Run*

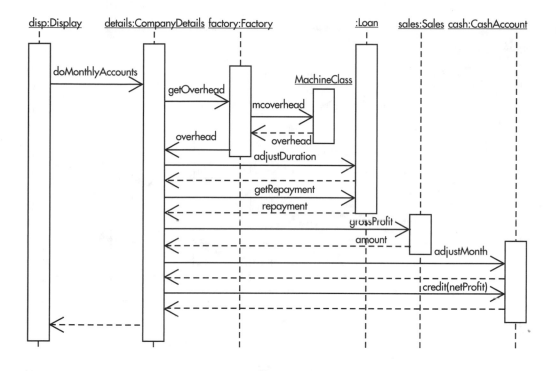

Figure 10-12   *Sequence diagram for use case #4—Processing the Company Accounts*

Summary

This chapter takes you through the documents used during the analysis phase of an application. Each of the documents is introduced in Chapter 2 and is shown here in a fully integrated example. This chapter shows how the information found in one area of analysis can be used in another. For instance, the static documents describe the interfaces of the classes, while the dynamic documents show these interfaces in use. Each of the documents used in this chapter, while seemingly covering the same information, does so in different ways and therefore provides different perspectives. As such, I would advise using each document type during the analysis phase to provide the fullest coverage and understanding.

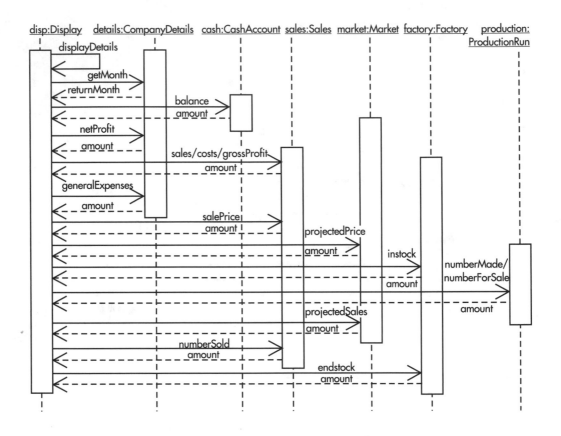

Figure 10-13 *Sequence diagram for use case #5—Displaying the Company Details*

Developing a Multithreaded Airport Simulation

IN THIS CHAPTER:

Learn How to Develop a Multithreaded Application

Understand the Problems Associated with Interacting Threads

This airport simulation case study allows us to develop the threading model required to expand a small, one-plane-per-day airport software application into something more substantial. The initial airport consists of one runway, one terminal, and one gate. The final model will allow for many more airplanes while avoiding crashes and deadlock.

One Airplane at a Time

This section details how the airport currently manages the aircraft using its facilities.

▶ **Landing Procedure**   An aircraft uses the runway, lands, and then taxis over to the terminal:

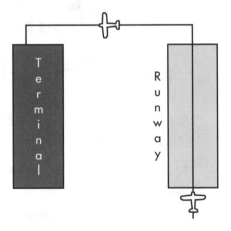

▶ **Take-Off Procedure**   An aircraft taxis to the runway and then takes off:

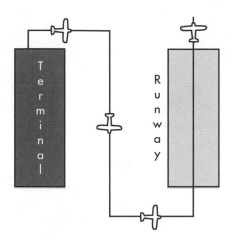

Java Code

Here is the basic outline of the Java code application used to simulate the airport.

Airport.java

```
/*
**   Name: Airport.java
**   This is the main class for the airport simulation.
**   It creates one thread to simulate a single aircraft usage of
**   the airport.
*/
```

Almost every Java program ever written includes these basic import files:

```
import java.awt.*;
import java.io.*;
import java.lang.*;
import java.util.*;
```

Airport class is the main class of the airport simulation application:

```
public class Airport
{
```

The airport map provides a graphical representation of the airport. It shows the runway, the terminal, as well as the aircraft, as they move about the airport:

```
    public AirportMap          airportMap;
```

A threadgroup allows threads to be manipulated as a group, as well as individually. The following statements declare the threadgroup. Although this is not required in this example, it is included for greater flexibility in future versions:

```
    protected ThreadGroup      threadGroup;

    public Airport()
    {
```

The following commands create and display the AirportMap. The AirportMap extends the **Canvas** class, and therefore needs to have a frame in which to be displayed. The AirportMap source code is shown after the source code for the airport:

```
        Frame          mapFrame;
        Panel          panel;

        mapFrame = new Frame ("Airport Map");
        airportMap = new AirportMap ();
        panel = new Panel ();
        panel.setLayout (new BorderLayout ());
        panel.add ("Center", airportMap);

        mapFrame.add ("Center", panel);
        mapFrame.setSize (100, 150);
        mapFrame.show ();
```

Next, we need to initialize the threadgroup:

```
        threadGroup = new ThreadGroup("Airports");
```

Although it is not necessary to have an array of aircraft, it will be useful later:

```
        Plane planes [] = new Plane [1];
```

Every thread must have a *run* method. This *run* method can be called from the creator of the thread, or, as in this example, each aircraft thread will invoke its own *run* method:

```
planes [0] = new Plane (threadGroup, 0, this);
```

The airport application uses the thread construct 'join' to wait for the threads that represent the planes, such that the airport application does not exit as long as there is a plane:

```
        try
        {
            planes [0].join();
        }
        catch (InterruptedException e) {}

        System.exit (0);
    }


    /*
    ** The main method of the application.
    ** Start the Airport
    */
    public static void main(String[] args)
    {
        Airport a = new Airport ();
    }
}
```

AirportMap.java

```
/*
**   Name: AirportMap.java
*/
import java.awt.*;
public class AirportMap extends Canvas
{
    public AirportMap ()
    {
    /*
    ** Create the airport map
    */
    }
```

Method Name: LandPlane
This method shows an aircraft coming into land and taxiing to the terminal gate.
Input: A handle for the aircraft to use
Output: None

```
public void LandPlane (Plane plane)
{
    /*
    ** Display the aircraft flying north as it uses the runway to
    ** land. Finally show the aircraft moving west and then south
    ** towards the terminal
    */
}
```

Method Name: Takeoff
This method shows an aircraft taxiing from the terminal gate onto the runway and
then taking off.
Input: A handle to the aircraft to use
Output: None

```
public void Takeoff (Plane plane)
{
    /*
    ** Display the aircraft moving away from the terminal, down
    ** the map as it taxis to the start of the runway, then
    ** finally north as it flies away from the airport
    */
}
}
```

Plane.java

```
/*
**   Name: Plane.java
**   This class is the aircraft, it dictates how the aircraft will
**   approach and use the airport
*/
import java.awt.*;
import java.io.*;
import java.lang.*;
import java.util.*;
public class Plane extends Thread
{
```

This line of code is the name of the thread used by the application to identify it:

```
String          threadName;
```

The Airport instance passes itself off as a reference to obtain a handle to other components of the application:

```
Airport         airport;
```

We use this statement to indicate how long an aircraft will remain at a gate:

```
static int              timeAtGate;
```

We next declare the variables used to display the aircraft on the AirportMap.

This is the main constructor for the aircraft. This method sets the thread names and creates the aircraft images. It also starts the thread.

```
public Plane
    (ThreadGroup threadGroup, int name, Airport theAirport)
{
    /*
    ** Create our server thread with a name.
    */
    super(threadGroup, "Plane-" + name);

    /*
    ** Save the reference to the Airport instance
    */
    airport = theAirport;

    /*
    ** Set the time at the terminal for this aircraft,
    ** to be 3 seconds
    */
    timeAtGate = 3000;

    /*
    ** Create the images and draw the aircraft
    */
    createImages ();

    /*
    ** name the thread
```

```
        */
        threadName = new String ("Plane-" + name);

        /*
        ** Start the thread
        */
        this.start ();
    }

    public void createImages ()
    {
        /*
        ** Create the polygon objects and draw the aircraft
        */
```

This illustration shows the polygons for the airplane objects:

```
    }

/*
**  Run
*/
    public void run()
    {
        System.out.println ("Waiting to land " + threadName);
        airport.airportMap.LandPlane (this);

        System.out.println ("At gate " + threadName);
        /* Spend some time at the gate */
        try
        {
            sleep (timeAtGate);
        }
        catch (InterruptedException e) {}

        System.out.println ("Waiting to takeoff " + threadName);
        airport.airportMap.Takeoff (this);
```

```
        System.out.println ("END " + threadName);
    }
}
```

Two Airplanes at a Time—One Terminal Gate

The model is now modified to support two aircraft trying to use the airport at the same time with a single terminal.

Landing Procedure

Here is a description of how two aircraft will land at the airport.

- ▶ **First Aircraft Landing**   As with the previous description, the aircraft uses the runway, lands, and then taxis over to the terminal.

- ▶ **Second Aircaft Landing**   The second aircraft follows exactly the same procedure as the first aircraft.

Problem #1—News Flash: "Aircraft crash into each other at terminal"

The problem is that the second aircraft follows exactly the same procedure as the first, even so far as to assume that the terminal is free and that it can blindly taxi up to it. How do you avoid the crash?

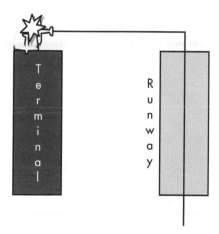

Solution #1

The terminal must provide a *mutex*, a lock that can only be held by one aircraft at a time. In this way, when the second aircraft tries to get the mutex, it will be informed that there is already an aircraft at the terminal, and that it must wait in the newly created landing area just off the runway. The mutex is shown as a padlock and the landing area is shown as a crossed circle in this diagram:

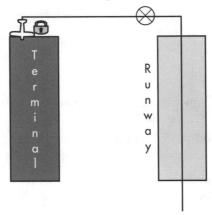

Revised Landing Procedure

Any aircraft uses the runway, lands, and then moves into the landing area. Once in the landing area it then requests the mutex on the terminal. If the mutex is free, the aircraft taxis over to the terminal. If the mutex is not free, the aircraft waits for it to become free.

Takeoff Procedure

Here is a description of how two aircraft will take off from the airport.

▶ **First Aircaft Taking Off**   As with the previous description, the aircraft taxis to the runway and takes off.

▶ **Second Aircraft Taking Off**   The second aircraft follows exactly the same procedure as the first aircraft.

Problem #2—News Flash: "Aircraft crash on runway"

This problem arises if the second aircraft is not on the ground when the first aircraft is trying to takeoff. The second aircraft is trying to land at the same time that the first aircraft is trying to takeoff. How do you avoid the crash?

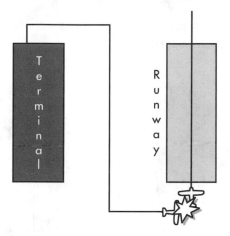

Solution #2

The runway must provide a *mutex*, a lock that can only be held by one aircraft at a time. In this way, when either aircraft tries to get the mutex, it will be informed that there is already an aircraft using it and that it must wait.

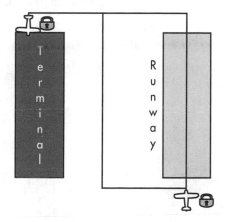

Revised Takeoff Procedure

An aircraft requests usage of the runway. Permission is given to use the runway and the aircraft then takes off.

Problem #3—News Flash: "Airport at a standstill"

Although mutexes have been implemented to avoid aircraft crashes, nobody has released them, causing deadlock. How do you avoid the deadlock?

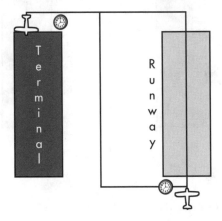

Solution #3

Make sure that when an aircraft no longer needs the runway mutex, it is released. Also, make sure that when an aircraft has finished with the terminal mutex, it is released.

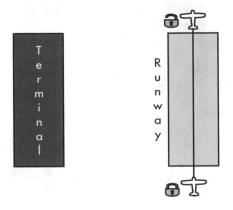

Revision of Landing/Takeoff Procedures

Here are the revised procedures for both landing and taking off.

Landing Procedure

The following is a list of steps that have to be adhered to so those airplanes can land safely.

1. The aircraft requests the mutex for the runway.
2. The aircraft acquires the mutex for the runway.
3. The aircraft lands.
4. The aircraft moves into the landing area.
5. The aircraft releases the mutex for the runway.
6. The aircraft requests the mutex for the terminal.
7. The aircraft acquires the mutex for the terminal.
8. The aircraft taxis to the terminal.

Takeoff Procedure

The following is a list of steps that have to be adhered to so those airplanes can take off safely.

1. The aircraft requests the mutex for the runway.
2. The aircraft acquires the mutex for the runway.
3. The aircraft taxis to the runway.
4. The aircraft takes off.
5. The aircraft releases the mutex for the terminal.
6. The aircraft releases the mutex for the runway.

Revised Java Code

This new code reflects the changes needed to support Solutions #1, #2, and #3 for landing and taking off.

Airport.java

```
public class Airport
{
    < code as before >
```

In order to provide solutions for the three problems so far encountered, it is necessary to declare the mutexes. The mutexes in this example are implemented as lists in the form of vectors. This method allows each thread to wait for the mutex to become free. When a thread releases the mutex, it removes itself from the head of the list and notifies the next thread in the list (now the first element in the list) that it has now acquired the mutex. The thread at the head of the list is deemed the active thread, while all other threads are deemed to be waiting.

```
/* Solution #2 - runway mutex */
private static Vector            runwayList = new Vector ();
/* Solution #1 - terminal gate mutex */
private static Vector            gatesList = new Vector ();

public Airport()
{
    /*
    ** Create and display the AirportMap
    */

    < code as before >

    /*
    ** In this example the array is constructed to hold two
    ** threads
    */
    Plane planes [] = new Plane [2];
    /*
    ** Create the threads
    */
    for (int j = 0; j < 2; j++)
    {
        planes [j] = new Plane (threadGroup, j, this);
```

As in real life, not all of the aircraft arrive at the airport at the same time. This delay adds a five-second wait between each aircraft.

```
        synchronized (this)
        {
           try
           {
               wait (5000);
           }
           catch (InterruptedException e) {}
        }
    }
```

As previously mentioned, so that the application does not exit as soon as the aircraft threads have started running, force it to wait here for the aircraft thread to finish.

```
        try
        {
            for (int j = 0; j < 2; j++)
            {
                planes [j].join();
            }
        }
        catch (InterruptedException e) {}

        System.exit (0);
    }

/* Start the Airport */
public static void main(String[] args)
{
    Airport a = new Airport ();
}
```

These methods provide solutions to problems #1 and #2; they use the runway and terminal gate mutexes. They request the lock. If the request fails, it will cause the thread to block. If the thread acquires the lock, set the value of the lock. When the thread releases the lock, reset the value of the lock. A generic method takes as arguments the thread and the lock.

```
public void RequestRunwayLock (Plane plane)
{
    RequestLock (plane, runwayList);
}
```

```
public void RequestGatesLock (Plane plane)
{
    RequestLock (plane, gatesList);
}
```

This generic *RequestLock* method takes as argument the calling thread, so that it knows which thread is requesting the lock, and the kind of lock being requested.

Synchronize usage of the parameter lockList so that only one thread has access. Set a flag to show the emptiness of the list, and then add the current aircraft thread to the list. If the list contains one element, then the lock is in use. If the list contains more than one element, then the lock is in use and there are other threads waiting to use it. If the list is empty, it shows that the lock is free, as it is not in use and there are no other threads waiting to use it.

```
private void RequestLock (Plane plane, Vector lockList)
{
    Boolean     empty;
    synchronized (lockList)
    {
        empty = lockList.isEmpty ();
        lockList.addElement (plane);
    }

    /*
    ** if the list is not empty, emulate C++ and wait
    */
    if (empty == false)
    {
        try {plane.wait ();}
        catch (InterruptedException e) {}
    }
    /*
    ** This method will exit if the list is empty or this
    ** thread has been woken up (unblocked)
    */
}
```

These methods are called when the active thread no longer requires the lock. These methods call a generic method, which takes as argument the thread and the lock.

```
public void ReleaseRunwayLock (Plane plane)
{
```

```
        ReleaseLock (plane, runwayList);
}

public void ReleaseGatesLock (Plane plane)
{
        ReleaseLock (plane, gatesList);
}
```

This generic *ReleaseLock* method takes as argument the calling thread, so that it knows which thread is releasing the lock and the lock being released.

Synchronize usage of the parameter lockList so that only one thread has access. Remove current aircraft thread from the list so that it contains only those threads waiting to use the lock. If the list is empty, then return. If the list is not empty, examine the first element and notify it that it now has the lock.

```
    private void ReleaseLock (Plane plane, Vector lockList)
    {
        /*
        ** This variable is assigned to the extracted list element.
        */
        Plane    peek;

        synchronized (lockList)
        {
            /*
            ** remove current aircraft thread from the list
            */
            lockList.removeElement (plane);
            /*
            ** If the list is not empty it means that there is
            ** another waiting to use this lock
            */
            if (lockList.isEmpty () == false)
            {
                try
                {
                    /*
                    ** Get the first element on the list
                    */
                    peek = (Plane)lockList.firstElement ();
                    /*
                    ** synchronize the thread, so that nothing else
```

```
             ** is trying to use it
             */
             synchronized (peek)
             {
                 /* Wake up the thread */
                 peek.notify ();
             }
         }
         catch (NoSuchElementException e) {}
     }
   }
  }
}
```

AirportMap.java

```
public class AirportMap extends Canvas
{
    < code as before >
```

This is a new *LandPlane* method, as the landing aircraft now has a landing area to taxi to if the terminal is busy:

```
    public void LandPlane (Plane plane)
    {
        /*
        ** Display the aircraft flying north as it uses the runway
        ** to land, then moves slightly to the west to the landing
        ** area
        */
    }
```

This is a new method; *TaxiToGate* takes the aircraft from the landing area to the terminal gate:

```
    public void TaxiToGate (Plane plane)
    {
        /*
        ** Display the aircraft moving west from the landing area and
        ** south towards the terminal gate
        */
    }
```

```
    public void Takeoff (Plane plane)
    {
        /*
        ** Display the aircraft moving away from the terminal, down
        ** the map as it taxis to the start of the runway, then
        ** finally north as it flies away from the airport
        */
    }
}
```

Plane.java

```
public class Plane extends Thread
{
        < code as before >
/*
**   Run
*/
    public void run()
    {
        System.out.println ("Waiting to land " + threadName);
```

Landing procedure (1, 2)—request and acquire the runway mutex:

```
        /* Solution #2 - runway mutex */
        airport.RequestRunwayLock (this);
        System.out.println ("Got use of runway " + threadName);
```

Landing procedure (3, 4)—aircraft lands and moves to the landing area:

```
        System.out.println ("Landing " + threadName);
        airport.airportMap.LandPlane (this);
        System.out.println ("Landed " + threadName);
```

Landing procedure (5)—release the runway mutex:

```
        /* Solution #3 - release mutex when no longer needed */
        airport.ReleaseRunwayLock (this);
```

Landing procedure (6, 7)—request and acquire the terminal gate:

```
        /* Solution #1 - terminal gate mutex */
        airport.RequestGatesLock (this);
        System.out.println ("Got a gate " + threadName);
```

Landing procedure (8)—taxi to the terminal gate:

```
airport.airportMap.TaxiToGate (this);
System.out.println ("At gate " + threadName);
```

Spend some time at the gate:

```
try
{
    sleep (timeAtGate);
}
catch (InterruptedException e) {}
System.out.println ("Waiting to leave " + threadName);
```

Takeoff procedure (1, 2)—request and acquire the runway mutex:

```
/* Solution #2 - runway mutex */
airport.RequestRunwayLock (this);
System.out.println ("Got runway for take-off " + threadName);
```

Takeoff procedure (3, 4)—the aircraft taxis to the runway and then takes off:

```
airport.airportMap.Takeoff (this);
```

Takeoff procedure (5, 6)—the aircraft releases all remaining locks:

```
/* Solution #3 - release mutex when no longer needed */
airport.ReleaseGatesLock (this);
airport.ReleaseRunwayLock (this);

System.out.println ("END " + threadName);
    }
}
```

Three Airplanes at a Time—One Terminal Gate

The model is now modified to support three aircraft trying to use the airport at the same time.

Landing Procedure

Here is a description of how aircraft will land at the airport.

▶ **First Aircraft Landing**   The following is a list of steps that have to be adhered to so this airplane can land safely.

1. The first aircraft requests the mutex for the runway.

2. The aircraft acquires the mutex for the runway.

3. The aircraft lands.

4. The aircraft releases the mutex for the runway.

5. The aircraft requests the mutex for the terminal.

6. The aircraft acquires the mutex for the terminal.

7. The aircraft taxis to the terminal.

▶ **Second Aircraft Landing**   The following is a list of steps that have to be adhered to so this airplane can land safely.

1. The second aircraft requests the mutex for the runway.

2. The aircraft acquires the mutex for the runway.

3. The aircraft lands.

4. The aircraft releases the mutex for the runway.

5. The aircraft requests the mutex for the terminal.

6. The aircraft waits.

Problem #4—News Flash: "Aircraft crash just off the runway"

When the second aircraft landed, it released the mutex for the runway. The third aircraft took this as a signal that it could land. Unfortunately, the second aircraft was sitting at the end of the runway waiting for the terminal to become free. How do you avoid the crash?

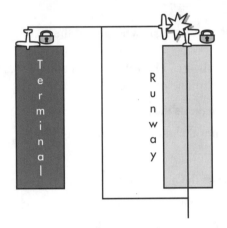

Solution #4

The solution is to provide a mutex at the end of the runway. This mutex is used to indicate that the landing area is in use and that another aircraft should not try to land. Once an aircraft has reached the terminal, it must release the landing area mutex to allow another aircraft to use it.

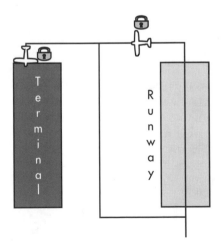

Problem #5—News Flash: "Airport at a standstill"

This is another deadlock problem. The incoming aircraft has acquired the runway mutex and is waiting to acquire the landing area mutex. But, there is another aircraft there waiting to acquire the terminal mutex, and there is an aircraft at the terminal waiting to acquire the runway mutex—circular deadlock. How do you avoid the deadlock?

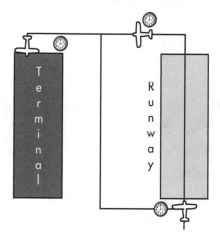

Solution #5

The incoming aircraft needs to acquire the landing area mutex before the runway mutex to make sure once it is landed. It is guaranteed to be moved to the landing area and free the runway. Once the incoming aircraft has landed and moved to the landing area, it should release the runway mutex, once again allowing the runway to be used for takeoffs.

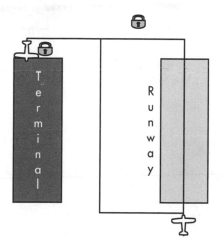

Takeoff Procedure

The takeoff procedure is as previously stated.

Revision of Landing Procedures

The following is a list of steps that have to be adhered to so airplanes can land safely.

1. The aircraft requests the mutex for the landing area.
2. The aircraft acquires the mutex for the landing area.
3. The aircraft requests the mutex for the runway.
4. The aircraft acquires the mutex for the runway.
5. The aircraft lands and moves to the landing area.
6. The aircraft releases the mutex for the runway.
7. The aircraft requests the mutex for the terminal.
8. The aircraft acquires the mutex for the terminal.
9. The aircraft releases the mutex for the landing area.
10. The aircraft taxis to the terminal.

Revised Java Code

This new code reflects the changes needed to support Solutions #1, #2, and #3.

Airport.java

```
public class Airport
{
```

In order to provide the solution for problem #4, it is necessary to declare another mutex. This mutex is again implemented as lists in the form of vectors:

```
< code as before >
/* Solution #4 - landing area mutex */
private static Vector          landingList = new Vector ();
/* Solution #2 - runway mutex */
private static Vector          runwayList = new Vector ();
/* Solution #1 - terminal gate mutex */
private static Vector          gatesList = new Vector ();
```

```
public Airport()
{
    < code as before accept now using three threads>
}

/* Start the Airport */
public static void main(String[] args)
{
    Airport a = new Airport ();
}
```

Additional methods provide solutions to problem #4. They use the landing area mutex.

```
public void RequestLandingLock (Plane plane)
{
    RequestLock (plane, landingList);
}

public void ReleaseLandingLock (Plane plane)
{
    ReleaseLock (plane, landingList);
}

< other mutex methods as before >
}
```

AirportMap.java

There is no change in this code.

Plane.java

```
public class Plane extends Thread
{
    < code as before >
/*
** Run
*/
    public void run()
    {
        System.out.println ("Waiting to land " + threadName);
```

Landing procedure (1, 2)—request and acquire the landing area mutex:

```
/* Solution #4 - landing area mutex */
/* Solution #5 - acquire landing area before runaway */
airport.RequestLandingLock (this);
System.out.println ("Got somewhere to land " + threadName);
```

Landing procedure (3, 4)—request and acquire the runway mutex:

```
/* Solution #2 - runway mutex */
airport.RequestRunwayLock (this);
System.out.println ("Got use of runway " + threadName);
System.out.println ("Landing " + threadName);
```

Landing procedure (5)—the aircraft lands and moves to the landing area:

```
airport.airportMap.LandPlane (this);
System.out.println ("Landed " + threadName);
```

Landing procedure (6)—release the runway lock:

```
/* Solution #3 - release mutex when no longer needed */
airport.ReleaseRunwayLock (this);
```

Landing procedure (7, 8)—request and acquire the terminal gate:

```
/* Solution #1 - terminal gate mutex */
airport.RequestGatesLock (this);
System.out.println ("Got a gate " + threadName);
```

Landing procedure (9)—release the landing area mutex:

```
/* Solution #4 - landing area mutex */
airport.ReleaseLandingLock (this);
```

Landing procedure (10)—taxi to the terminal gate:

```
airport.airportMap.TaxiToGate (this);
System.out.println ("At gate " + threadName );
```

Spend some time at the gate:

```
try
{
    sleep (timeAtGate);
}
catch (InterruptedException e) {}
System.out.println ("Waiting to leave " + threadName);
```

Takeoff procedure (1, 2)—request and acquire the runway mutex:

```
/* Solution #2 - runway mutex */
airport.RequestRunwayLock ();
System.out.println ("Got runway for take-off " + threadName);
```

Takeoff procedure (3, 4)—the aircraft taxis to the runway and then takes off:

```
airport.airportMap.Takeoff (this);
```

Takeoff procedure (5, 6)—the aircraft releases all remaining locks:

```
/* Solution #3 - release mutex when no longer needed */
airport.ReleaseGatesLock (this);
airport.ReleaseRunwayLock (this);

System.out.println ("END " + threadName);
    }
}
```

More Aircraft—Additional Gates

As the traffic through the airport was expected to rise dramatically, additional gates were built at the terminal. The terminal now houses four gates.

Landing Procedure

The landing procedure is as previously stated.

Problem #6—News Flash: "Aircraft crash while taxiing"

The problem is that one aircraft could be taxiing towards the terminal and its gate while another could be taxiing towards the runway wanting to take off. How do you avoid a crash?

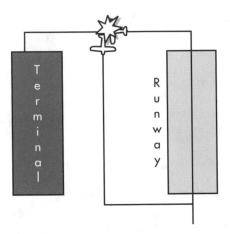

Solution #6

The solution is to provide a mutex for taxiing. This mutex is used to allow only one aircraft at a time permission to taxi anywhere around the airport.

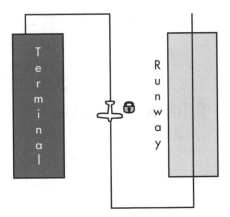

Problem #7—News Flash: "Airport at a standstill, waiting for departing aircraft"

The problem is that in order for an aircraft to take off, it must acquire the mutex for the runway and acquire the taxiing mutex. While the plane is taxiing to the runway and during takeoff, the airport comes to a standstill and waits. The runway mutex and the taxiing mutex are the most important and widely used mutexes within the airport. If one single aircraft has both of them, nothing else can happen.

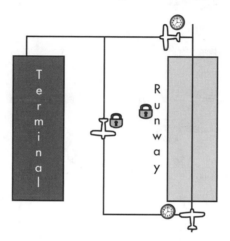

Solution #7

The solution is to provide another waiting area. This time it will be used for takeoffs. Once an aircraft has reached the takeoff area it can release the taxiing mutex and then request the runway mutex.

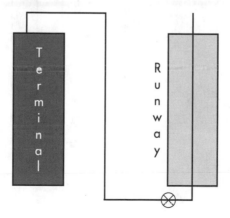

Problem #8—News Flash: "Aircraft crash as they try to take off at the same time"

The problem is similar to problem #4—Multiple Landings. As soon as an aircraft reaches the takeoff area and releases the taxiing mutex, another aircraft might take this as a signal that it can now taxi towards the runway for takeoff.

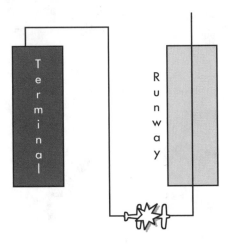

Solution #8

As with solution #4, provide a mutex, such that an aircraft can only taxi to the landing area if it has the mutex, if, for example, there is no other aircraft already in the takeoff area.

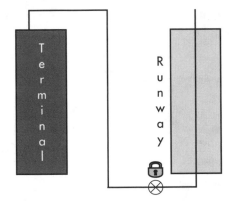

Also as with solution #5, to avoid deadlock an aircraft needs to acquire the mutex for the landing area before it should try to acquire the taxiing mutex.

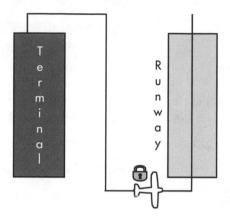

Full Aircraft Life Cycle

This illustration shows where the mutexes are and the areas they control:

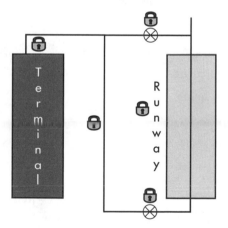

▶ **Landing**   The following is a list of steps that have to be adhered to so airplanes can land safely.

   1. Request the landing area mutex.

   2. Acquire the landing area mutex.

3. Request the runway mutex.

4. Acquire the runway mutex.

5. <Landing + move to landing area>.

6. Release the runway mutex.

7. Request a terminal gate mutex.

▶ **Moving to Terminal Gate**   The following is a list of steps that have to be adhered to so airplanes can move safely to the terminal gate.

1. Acquire a terminal gate mutex.

2. Request the taxiing mutex.

3. Acquire the taxiing mutex.

4. Release the landing area mutex.

5. <Taxi to assigned terminal gate>.

6. Release the taxiing mutex.

▶ **Ready for Takeoff**   The following is a list of steps that have to be adhered to so airplanes can get ready for takeoff.

1. Request the holding area mutex.

2. Acquire the holding area mutex.

3. Request the taxiing mutex.

4. Acquire the taxiing mutex.

5. <Taxi to holding area>.

6. Release the terminal gate mutex.

7. Release the taxiing mutex.

▶ **Takeoff**   The following is a list of steps that have to be adhered to so airplanes can take off.

1. Request the runway mutex.

2. Acquire the runway mutex.

3. Release the holding area mutex.

4. <Takeoff>.

5. Release the runway mutex.

This illustration shows the airport with many aircraft and four terminal gates:

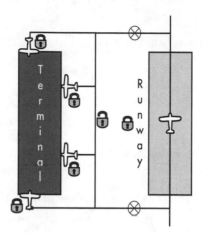

Revised Java Code

This new code reflects the changes needed to support solutions #6, #7, and #8.

Airport.java

```
static Vector     gatesLock = new Vector ();
static Integer    gate1 = new Integer (1);
static Integer    gate2 = new Integer (2);
static Integer    gate3 = new Integer (3);
static Integer    gate4 = new Integer (4);

/* Solution #6 - taxiing area mutex */
static Vector     taxiList = new Vector ();

/* Solution #8 - holding area mutex */
static Vector     holdingList = new Vector ();
```

Synchronize the 'gatesLock' vector so that the four terminal gates can be added to it:

```
synchronized (gatesLock)
{
    gatesLock.addElement (gate1);
    gatesLock.addElement (gate2);
    gatesLock.addElement (gate3);
```

```
        gatesLock.addElement (gate4);
}
```

Previously, the code was implemented as follows:

```
public void RequestGatesLock (Plane plane)
{
    RequestLock (plane, gatesList);
}
```

The previous 'RequestGatesLock' method was concerned with only one terminal gate. This new implementation has been designed to handle four terminal gates:

```
public Integer RequestGatesLock (Plane plane)
{
    boolean    empty;

    Integer    atGate;

    synchronized (gatesLock)
    {
        empty = gatesLock.isEmpty ();

        synchronized (gatesList)
        {
            gatesList.addElement (plane);
        }
    }
    if (empty == true)
    {
        try {plane.wait ();}
            catch (InterruptedException e) {}
    }

    synchronized (gatesLock)
    {
        atGate = (Integer)gatesLock.firstElement ();
        gatesLock.removeElement (atGate);

        synchronized (gatesList)
        {
```

```
            gatesList.removeElement (plane);
        }
    }

    return (atGate);
}
```

Here are the implementations of the additional request methods:

```
public void RequestTaxiLock (Plane plane)
{
    RequestLock (plane, taxiList);
}


public void RequestHoldingLock (Plane plane)
{
    RequestLock (plane, holdingList);
}
```

Previously, here is how the code was implemented:

```
/* old code */
public void ReleaseGatesLock (Plane plane)
{
    ReleaseLock (plane, gatesList);
}
```

The previous 'ReleaseGatesLock' method was concerned with only one terminal gate. This new implementation has been designed to handle four terminal gates.

```
public void ReleaseGatesLock (Integer atGate)
{
    Plane      peek;

    synchronized (Airport.gatesLock)
    {
        Airport.gatesLock.addElement (atGate);

        synchronized (Airport.gatesList)
        {
            if (Airport.gatesList.isEmpty () == false)
```

```
            {
                try
                {
                    peek = (Plane)Airport.gatesList.firstElement ();
                    synchronized (peek)
                    {
                        peek.notify ();
                    }
                }
                catch (NoSuchElementException e) {}
            }
        }
    }
}
```

Here are the implementations of the addiitonal release methods:

```
/* new code */
public void ReleaseTaxiLock (Plane plane)
{
    ReleaseLock (plane, taxiList);
}

public void ReleaseHoldingLock (Plane plane)
{
    ReleaseLock (plane, holdingList);
}
```

AirportMap.java

```
/*
**   TaxiToGateOne
*/
public void TaxiToGateOne (Plane plane)
{
    /*
    ** Display the aircraft moving west from the landing area and
    ** south towards the terminal
    ** Gate 1 is at the northern end of the terminal
    */
}
```

```
/*
**   TaxiToGateTwo
*/
public void TaxiToGateTwo (Plane plane)
{
    /*
    ** Display the aircraft moving west from the landing area and
    ** south towards the terminal
    ** Gate 2 is the topmost gate on the eastern side of the terminal
    */
}


/*
**   TaxiToGateThree
*/
public void TaxiToGateThree (Plane plane)
{
    /*
    ** Display the aircraft moving west from the landing area and
    ** south towards the terminal Gate 3 is the bottommost gate on
    ** the eastern side of the terminal
    */

}


/*
**   TaxiToGateFour
*/
public void TaxiToGateFour (Plane plane)
{
    /*
    ** Display the aircraft moving west from the landing area and
    ** south towards the terminal
    ** Gate 2 is at the southern end of the terminal
    */
}


/*
**   TaxiFromGateOne
*/
public void TaxiFromGateOne (Plane plane)
{
```

```
    /*
    ** Display the aircraft moving up and around the terminal,
    ** towards the holding area just to the west of the southern
    ** end of the runway
    */
}


/*
**   TaxiFromGateTwo
*/
public void TaxiFromGateTwo (Plane plane)
{
    /*
    ** Display the aircraft moving away from the terminal, and south
    ** towards the holding area just to the west of the southern end
    ** of the runway
    */
}


/*
**   TaxiFromGateThree
*/
public void TaxiFromGateThree (Plane plane)
{
    /*
    ** Display the aircraft moving away from the terminal, and south
    ** towards the holding area just to the west of the southern end
    ** of the runway
    */
}


/*
**   TaxiFromGateFour
*/
public void TaxiFromGateFour (Plane plane)
{
    /*
    ** Display the aircraft moving away from the terminal, towards
    ** the holding area just to the west of the southern end of the
    ** runway
    */
}
```

```
/*
** Method Name: Takeoff
** This method is used to show an aircraft taxiing from the
** terminal gate onto the runway and then taking off
**
** Input: A handle to the aircraft to use
** Output: none
*/
public void TakeOff (Plane plane)
{
    /*
    ** Display the aircraft moving east away from the holding area
    ** to the start of the runway, then finally north as it flies
    ** away from the airport
    */
}
```

Plane.java

```
public class Plane extends Thread
{
        < code as before >
/*
**    Run
*/
public void TaxiToGate (int gateNo)
{
    if (gateNo == 1)
    {
        airport.airportMap.TaxiToGateOne (this);
    }
    else if (gateNo == 2)
    {
        airport.airportMap.TaxiToGateTwo (this);
    }
    else if (gateNo == 3)
    {
        airport.airportMap.TaxiToGateThree (this);
    }
    else
    {
        airport.airportMap.TaxiToGateFour (this);
```

```
        }
}
/*
**
*/
public void TaxiFromGate (int gateNo)
{
    if (gateNo == 1)
    {
        airport.airportMap.TaxiFromGateOne (this);
    }
    else if (gateNo == 2)
    {
        airport.airportMap.TaxiFromGateTwo (this);
    }
    else if (gateNo == 3)
    {
        airport.airportMap.TaxiFromGateThree (this);
    }
    else
    {
        airport.airportMap.TaxiFromGateFour (this);
    }
}
/*
**   Run
*/
public void run()
{
    Integer     atGate;

    System.out.println ("Waiting to land " + threadName);
```

Landing procedure (1, 2)—request and acquire the landing area mutex:

```
    /* Solution #4 - landing area mutex */
    /* Solution #5 - acquire landing area before runaway */
    airport.RequestLandingLock (this);
    System.out.println ("Got somewhere to land " + threadName);
```

Landing procedure (3, 4)—request and acquire the runway mutex:

```
/* Solution #2 - runway mutex */
airport.RequestRunwayLock (this);
System.out.println ("Got use of runway " + threadName);
System.out.println ("Landing " + threadName);
```

Landing procedure (5)—aircraft lands and moves to the landing area:

```
airport.airportMap.LandPlane (this);
System.out.println ("Landed " + threadName);
```

Landing procedure (6)—release the runway mutex:

```
/* Solution #3 - release mutex when no longer needed */
airport.ReleaseRunwayLock (this);
```

Landing procedure (7)—request the terminal gate mutex:
Moving to terminal gate procedure (1)—acquire the terminal gate mutex:

```
/* Solution #1 - terminal gate mutex */
atGate = airport.RequestGatesLock (this);
System.out.println ("Got a gate " + threadName);
```

Moving to terminal gate procedure (2)—request and acquire the taxiing mutex:

```
/* Solution #6 - taxiing mutex */
airport.RequestTaxiLock (this);
System.out.println ("Got use of taxiway " + threadName + "\n");
System.out.println ("Taxiing " + threadName + "\n");
```

Moving to terminal gate procedure (4)—release the landing area mutex:

```
/* Solution #4 - landing area mutex */
airport.ReleaseLandingLock (this);
```

Moving to terminal gate procedure (5)—taxi to the assigned terminal gate:

```
TaxiToGate (atGate.intValue ());
System.out.println ("At gate " + threadName + "\n");
```

Moving to terminal gate procedure (6)—release the taxiing mutex:

```
/* Solution #5 - release lock to avoid deadlock*/
airport.ReleaseTaxiLock (this);
```

Spend some time at the gate:

```
try
{
    sleep (timeAtGate);
}
catch (InterruptedException e) {}
System.out.println ("Waiting to leave " + threadName + "\n");
```

Ready for takeoff procedure (1, 2)—request and acquire the holding area mutex:

```
/* Solution #5 - holding lock */
airport.RequestHoldingLock (this);
System.out.println
    ("Got holding area lock " + threadName + "\n");
```

Ready for takeoff procedure (3, 4)—request and acquire the taxiing mutex:

```
/* Solution #8 - the order in which mutexes are acquired */
/* Solution #6 - taxiing lock */
airport.RequestTaxiLock (this);
System.out.println ("Got use of taxiway " + threadName + "\n");
System.out.println ("Taxiing " + threadName + "\n");
```

Ready for takeoff procedure (5)—taxi from the terminal gate to the holding area:

```
TaxiFromGate (atGate.intValue ());
System.out.println ("At holding area " + threadName + "\n");
```

Ready for takeoff procedure (6)—release the terminal gate mutex:

```
/* Solution #3 - release mutex when no longer needed */
airport.ReleaseGatesLock (atGate);
```

Ready for takeoff procedure (7)—release the taxiing mutex:

```
/* Solution #5 - taxiing lock */
airport.ReleaseTaxiLock (this);
System.out.println ("At holding area " + threadName + "\n");
```

Takeoff procedure (1, 2)—request and acquire the runway mutex:

```
/* Solution #2 - runway lock */
airport.RequestRunwayLock (this);
System.out.println ("Got runway " + threadName + "\n");
```

Takeoff procedure (3)—release the holding area mutex:

```
airport.ReleaseHoldingLock (this);
```

Takeoff procedure (4)—aircraft takes off:

```
System.out.println ("Taking off " + threadName + "\n");
airport.airportMap.TakeOff (this);
```

Takeoff procedure (5)—release the runway lock:

```
/* Solution #3 - release mutex when no longer needed */
airport.ReleaseRunwayLock (this);

System.out.println ("END " + threadName + "\n");
}
```

Final Solution

This final solution adds three more classes:

▶ **AirportDetails** to act as the display on which each aircraft is shown. The details show which aircraft is requesting, acquiring, and releasing which mutexes. It also shows what each aircraft is doing having acquired a particular mutex.

▶ **MediumPlane** and **SmallPlane** have been added to provide variety. **SmallPlane** is half the size and also waits at the terminal gates for half the time.

The Airport Details Window

This illustration shows the all of the airplanes in their various states as they approach, use, and take off from the airport:

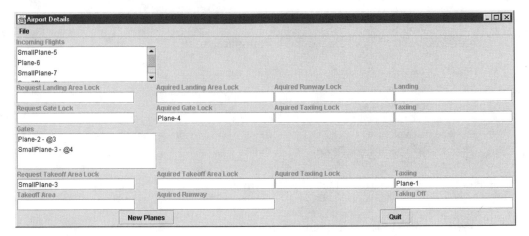

Java Code

This new code reflects the changes made to support the Airport Details window and the derived aircraft classes.

Airport.java

```
public class Airport
{
    public AirportDetails    airportDetails;
    ...
    private Random generator =
        new Random(System.currentTimeMillis());
...
    public Airport()
    {
        airportDetails = new AirportDetails ("Airport Details");
        ...
        Plane planes [] = new Plane [10];
```

```
    /* Create the threads */
    for (int j = 0; j < 10; j++)
    {
        if (generator.nextInt (2) < 1)
        {
            planes [j] = new Plane (threadGroup, j, this);
        }
        else
        {
            planes [j] = new Plane (threadGroup, j, this);
        }
    }
    ...
    }
}
```

Summary

From the initial example of a single aircraft at a single terminal configuration, to multiple aircraft at multiple terminals, there are numerous areas in which accidents and errors cause the airport to come to a standstill. Even now there are improvements that could be made to make better use of the taxiing mutex. For instance, modifications could be made to allow an aircraft to go to Gate #1, closest to the landing area, while another aircraft departs from Gate #4, closest to the takeoff area. Those improvements can be left for another time.

Philosopher Source Code

ere is an implementation of the philosopher program, referenced in earlier chapters, developed using Visual C++®.

Windows Visual C++®

phils.cc

```
/*
**  Name: phils.cc - Dining Philosophers
**
** Description:
**  There are 10 philosophers who spend their lives either eating or
**  thinking.
**  Each philosopher has his own place at a circular table, in the
**  center of which is a large bowl of rice.  To eat rice requires
**  two chopsticks, but only 10 chopsticks are provided, one between
**  each pair of philosophers. The only chopsticks a philosopher can
**  pick up are those on his immediate right and left.
**  Each philosopher is identical in structure, alternately eating
**  then thinking. The problem is to simulate the behaviour of the
**  philosophers while avoiding deadlock (the request by a philosopher
**  for a chopstick can never be granted) and indefinite postponement
**  (the request by a philosopher is continually denied), known
**  colloquially as "starvation."
**
**  Created by : Andrew Haigh
**  Change history
**      20-mar-2001 (Andrew Haigh)
**          created
*/

/*
**  system include files
*/
#include <windows.h>
#include <stdlib.h>
#include <string.h>
#include <stdio.h>
#include <conio.h>
#include <process.h>

/*
**  local variables
```

```
*/
HANDLE  hChopsticksMutex [numPhilosophers];
HANDLE  hSyncEvent;
int     ThreadNr;                       /* Number of threads started */

/*
**   local defines
*/
#define numPhilosophers 10     // number of philosophers
#define numBites        5      // number of bites to take

/*
** getrandom returns a random number between min and max,
** which must be in integer range.
*/
#define getrandom( min, max ) ((rand() % (int) \
              (((max) + 1) - (min))) + (min))

/*
**   forward declaration of methods
*/
void main( void );                      /* Thread 1: main */
void PhilosopherProc (int * MyID);      /* Threads 2 to n: display */

/*
**   Psem
**   Purpose of method
**       This method will lock the mutex and return
**       If the mutex is not free, it will wait until it is
**   Input
**       mutex - handle of the mutex
**       seq - number to be printed in the message
**   Output/Return
**       method is void
**   Change History
**       20-mar-2001 (Andrew Haigh)
**           created
*/
void
Psem (HANDLE mutex, int seq)
{
    DWORD stat;
    stat = WaitForSingleObject( mutex, INFINITE );
    if(stat == WAIT_FAILED)
    {
      printf ("Error lock - %d = %d\n", seq, stat);
      exit(1);
```

```
    }
}


/*
**  Psem_try
**  Purpose of method
**      This method will try to lock the mutex
**      If the mutex if free, acquire it and return
**      If the mutex is already locked it will return WAIT_TIMEOUT
**  Input
**      mutex - handle of the mutex
**      time - period to wait for the mutex to become free
**      seq - number to be printed in the message
**  Output/Return
**      return 0 - when it succeeds
**      return WAIT_TIMEOUT - when it timed-out
**      exit 1 - when it fails
**  Change History
**      20-Mar-2001 (Andrew Haigh)
**          created
*/
DWORD
Psem_try (HANDLE mutex, DWORD time, int seq)
{
    DWORD stat;
    stat = WaitForSingleObject( mutex, time );
    if(stat == WAIT_TIMEOUT)
    {
        return WAIT_TIMEOUT;
    }
    else if (stat == WAIT_FAILED)
    {
        printf ("Error trylock - %d = %d\n", seq, stat);
        exit(1);
    }
    else
        return 0;
}


/*
**  Vsem
**  Purpose of method
**      Release the mutex
**  Input
**      mutex - handle of the mutex
**      seq - number to be printed in the message
**  Output/Return
```

```
**      method is void
**   Change History
**      20-mar-2001 (Andrew Haigh)
**          created
*/
void
Vsem (HANDLE mutex, int seq)
{
    DWORD stat;
    stat = ReleaseMutex ( mutex );
    if(stat == 0)
    {
        printf ("Error unlock - %d = %d\n", seq, stat);
        exit(1);
    }
}


/*
**   main
**   Purpose of method
**      This method controls the program,
**      it creates the mutexes, it then creates the threads,
**      starts the threads and then waits for them to finish
**   Input
**      argc - number of command line arguments
**      argv - the command line arguments
**   Output/Return
**      method is void
**   Change History
**      20-mar-2001 (Andrew Haigh)
**          created
*/
void
main(int argc, char **argv)                        /* Thread One */
{
    int    i;
    int    *buffer;

    /* Create the mutexes and reset thread count. */
    hSyncEvent = CreateEvent (NULL,TRUE, FALSE, "SyncCond");
    for (i = 0; i < numPhilosophers; i ++)
        hChopsticksMutex [i] = CreateMutex (NULL, FALSE, NULL);

    ThreadNr = 10;

    /*
    ** Start waiting for keyboard input to dispatch threads or exit
```

```
    */
    for (i = 0; i < numPhilosophers; i++)
    {
        buffer = calloc (2, sizeof (int));
        *buffer = i;
        _beginthread (PhilosopherProc, 0, buffer);
    }
    SetEvent (hSyncEvent);

    /*
    **  wait to be signalled that the threads have finished
    */
    do
    {
        Sleep (2000L);
        Psem (hSyncEvent, 99);
        ResetEvent (hSyncEvent);
    }
    while (ThreadNr != 0);

    /*
    ** All threads done. Clean up handles
    */
    for (i = 0; i < numPhilosophers; i ++)
    {
        CloseHandle (hChopsticksMutex [i]);
    }
    CloseHandle (hSyncEvent);
}


/*
**   PhilosopherProc
**   Purpose of method
**       This is the process run by each philosopher thread
**   Input
**       MyId - unique thread identifier
**   Output/Return
**       method is void
**   Change History
**       20-mar-2001 (Andrew Haigh)
**           created
*/
void
PhilosopherProc( int *MyID )
{
    int    I, nextstick;
```

```
    Psem (hSyncEvent, 0);

    nextstick = (*MyID+1)%numPhilosophers;

    for (i = 0; i < numBites; i++)
    {
        printf ("Philosopher %d thinking\n", *MyID);
        Sleep (0);  // yield

        // hungry, so picks up chopsticks
        Psem (hChopsticksMutex[*MyID], 3);

        while (Psem_try (hChopsticksMutex[nextstick], 0, 4) == 1)
        {
            printf ("Philosopher %d waiting\n", *MyID);
            Vsem (hChopsticksMutex[*MyID], 3);
            Sleep (getrandom (1, 100));
            Psem (hChopsticksMutex[*MyID], 3);
        }

        // eating
        printf ("Philosopher %d eating bite %d\n", *MyID, i);
        Sleep (100L);  // yield

        Vsem (hChopsticksMutex[(*MyID+1)%numPhilosophers], 4);
        Vsem (hChopsticksMutex[*MyID], 3);

        Sleep (getrandom (500, 1000));  // yield
    }

    printf ("Thread %d ending\n", *MyID);
    ThreadNr--;
    SetEvent (hSyncEvent);
    return;
}
```

UNIX C++

Here is an implementation of the philosopher program written to work against Unix C++ and Unix Posix threads.

phils.cpp

```
/*
** Name: phils.cc - Dining Philosophers
```

```
**
**   Description:
**   There are 10 philosophers who spend their lives either eating or
**   thinking.
**   Each philosopher has his own place at a circular table, in the
**   center of which is a large bowl of rice.  To eat rice requires
**   two chopsticks, but only 10 chopsticks are provided, one between
**   each pair of philosophers. The only chopsticks a philosopher can
**   pick up are those on his immediate right and left.
**   Each philosopher is identical in structure, alternately eating
**   then thinking. The problem is to simulate the behaviour of the
**   philosophers while avoiding deadlock (the request by a philosopher
**   for a chopstick can never be granted) and indefinite postponement
**   (the request by a philosopher is continually denied), known
**   colloquially as "starvation."
**
**   Created by : Andrew Haigh
**   Change history
**       20-mar-2001 (Andrew Haigh)
**           created
*/

/*
**   system include files
*/
# include <stdlib.h>
# include <iostream.h>
# include <sys/errno.h>
# include <unistd.h>

/*
** local include files
*/
# define  POSIX_THREADS
# include <PortableThreads.h>

/*
**   local variables
*/
const int  numPhilosophers = 10;     // number of philosophers
const int  numBites = 5;             // number of bites to take

// Setup the chopsticks as mutexs
PM_t       chopsticks[numPhilosophers];

// Provide a mutex to the resource 'threadCount'
int        threadCount = 0;
```

```
PM_t          threadCountMutex;

// Provide a condition variable and Boolean to allow the threads
// to have a synchronized start, and a mutex to setup the condition
PM_t          syncCondMutex;
int           syncBit;
PC_t          syncCond;

/*
**    Psem
**    Purpose of method
**        This method will lock the mutex and return
**        If the mutex is not free, it will wait until it is
**    Input
**        mutex - handle of the mutex
**        seq - number to be printed in the message
**    Output/Return
**        method is void
**    Change History
**        20-mar-2001 (Andrew Haigh)
**             created
*/
void
Psem (PM_t *mutex, int seq)
{
    int stat;
    // request a lock on a specific mutex
    stat = PM_lock (mutex);
    if(stat)
    {
        // if the request fails, report error to the user
        // do not try and recover
        cout << "Error PM_lock - " << seq << " = " << stat << endl;
        exit(1);
    }
}


/*
**    Psem_try
**    Purpose of method
**        This method will try to lock the mutex
**        If the mutex if free, acquire it and return
**        If the mutex is already locked it will return WAIT_TIMEOUT
**    Input
**        mutex - handle of the mutex
**        seq - number to be printed in the message
**    Output/Return
```

```
**      return 0 - when it succeeds
**      return 1 - when the mutex is not free
**      exit 1 - when it fails
**  Change History
**      20-Mar-2001 (Andrew Haigh)
**          created
*/
int
Psem_try (PM_t *mutex, int seq)
{
    int stat;
    // try and get the lock on the mutex
    stat = PM_trylock (mutex);
    if(stat == EBUSY)
    {
        return 1;
    }
    else if (stat != 0)
    {
        cout << "Error PM_lock - " << seq << " = " << stat << endl;
        exit(1);
    }
    else
        return 0;
}


/*
**  Vsem
**  Purpose of method
**      Release the mutex
**  Input
**      mutex - handle of the mutex
**      seq - number to be printed in the message
**  Output/Return
**      method is void
**  Change History
**      20-mar-2001 (Andrew Haigh)
**          created
*/
void
Vsem (PM_t *mutex, int seq)
{
    // release the lock on a specific mutex
    if (PM_unlock (mutex))
    {
        // if the release fails, report error to the user
        // do not try and recover
```

```
            cout << "Error PM_unlock - " << seq << " = " << stat << endl;
            exit(1);
        }
    }


/*
**   PhilosopherThread
**   Purpose of method
**       This is the process run by each philosopher thread
**       Each philosopher tries to pick up both chopsticks
**       When they have both chopsticks, they eat and return the
**       chopsticks and wait/think. This is repeated 'numBites' times
**   Input
**   Output/Return
**       method is void *
**       return value 0 - when it succeeds
**   Change History
**       20-mar-2001 (Andrew Haigh)
**           created
*/
void *
PhilosopherThread()
{
    int thrid, stat;
    int nextstick;
    PT_t self = PT_get_thread_id();

    Psem (&threadCountMutex, 1);

    thrid = threadCount;
    threadCount++;
    cout << "Thread " << thrid << " entry point self=" << self
        << " addr = "<< &chopsticks << endl;

    Vsem (&threadCountMutex, 1);

    cout << "Local thread id = " << thrid << endl;

    // wait on a condition broadcast to start thread
    Psem (&syncCondMutex, 2);

    while (!syncBit)
    {
        stat = pthread_cond_wait(&syncCond, &syncCondMutex);
        if(stat)
        {
            cout << "Error pthread wait1 = " << stat << endl;
```

```
                exit(1);
        }
    }

    cout << "Thread " << thrid <<
        " released and beginning run." << endl;

    Vsem (&syncCondMutex, 2);

    for ( int bites = 1; bites <= numBites; bites++ )
    {
        // thinking
        cout << "Philosopher " << thrid << " thinking" << endl;
        PT_yield();

        // hungry, so picks up chopsticks
        Psem (&chopsticks[thrid], 3);

        Psem_try (thrid, &chopsticks[thrid],
            &chopsticks[(thrid+1)%numPhilosophers], 4);

        // eating
        cout << "Philosopher " << thrid << " eating" <<
            " bite " << bites << endl;
        PT_yield();

        // done eating
        Vsem (&chopsticks[(thrid+1)%numPhilosophers], 4);

        PT_yield();

        Vsem (&chopsticks[thrid], 3);
    }
    cout << "Thread " << thrid << " ending self=" << self << endl;
    return 0;
}

/*
**  main
**  Purpose of method
**      This method controls the program,
**      it creates the mutexes, it then creates the threads,
**      starts the threads and then waits for them to finish
**  Input
**      argc - number of command line arguments
**      argv - the command line arguments
**  Output/Return
```

```
**      return 0 - is successful finish
**      exit (1) - is a failure
**   Change History
**      20-mar-2001 (Andrew Haigh)
**          created
*/
int
main (int argc, char **argv)
{
    PT_t phils[numPhilosophers];
    int i, stat;
    void *ret;

    /*
    ** initialize the thread counter and the chopsticks
    */
    stat = PM_init(&threadCountMutex,NULL);
    Psem (&threadCountMutex, 0);
    for ( i=0; i < numPhilosophers; i++ )
    {
        cout << "Init mutex no.=" << i << " addr=" <<
            &chopsticks[i] << endl;
        stat = PM_init(&chopsticks[i],NULL);
        if(stat)
        {
            cout << "Error PT_init:1 = " << stat << endl;
            exit(1);
        }
    }


    /*
    ** initialize the synchronization flag
    ** that starts the threads running
    */
    syncBit = 0;
    stat = PM_init(&syncCondMutex, NULL);
    if(stat)
    {
        cout << "Error PT_init:2 = " << stat << endl;
        exit(1);
    }
    stat = PC_init(&syncCond, NULL);
    if(stat)
    {
        cout << "Error PC_init = " << stat << endl;
        exit(1);
    }
```

```
    // Create the philosopher threads
    for ( i=0; i < numPhilosophers; i++ )
    {
        // create the philosopher threads
        PT_create(NULL, NULL, (void *(*)(void*))PhilosopherThread,
            NULL, &phils[i], PTHREAD_CREATE_JOINABLE, &stat);
    }
    cout << numPhilosophers << " threads created." << endl;

    Vsem (&threadCountMutex, 6);

    // now wake them all up at once
    Psem (&syncCondMutex, 7);

    syncBit = 1;
    stat = PC_broadcast(&syncCond);
    if(stat)
    {
        cout << "Error PC_broadcast = " << stat << endl;
        exit(1);
    }
    cout << "Startup condition signaled." << endl;

    Vsem (&syncCondMutex, 7);

    // wait for all threads to finish execution
    for ( i = 0; i < numPhilosophers; i++ )
    {
        stat =  PT_join( phils[i], &ret );
        if(stat)
        {
            cout << "Error PT_join" << i <<"  = " << stat << endl;
            exit(1);
        }
    }

    cout << "Normal shutdown" <<endl;

    return 1;
}
```

Java

The first of these Java files is the controller for the other file that contains the
running code for the Java threads.

Dinner.java

```
/*
**   Name: Dinner.java - Dining Philosophers
**
**   Description:
**   There are 10 philosophers who spend their lives either eating or
**   thinking.
**   Each philosopher has his own place at a circular table, in the
**   center of which is a large bowl of rice.  To eat rice requires
**   two chopsticks, but only 10 chopsticks are provided, one between
**   each pair of philosophers. The only chopsticks a philosopher can
**   pick up are those on his immediate right and left.
**   Each philosopher is identical in structure, alternately eating
**   then thinking. The problem is to simulate the behaviour of the
**   philosophers while avoiding deadlock (the request by a philosopher
**   for a chopstick can never be granted) and indefinite postponement
**   (the request by a philosopher is continually denied), known
**   colloquially as "starvation."
**
**   Created by : Andrew Haigh
**   Change history
**       20-mar-2001 (Andrew Haigh)
**           created
*/

import java.io.*;
import java.lang.*;
import java.util.*;

public class Dinner
{
    protected ThreadGroup    threadGroup;
    static Boolean           chopstickLock [] = new Boolean [10];
    static int               numPhils = 5;

    /*
    **   Dinner
    **   Purpose of method
    **       This method controls the program,
    **       it creates the mutexes, it then creates the threads,
    **       starts the threads and then waits for them to finish
    **   Input
    **   Output/Return
    **       method is the class constructor
    **   Change History
```

```
**      20-mar-2001 (Andrew Haigh)
**          created
*/
public Dinner()
{
    // Create the threadgroup.
    threadGroup = new ThreadGroup("Dinner");

    synchronized (chopstickLock)
    {
        for (int j = 0; j < numPhils; j++)
        {
            chopstickLock [j] = new Boolean (false);
        }
    }

    Phils phils [] = new Phils [numPhils];

    try
    {
        // Start the thread
        for (int j = 0; j < numPhils; j++)
        {
            phils [j] = new Phils (threadGroup, j, this);
            phils [j].start ();
        }

        for (int j = 0; j < numPhils; j++)
        {
            phils [j].join ();
        }
    }
    catch(InterruptedException e){}
}

// Start the application
public static void main(String[] args)
{
    Dinner a = new Dinner ();
}
}
```

Phils.java

```
/*
**  Name: Phils.java - Philosophers thread
```

```
**
**  Description:
**      This is the process run by each philosopher thread
**      Each philosopher tries to pick up both chopsticks
**      When they have both chopsticks, they eat and return the
**      chopsticks and wait/think. This is repeated 'numBites' times
*/

import java.io.*;
import java.lang.*;
import java.util.*;

public class Phils extends Thread
{
    String     threadName;
    int        thrid;
    Dinner     dinner;

    /*
    **  Phils
    **      Each philosopher tries to pick up both chopsticks
    **      When they have both chopsticks, they eat and return the
    **      chopsticks and wait/think. This is repeated 'numBites' times
    **  Input
    **      threadGroup - group to which the thread belongs, a group
    **                      allows to be manipulated as a unit
    **      name - unique thread identifier
    **      parent - handle back to the thread owner
    **  Output/Return
    **      method is the class constructor
    **  Change History
    **      20-mar-2001 (Andrew Haigh)
    **          created
    */
    public Phils (ThreadGroup threadGroup, int name, Dinner parent)
    {
        // Create our server thread with a name.
        super(threadGroup, "Philosopher-" + name);

        dinner = parent;

        threadName = new String ("Philosopher-" + name);
        thrid = name;
    }

    /*
    **  Psem
```

```
**   Purpose of method
**       This method will lock the mutex and return
**       If the mutex is not free, it will wait until it is
**   Input
**       pos - the number of the mutex
**   Output/Return
**       method is void
**   Change History
**       20-mar-2001 (Andrew Haigh)
**           created
*/
public void Psem (int pos)
{
    boolean    flag;

    /*
    ** lock the mutex variable for single thread access
    */
    System.out.println (threadName + " RequestLock");
    synchronized (Dinner.chopstickLock [pos])
    {
        /*
        ** if the mutex is free acquire it and return
        */
        flag = Dinner.chopstickLock [pos].booleanValue ();
        if (flag == false)
        {
            Dinner.chopstickLock [pos] = new Boolean (true);
            System.out.println (threadName + " AcquiredLock");
            return;
        }
    }

    /*
    ** the mutex was already locked
    ** loop and keep testing the mutex availability
    ** until it becomes free
    */
    while (flag == true)
    {
        synchronized (Dinner.chopstickLock [pos])
        {
            flag = Dinner.chopstickLock [pos].booleanValue ();
            if (flag == false)
            {
                Dinner.chopstickLock [pos] = new Boolean (true);
                System.out.println (threadName + " AcquiredLock");
```

```
                    return;
                }
            }
        try {sleep (20);}
        catch (InterruptedException e) {}
        }
}


/*
**   Psem_try
**   Purpose of method
**       This method will try to lock the mutex
**       If the mutex if free, acquire it and return
**       If the mutex is already locked it will return WAIT_TIMEOUT
**   Input
**       pos - the number of the mutex
**   Output/Return
**       return value 0 - when it succeeds
**       return value 1 - when it fails
**   Change History
**       20-Mar-2001 (Andrew Haigh)
**           created
*/
public int Psem_try (int pos)
{
    System.out.println (threadName + " Psem_try " + pos);
    synchronized (Dinner.chopstickLock [pos])
    {
        if (Dinner.chopstickLock [pos].booleanValue () == false)
        {
            Dinner.chopstickLock [pos] = new Boolean (true);
            System.out.println (threadName + " AcquiredLock");
            return 0;
        }
        else
        {
            System.out.println (threadName + " Lock - waiting");
            return 1;
        }
    }
}


/*
**   Vsem
**   Purpose of method
**       Release the mutex
**   Input
```

```
**       pos - the number of the mutex
**   Output/Return
**       method is void
**   Change History
**       20-mar-2001 (Andrew Haigh)
**           created
*/
public void Vsem (int pos)
{
    System.out.println (threadName + " Vsem " + pos);
    synchronized (Dinner.chopstickLock [pos])
    {
        Dinner.chopstickLock [pos] = new Boolean (false);
    }
}


/*
**   Run
**   Purpose of method
**       This is the process run by each philosopher thread
**       Each philosopher tries to pick up both chopsticks
**       When they have both chopsticks, they eat and return the
**       chopsticks and wait/think. This is repeated 'numBites' times
**   Input
**   Output/Return
**       method is void *
**   Change History
**       20-mar-2001 (Andrew Haigh)
**           created
*/
public void run()
{
    int    next = thrid + 1;

    if (next == Dinner.numPhils)
        next = 0;

    System.out.println ("Go " + threadName);

    for (int i = 0; i < 5; i++)
    {
        Psem (thrid);

        while (Psem_try (next) == 1)
        {
            Vsem (thrid);
            try {sleep (20);}
```

```
                catch (InterruptedException e) {}
                Psem (thrid);
            }

        System.out.println ("All chopsticks acquired " +
            threadName);

        try {sleep (20);}
        catch (InterruptedException e) {}

        Vsem (next);
        Vsem (thrid);

        try {sleep (20);}
        catch (InterruptedException e) {}
    }

    System.out.println ("END " + threadName);
    }
}
```

Java JNI (C++)

The files that follow are very similar to the previous versions of the philosophers
program written in a Java and Unix C++. The only difference is that instead of the
C++ being called from a main routine, it is being called from Java. It is necessary to
initialize to threading environment before the C++ threads start; hence, the routines
'StartUp' and 'ShutDown'.

Dinner.java

```
/*
** Name: Dinner.java - Dining Philosophers
**
** Description:
** There are 10 philosophers who spend their lives either eating or
** thinking.
** Each philosopher has his own place at a circular table, in the
** center of which is a large bowl of rice.  To eat rice requires
** two chopsticks, but only 10 chopsticks are provided, one between
** each pair of philosophers. The only chopsticks a philosopher can
** pick up are those on his immediate right and left.
** Each philosopher is identical in structure, alternately eating
```

```
**   then thinking. The problem is to simulate the behaviour of the
**   philosophers while avoiding deadlock (the request by a philosopher
**   for a chopstick can never be granted) and indefinite postponement
**   (the request by a philosopher is continually denied), known
**   colloquially as "starvation."
**
**   Created by : Andrew Haigh
**   Change history
**       20-mar-2001 (Andrew Haigh)
**           created
*/
import java.io.*;
import java.lang.*;
import java.util.*;

public class Dinner
{
    protected static ThreadGroup    threadGroup;

    /*
    **   Purpose of method
    **       load the JNI libraries
    **   Input
    **   Output/Return
    **   Change History
    **       20-mar-2001 (haian02)
    **           created
    */
    static
    {
        System.loadLibrary("phil_java");
    }

    /*
    **   main
    **   Purpose of method
    **       This method controls the program,
    **       it creates the mutexes, it then creates the threads,
    **       starts the threads and then waits for them to finish
    **       It uses two JNI methods to initialize and cleanup the JNI code
    **   Input
    **       args - command line arguments
    **   Output/Return
    **       method is void
    **   Change History
    **       20-mar-2001 (Andrew Haigh)
    **           created
```

```
    */
    public static void main(String args[])
    {
        int     numPhils = 1;
        Dinner bigMeal = new Dinner();
        bigMeal.StartUp();
        // Create the threadgroup.
        threadGroup = new ThreadGroup("Philosophers");

        Phils [] phils = new Phils [numPhils];

        try
        {
            for (int j = 0; j < numPhils; j++)
            {
                System.out.println("new philosopher");
                phils [j] = new Phils(threadGroup, j);
                phils [j].start ();
            }

            for (int j = 0; j < numPhils; j++)
            {
                phils [j].join ();
            }
        }
        catch(InterruptedException e) {}

        bigMeal.ShutDown();
    }

    public native void StartUp();
    public native void ShutDown();
}
```

Dinner.h

```
/* DO NOT EDIT THIS FILE - it is machine generated */
#include <jni.h>
/* Header for class Dinner */

#ifndef _Included_Dinner
#define _Included_Dinner
#ifdef __cplusplus
extern "C" {
#endif
/* Inaccessible static: threadGroup */
```

```
/*
 * Class:      Dinner
 * Method:     ShutDown
 * Signature: ()V
 */
JNIEXPORT void JNICALL Java_Dinner_ShutDown
  (JNIEnv *, jobject);

/*
 * Class:      Dinner
 * Method:     StartUp
 * Signature: ()V
 */
JNIEXPORT void JNICALL Java_Dinner_StartUp
  (JNIEnv *, jobject);

#ifdef __cplusplus
}
#endif
#endif
```

Phils.java

```
/*
** Name: Phils.java - Philosophers thread
**
** Description:
**      This is the process run by each philosopher thread
**      It calls the JNI code to execute the philosophers actions
*/
import java.io.*;
import java.lang.*;
import java.util.*;

public class Phils extends Thread
{
    String     threadName;

    /*
    ** Phils
    ** Purpose of method
    **      Adds the thread to the thread group and names the thread
    ** Input
    **      threadGroup - handle of the mutex
    **      name - unique thread identifier
    ** Output/Return
```

```
**      method is the class constructor
**   Change History
**       20-mar-2001 (Andrew Haigh)
**           created
*/
public Phils (ThreadGroup threadGroup, int name)
{
    // Create our server thread with a name.
    super(threadGroup, "Philosopher-" + name);

    threadName = new String ("Java-" + name);
}


/*
**   run
**   Purpose of method
**       Call the JNI method
**   Input
**   Output/Return
**       method is void
**   Change History
**       20-mar-2001 (Andrew Haigh)
**           created
*/
public void run()
{
    System.out.println("start Jphil " + threadName);
    this.eatDinner(threadName);
    System.out.println("end Jphil " + threadName);
}

    public native void eatDinner(String ThrdName);
}
```

Phils.h

```
/* DO NOT EDIT THIS FILE - it is machine generated */
#include <jni.h>
/* Header for class Phils */

#ifndef _Included_Phils
#define _Included_Phils
#ifdef __cplusplus
extern "C" {
#endif
/* Inaccessible static: threadInitNumber */
```

```
/* Inaccessible static: stopThreadPermission */
#undef Phils_MIN_PRIORITY
#define Phils_MIN_PRIORITY 1L
#undef Phils_NORM_PRIORITY
#define Phils_NORM_PRIORITY 5L
#undef Phils_MAX_PRIORITY
#define Phils_MAX_PRIORITY 10L
/*
 * Class:     Phils
 * Method:    eatDinner
 * Signature: (Ljava/lang/String;)V
 */
JNIEXPORT void JNICALL Java_Phils_eatDinner
  (JNIEnv *, jobject, jstring);

#ifdef __cplusplus
}
#endif
#endif
```

phils.cpp

```
/*
** Name: phils.cpp - Dining Philosophers
**
** Description:
**   There are 10 philosophers who spend their lives either eating or
**   thinking.
**   Each philosopher has his own place at a circular table, in the
**   center of which is a large bowl of rice.  To eat rice requires
**   two chopsticks, but only 10 chopsticks are provided, one between
**   each pair of philosophers. The only chopsticks a philosopher can
**   pick up are those on his immediate right and left.
**   Each philosopher is identical in structure, alternately eating
**   then thinking. The problem is to simulate the behaviour of the
**   philosophers while avoiding deadlock (the request by a philosopher
**   for a chopstick can never be granted) and indefinite postponement
**   (the request by a philosopher is continually denied), known
**   colloquially as "starvation."
*/

/*
**   system include files
*/
# include <stdlib.h>
# include <iostream.h>
```

```
# include <sys/errno.h>

/*
**  local include files
*/
# include "Dinner.h"
# include "Phils.h"
# define   POSIX_THREADS
# include <PortableThreads.h>
# include <unistd.h>

/*
**  local variables
*/
const int  numPhilosophers = 10;     // number of philosophers
const int  numBites = 5;             // number of bites to take

// Setup the chopsticks as mutexs
PM_t        chopsticks[numPhilosophers];

// Provide a mutex to the resource 'threadCount'
int         threadCount = 0;
PM_t        threadCountMutex;

// Provide a condition variable and Boolean to allow the threads
// to have a synchronized start, and a mutex to setup the condition
PM_t        syncCondMutex;
int         syncBit;
PC_t        syncCond;

/*
**  Java_Dinner_StartUp
**  Purpose of method
**      Initialize the JNI philosophers environment
**  Input
**      *env - java environment
**      obj - java object
**  Output/Return
**      method is void
**  Change History
**      20-mar-2001 (Andrew Haigh)
**          created
*/
JNIEXPORT void JNICALL
Java_Dinner_StartUp( JNIEnv *env, jobject obj )
{
    int i, stat;
```

```
    printf ("in Phils_Startup\n");

    stat = PM_init(&threadCountMutex,NULL);
    stat = PM_lock(&threadCountMutex);
    for ( i=0; i < numPhilosophers; i++ )
    {
        cout << "Init mutex no.=" << i << " addr=" <<
            &chopsticks[i] << endl;
        stat = PM_init(&chopsticks[i%numPhilosophers],NULL);
        if(stat)
        {
            printf ("Error PT_init:1 = %d\n", stat);
            exit(1);
        }
    }

    syncBit = 0;
    stat = PM_init(&syncCondMutex, NULL);
    if(stat)
    {
        printf ("Error PM_init:2 = %d\n", stat);
        exit(1);
    }
    stat = PC_init(&syncCond, NULL);
    if(stat)
    {
        printf ("Error PC_init:3 = %d\n", stat);
        exit(1);
    }
    printf ("in Phils_Startup\n");
}


/*
**  Java_Dinner_Shutdown
**  Purpose of method
**      Release the JNI philosophers environment
**  Input
**      *env - java environment
**      obj - java object
**  Output/Return
**      method is void
**  Change History
**      20-mar-2001 (Andrew Haigh)
**          created
*/
JNIEXPORT void JNICALL
Java_Dinner_ShutDown( JNIEnv *env, jobject obj )
```

```
{
    int i, stat;
    printf ("in Phils_Shutdown\n");

    stat = PM_destroy(&threadCountMutex);
    for ( i=0; i < numPhilosophers; i++ )
    {
        stat = PM_destroy(&chopsticks[i%numPhilosophers]);
    }

    stat = PM_destroy(&syncCondMutex, NULL);
    stat = PC_destroy(&syncCond, NULL);

    printf ("in Phils_Shutdown\n");
}

/*
**   Psem
**   Purpose of method
**       This method will lock the mutex and return
**       If the mutex is not free, it will wait until it is
**   Input
**       mutex - handle of the mutex
**       seq - number to be printed in the message
**   Output/Return
**       method is void
**       return value 1 - when it succeeds
**       return value 2 - when it fails
**   Change History
**       20-mar-2001 (Andrew Haigh)
**           created
*/
void Psem (PM_t *mutex, int seq)
{
    int stat;
    // request a lock on a specific mutex
    stat = PM_lock (mutex);
    if(stat)
    {
        // if the request fails, report error to the user
        // do not try and recover
        cout << "Error PM_lock - " << seq << " = " << stat << endl;
        exit(1);
    }
}

/*
```

```
**   Psem_try
**   Purpose of method
**       This method will try to lock the mutex
**       If the mutex if free, acquire it and return
**       If the mutex is already locked it will return WAIT_TIMEOUT
**   Input
**       mutex - handle of the mutex
**       seq - number to be printed in the message
**   Output/Return
**       return 0 - when it succeeds
**       return WAIT_TIMEOUT - when it timed-out
**       exit 1 - when it fails
**   Change History
**       20-Mar-2001 (Andrew Haigh)
**           created
*/
int
Psem_try (PM_t *mutex, int seq)
{
    int stat;
    // try and get the lock on the mutex
    stat = PM_trylock (mutex);
    if(stat == EBUSY)
    {
        return 1;
    }
    else if (stat != 0)
    {
        cout << "Error PM_lock - " << seq << " = " << stat << endl;
        exit(1);
    }
    else
        return 0;
}


/*
**   Vsem
**   Purpose of method
**       Release the mutex
**   Input
**       mutex - handle of the mutex
**       seq - number to be printed in the message
**   Output/Return
**       method is void
**   Change History
**       20-mar-2001 (Andrew Haigh)
**           created
```

```
*/
void
Vsem (PM_t *mutex, int seq)
{
    // release the lock on a specific mutex
    if (PM_unlock (mutex))
    {
        // if the release fails, report error to the user
        // do not try and recover
        cout << "Error PM_unlock - " << seq << " = " << stat << endl;
        exit(1);
    }
}


/*
** PhilosopherThread
** Purpose of method
**     This is the process run by each philosopher thread
**     Each philosopher tries to pick up both chopsticks
**     When they have both chopsticks, they eat and return the
**     chopsticks and wait/think. This is repeated 'numBites' times
** Input
** Output/Return
**     method is void *
**     return value 0 - when it succeeds
** Change History
**     20-mar-2001 (Andrew Haigh)
**          created
*/
void *PhilosopherThread()
{
    int thrid, stat;
    int nextstick;
    PT_t self = PT_get_thread_id();

    Psem (&threadCountMutex, 1);

    thrid = threadCount;
    nextstick = (thrid+1)%numPhilosophers;
    threadCount++;
    cout << "Thread " << thrid << " entry point self=" << self
        << " addr = "<< &chopsticks << endl;

    Vsem (&threadCountMutex, 1);

    cout << "Local thread id = " << thrid << endl;
```

```cpp
// wait on a condition broadcast to start thread
Psem (&syncCondMutex, 2);

while (!syncBit)
{
    stat = pthread_cond_wait(&syncCond, &syncCondMutex);
    if(stat)
    {
        cout << "Error pthread wait1 = " << stat << endl;
        exit(1);
    }
}

cout << "Thread " << thrid <<
    " released and beginning run." << endl;

Vsem (&syncCondMutex, 2);

for ( int bites = 1; bites <= numBites; bites++ )
{
    // thinking
    cout << "Philosopher " << thrid << " thinking" << endl;
    PT_yield();

    // hungry, so picks up chopsticks
    Psem (&chopsticks[thrid], 3);

    while (Psem_try (&chopsticks[nextstick], 4) == 1)
    {
        Vsem (&chopsticks [third], 3);
        PT_yield ();
        Psem (&chopsticks [third], 3);
    }

    // eating
    cout << "Philosopher " << thrid << " eating" <<
        " bite " << bites << endl;
    PT_yield();

    // done eating
    Vsem (&chopsticks[(thrid+1)%numPhilosophers], 4);

    PT_yield();

    Vsem (&chopsticks[thrid], 3);
}
cout << "Thread " << thrid << " ending self=" << self << endl;
```

```
        return 0;
}


/*
**   Java_Phils_eatDinner
**   Purpose of method
**       This is the process run by each philosopher thread
**       Each philosopher tries to pick up both chopsticks
**       When they have both chopsticks, they eat and return the
**       chopsticks and wait/think. This is repeated 'numBites' times
**   Input
**       *env - java environment
**       obj - java object
**   Output/Return
**       method is void
**   Change History
**       20-mar-2001 (Andrew Haigh)
**           created
*/
JNIEXPORT void JNICALL
Java_Phils_eatDinner(JNIEnv *env, jobject obj )
{
    PT_t    phils[numPhilosophers];

    int i,  stat;
    void    *ret;

    // Create the philosopher threads
    for ( i=0; i < numPhilosophers; i++ )
    {
        // create the philosopher threads
        PT_create(NULL, NULL, (void *(*)(void*))PhilosopherThread,
            NULL, &phils[i], PTHREAD_CREATE_JOINABLE, &stat);
    }
    cout << numPhilosophers << " threads created." << endl;

    Vsem (&threadCountMutex, 6);

    // now wake them all up at once
    Psem (&syncCondMutex, 7);

    syncBit = 1;
    stat = PC_broadcast(&syncCond);
    if(stat)
    {
        cout << "Error PC_broadcast = " << stat << endl;
        exit(1);
```

```
    }
    cout << "Startup condition signaled." << endl;

    Vsem (&syncCondMutex, 7);

    // wait for all threads to finish execution
    for ( i = 0; i < numPhilosophers; i++ )
    {
        stat =  PT_join( phils[i], &ret );
        if(stat)
        {
            cout << "Error PT_join" << i <<"  = " << stat << endl;
            exit(1);
        }
    }

    cout << "Normal shutdown" <<endl;

    return 1;
}
```

Index

INTERNATIONAL CONTACT INFORMATION

AUSTRALIA
McGraw-Hill Book Company Australia Pty. Ltd.
TEL +61-2-9417-9899
FAX +61-2-9417-5687
http://www.mcgraw-hill.com.au
books-it_sydney@mcgraw-hill.com

CANADA
McGraw-Hill Ryerson Ltd.
TEL +905-430-5000
FAX +905-430-5020
http://www.mcgrawhill.ca

**GREECE, MIDDLE EAST,
NORTHERN AFRICA**
McGraw-Hill Hellas
TEL +30-1-656-0990-3-4
FAX +30-1-654-5525

MEXICO (Also serving Latin America)
McGraw-Hill Interamericana Editores S.A. de C.V.
TEL +525-117-1583
FAX +525-117-1589
http://www.mcgraw-hill.com.mx
fernando_castellanos@mcgraw-hill.com

SINGAPORE (Serving Asia)
McGraw-Hill Book Company
TEL +65-863-1580
FAX +65-862-3354
http://www.mcgraw-hill.com.sg
mghasia@mcgraw-hill.com

SOUTH AFRICA
McGraw-Hill South Africa
TEL +27-11-622-7512
FAX +27-11-622-9045
robyn_swanepoel@mcgraw-hill.com

**UNITED KINGDOM & EUROPE
(Excluding Southern Europe)**
McGraw-Hill Education Europe
TEL +44-1-628-502500
FAX +44-1-628-770224
http://www.mcgraw-hill.co.uk
computing_neurope@mcgraw-hill.com

ALL OTHER INQUIRIES Contact:
Osborne/McGraw-Hill
TEL +1-510-549-6600
FAX +1-510-883-7600
http://www.osborne.com
omg_international@mcgraw-hill.com